WEDDING ETIQUETTE

Cherished Traditions and Contemporary
Ideas for a Joyous Celebration

Peggy Post

Fourth Edition

HarperResource
An Imprint of HarperCollinsPublishers

HarperCollins books may be purchased for educational, business, or sales promotional use. For information please write: Special Markets Department, HarperCollins Publishers, Inc., 10 East 53rd Street, New York, NY 10022.

FOURTH EDITION

Designed by Richard Oriolo
Illustrations by Melanie Marder Parks

LIBRARY OF CONGRESS CATALOGING-IN-PUBLICATION DATA
HAS BEEN APPLIED FOR.

ISBN 0-06-019883-4

04 05 RRD 10

CONTENTS

ACKNOWLEDGMENTS ix

INTRODUCTION xi

CHAPTER ONE 1

ENGAGEMENT ETIQUETTE

Engagement Etiquette Guidelines ÷ *Sharing the Good News* ÷ *Welcome to the Family*
÷ *Spreading the News* ÷ *The Etiquette of Engagement Parties* ÷
When Families Disapprove ÷ *The Engagement Ring*

CHAPTER TWO 21

THE BIG DECISIONS

The Top-Priority Decisions ÷ *The Second Level of Decisions* ÷ *The Third Level
of Decisions* ÷ *Is a Wedding Consultant for You?* ÷ *Destination Weddings* ÷
Choosing Wedding Rings ÷ *The Joy of Coping* ÷ *Planning the Honeymoon*

CHAPTER THREE 41

EXPENSES AND LEGALITIES

Who Pays the Wedding Costs? ÷ *Traditional Division of Costs* ÷
Determining a Budget ÷ *Tips on Tipping* ÷ *All About Contracts* ÷
Marriage Legalities ÷ *The Who, What, When, and Where of Getting Married* ÷
Premarital Counseling ÷ *Name Changes* ÷ *Pre– and Postnuptial Agreements*
÷ *Wills and Finances* ÷ *Wedding Insurance*

CHAPTER FOUR 71

ATTENDANTS

The Etiquette of Choosing Your Attendants ÷ *Dispatches and Updates* ÷
Attendant Duties and Responsibilities

CHAPTER FIVE   87

FAMILY, FRIENDS, AND A CAREFULLY
PLANNED GUEST LIST

Guest List Survival Guide ÷ *Nuts and Bolts: The Guest List* ÷ *Trimming an Over-ambitious Guest List* ÷ *Organizing a Carefully Planned Master Guest List* ÷ *All About Children* ÷ *Help! What Do I Do About . . .* ÷ *Out-of-Town Guests* ÷ *Guest Etiquette* ÷ *The Good Guest's Pledge*

CHAPTER SIX   103

INVITATION ETIQUETTE

Invitation Styles ÷ *Invitation Wording* ÷ *Sample Invitations* ÷ *Wedding Announcements* ÷ *All About Envelopes* ÷ *Insertions* ÷ *Stuffing the Envelopes* ÷ *A Change in Plans* ÷ *Invitation Dos* ÷ *Invitation Don'ts* ÷ *Miscellaneous Stationery Items* ÷ *Newspaper Wedding Notice*

CHAPTER SEVEN   149

GIFTS OF LOVE

All About Bridal Registries ÷ *Wedding Celebration Gifts* ÷ *All About Wedding Gifts* ÷ *Gifts Among the Wedding Party* ÷ *All About Thank-you Notes* ÷ *Monogramming and Engraving*

CHAPTER EIGHT   169

WEDDING CELEBRATIONS

Wedding Showers ÷ *Bridesmaids' Luncheon* ÷ *Bachelor and Bachelorette Parties* ÷ *And the Party Never Ends . . .* ÷ *The Wedding Rehearsal* ÷ *The Rehearsal Dinner* ÷ *Wedding Night Afterglow* ÷ *The Wedding Party: A Belated Reception*

CHAPTER NINE   185

PLANNING THE CEREMONY

First Things First ÷ *Nuts and Bolts: Questions to Ask at the Ceremony Site* ÷ *Arrangements for a Ceremony at Another Site* ÷ *A Civil Ceremony* ÷ *Religious Ceremonies* ÷ *Commitment Ceremonies* ÷ *Military Weddings* ÷ *Double Weddings* ÷ *Special Ceremonial Tributes* ÷ *Blessing a Civil Marriage* ÷ *Reaffirmation of Vows*

CHAPTER TEN 217

MULTICULTURAL WEDDINGS

The Universality of Love ÷ *Weddings Around the World*

CHAPTER ELEVEN 227

ENCORE WEDDINGS

Essential Etiquette for Encore Weddings

CHAPTER TWELVE 239

WEDDING ATTIRE

How Formal Is Formal? ÷ *The Wedding Gown: Tip to Toe* ÷ *The Bridal Attendants*
÷ *Young Attendants* ÷ *The Groom and His Attendants* ÷
The Mothers of the Bride and Groom ÷ *The Fathers of the Bride and Groom*

CHAPTER THIRTEEN 257

PLANNING THE RECEPTION

The Wedding Team: Forming a Successful Partnership ÷ *Finding the Perfect Place* ÷
Checking Out the Site ÷ *A World of Receptions* ÷ *Reception Food and Drink* ÷ *Serve
It Up: Types of Reception Service* ÷ *Do You Need a Caterer?* ÷ *Selecting the Caterer
for You* ÷ *Nuts and Bolts: Questions for the Caterer* ÷ *The Wedding Drinks* ÷
The Fine Art of Seating Arrangements: Who Sits Where? ÷ *Planning Transportation*

CHAPTER FOURTEEN 279

FLOWERS FOR YOUR WEDDING

How to Choose Your Flowers ÷ *Wedding Flowers Checklist* ÷ *Floral Themes* ÷
Selecting the Florist for You ÷ *Nuts and Bolts: Questions for the Florist* ÷ *Flowers for
the Ceremony* ÷ *Flowers for the Reception* ÷ *Flowers for the Bride and Her Attendants*
÷ *Flowers for the Hair and Veil* ÷ *Flowers for the Groom and His Attendants*
÷ *Flowers for Children*

CHAPTER FIFTEEN 301

MUSIC

Music at the Ceremony ÷ *The Order of Ceremony Music* ÷ *Music at the Reception* ÷
Selecting the Musicians for You ÷ *Nuts and Bolts: Questions for the Reception Musicians*

CHAPTER SIXTEEN 313
PHOTOGRAPHY AND VIDEOGRAPHY

Photography: What's Your Style? ÷ *Selecting the Photographer for You* ÷
Nuts and Bolts: Questions for the Photographer ÷ *Getting the Photographs You Want* ÷
Videography: What's Your Style? ÷ *Video Options* ÷ *Selecting the Videographer for You*
÷ *Nuts and Bolts: Questions to Ask a Videographer* ÷ *Getting the Footage You Want*

CHAPTER SEVENTEEN 331
THE WEDDING CAKE

Who'll Make the Wedding Cake? ÷ *Cake Vocabulary* ÷
The Wedding Cake Display ÷ *The Art of Cutting the Cake*

CHAPTER EIGHTEEN 341
AT THE CEREMONY

Getting Ready ÷ *Seating Family* ÷ *The Ceremony* ÷ *The Celebration Begins*

CHAPTER NINETEEN 359
AT THE RECEPTION

The Etiquette of the Receiving Line ÷ *Toasts* ÷ *Blessing the Meal* ÷ *Dancing*
÷ *Closing Activities*

CHAPTER TWENTY 371
AFTER THE WEDDING:
FROM THIS DAY FORWARD

Thank-yous ÷ *Honeymoon Etiquette* ÷ *The Two of You: Life After the Honeymoon*
÷ *Anniversaries*

INDEX 379

ACKNOWLEDGMENTS

With appreciation, I'd like to recognize the following people for their contributions to this book.

The many brides and grooms who have shared their wedding experiences with me;

Toni Sciarra and Greg Chaput of HarperCollins, for their insights and hard work;

Alexis Flippin, Cindy Senning, and Katherine Cowles, for their diligence and creativity;

Caterer David Shields, florist Michael Piccioni, photographer Dan Bigelow, and events planner Laurie Barnett . . . for passing along their professional wedding planning expertise;

And the legacy of Emily Post, whose considerate spirit and timeless wisdom still serve as relevant foundations for today's weddings.

PEGGY POST
December 2000

INTRODUCTION

You're engaged! As the couple of the moment, you're in the throes

of rejoicing with your parents and friends, picturing a life of married bliss.

With all the excitement comes another wish—that of a perfect wedding. But

what does "perfect" mean? For one thing, it no longer describes only the story-

book formal event with six bridesmaids and yards of white tulle. (Indeed,

simple weddings are some of the most beautiful.) In truth, the ideal is a wed-

ding that personalizes style and surroundings to reflect who you are, where

you have been, and the direction you intend to go. The ideal is a celebration wherein the interests of all concerned—you, your family, your wedding party, your guests—are given utmost care and attention. It is about planning your wedding celebration with the following tenets in mind:

+ Let consideration be your guide. Make decisions based on preserving and enhancing the important relationships in your lives.
+ Give thought to the kind of occasion that you, your family, and your friends will feel comfortable with.
+ Forgo a tradition if you think that tradition threatens to cause a family rift. Or try to include a tradition that means a great deal to someone important to you.
+ Rely on tact and sensitivity when involving all concerned—even stepparents and extended family members.
+ Be considerate of the needs of the elderly or infirm guest. And find ways to give children special roles if they're included.
+ Anticipate potential problems in advance that may lead to discord.

The same attention and care applies to your relationship with suppliers and contractors, whether they include the all-purpose caterers and musicians who come with an elaborate event, or the florist and stationer who alone satisfy the needs of a smaller informal wedding.

For my own wedding, my husband and I put on a casual clambake reception—complete with seafood and corn on the cob—because we decided it just felt right for us. But what, you might wonder, would my great-grandmother-in-law Emily Post have made of our decision? That's easy: She'd have been there with bells on! Emily Post was one to change with the times, understanding that "etiquette" is first and foremost about making people feel comfortable with one another, whether they're going about the business of their daily lives or readying a wedding ceremony. Also, she knew that the magic of a wedding lay less in the details than in the tender quality of the occasion and the radiance of the bride—*and* the groom. "The radiance of a truly happy bride is so beautifying that even a plain girl is made pretty, and a pretty one, divine," she wrote in *Etiquette* in 1922. "She and the groom both look as though there were sunlight behind their eyes, as though their mouths irresistibly turned to smiles."

While that sentiment has stayed the same, weddings themselves haven't. Changes in society, from a more culturally diverse population to the redefinition of the family, have revolutionized the rite, giving rise to more informal ceremonies, a revival of ethnic customs, and a more active role for the groom. Beyond that, weddings have become more adventurous and imaginative, with destination and theme weddings sometimes part of the evolution.

It goes without saying that these changes can be confusing and stressful to sort through—a truth that is constantly driven home to me whenever I'm working on my monthly "Etiquette for Today" column in *Good Housekeeping* magazine. I find that wedding questions come from all quarters—brides, grooms, parents, attendants, guests, contractors—and that the queries reflect changing family structures and the relaxing of traditional rules. One future bride wonders, "Which of my fathers can walk me down the aisle? And can my mother?" Another, deciding on gift registries, asks, "Is it okay for us to register at a camping goods store?"

The flood of questions points out the differences in weddings today. First, the questions are more personal, with brides and grooms bending tradition to suit their backgrounds, preferences, and tastes. Multicultural customs are playing a big role in celebrations; African American brides are "jumping the broom" into wedded bliss, Irish American couples are dancing to spirited Celtic folk tunes, and Chinese American women are changing into traditional red cheongsams (for good luck) at their wedding banquets. Second, today's two-career couples take a different attitude toward how expenses should be divided and who will foot the bills. Third, the groom and sometimes his parents are more involved in the planning and organization than ever before. (Happily, the old saying "A man never knows how unimportant he is until he attends his own wedding" has mostly fallen by the wayside.) Fourth, the phenomenon of encore marriages—people marrying for the second time (or more)—has changed the way remarriages are celebrated. The old rules that said an encore bride may have only a small ceremony or should not wear white simply don't hold true in these modern times. Finally, the changes in family structure post a host of complicated questions: When parents are divorced and remarry and family trees branch out in all directions, who is responsible for what, and who is seated with whom—and who keeps track of it all while making sure everybody stays happy?

To address these ever-evolving issues, this edition of *Emily Post's Wedding*

Etiquette has greatly expanded its coverage on issues such as encore weddings, multicultural ceremonies, ethnic customs, postwedding duties, and how to work successfully with wedding consultants and the others on your wedding team. In addition, to better address the often complicated relationship issues of modern life as well as specific etiquette questions, there are new sidebars and boxes sprinkled throughout the text. These include:

- Etiquette Fine Points: Provides the lowdown on specific etiquette guidelines, such as how to have the ring placed on your finger if you're wearing gloves, or tips on how to arrange place cards.
- A Question for Peggy: Frequently asked questions are answered for brides, grooms, and others planning and attending their weddings.
- Another Viewpoint: Questions from someone other than the bride or groom.
- Behind the Tradition: The story behind a tradition.
- The Personal Touch: Thoughtful ways to personalize your wedding.
- The Wedding Team: Ways to work most successfully and develop satisfying relationships with consultants and vendors, using the expert advice of top wedding florists, photographers, and caterers.

Whatever questions and challenges come your way, I hope this book will give you the guidance relevant to today. Most important, I hope you'll have *fun,* whether your wedding is small and informal or grand and traditional. Really, all that's needed for the "perfect" wedding is the bride and groom's love for each other, the confidence to make decisions, and a careful effort to ensure that everyone involved is treated with courtesy. A sense of humor comes in handy, too, to help you negotiate any unexpected bumps along the way.

The date is set, the time is nigh, and it's time to get busy. As the two of you approach one of the most important days of your lives, just remember to keep the details in perspective and your happiness and joy in the forefront. May it all turn out beautifully—the perfect wedding for *you.*

—PEGGY POST
December 2000

CHAPTER ONE

This is the time to make

ENGAGEMENT

certain that marriage is the

ETIQUETTE

right decision for both

of you.

For the betrothed couple and family and friends, the engagement can be a time of unequaled euphoria. The goodwill that engagements engender is both thrilling and contagious. The generous opening of hearts by others in celebrating your happiness is a touching testament to the power of love.

The engagement period is an essential time, both to fully plan your celebrations and to acclimate yourselves to the idea of becoming a couple. The engagement period may be most valuable as a time of adjusting to the fact that you are committed to sharing your life with another person. It's when the romantic fantasy of perfect love hits the bedrock of reality. This is the time to make certain that marriage is the right decision for both of you and to think through potential obstacles to your happiness and how you plan to deal with them.

Perhaps you are wondering whether the engagement is right for you. While there is potentially less pain for all concerned in the breaking of an engagement than in the ending of a marriage, there is nonetheless a sense of loss. A broken engagement affects not just your own emotions, but those of the people dear to you as well. Think it through carefully; once family and friends are told, your commitment becomes real. Ideally you will find that you briefly had "cold feet," and that working through possible conflicts now will only strengthen the bonds of your love and commitment to one another.

Finally, your engagement is also a time of overwhelming detail—and enough stress to derail the most solid of unions. Don't give in to pressures to stage a celebration that is more about the festivities and less about you. Stay focused on your vision. Delegate chores to others who have offered to help. Stick to the day-to-day routine activities of your life. And whether the time between your engagement and your wedding is six weeks or six months, remember to take time off from organizing every now and then to enjoy each other and to immerse yourself in the fun and happiness your engagement brings.

❦ ENGAGEMENT ETIQUETTE ❧ GUIDELINES

Engagements require only a few simple guidelines. First, there are *no papers to sign or tests to take* to become engaged. You have only to say "yes" for an engagement to become official. Second, there is *no prescribed length of time* for an engagement. Some people might consider six months a long engagement; others take their time and stretch it out to three years. It may be as brief or as long as the couple requires to make their arrangements, save for their life together, or complete schooling, work, or a period of mourning. What's typical? The average length for an engagement in the United States is fourteen months. Many couples say that six months to one year is a comfortable length of time for them to be engaged.

Third, *do not become officially engaged until you are divorced.* Many a couple has jumped the gun and announced their engagement when a divorce is still in process. Even if an annulment or divorce is imminent, an engagement to another person should not be announced until the former union has been dissolved. Finally, a certain protocol should be followed in getting the news out about your betrothal. In sharing your engagement plans, *certain family members and close friends should hear the news first.*

❧ SHARING THE GOOD NEWS ❧

The guidelines of when, how, and to whom the news is spread have to do with people's feelings. Always let thoughtfulness be your guide.

Old Ways, New Ways

Historically, if the marriage had not been arranged by the two families in the first place, it was up to the groom to ask the young woman's father for permission to propose. If permission was granted, the groom would then, on bended knee, formally propose.

Today, in most cultures, things are very different. The bride and groom themselves usually make the decision to marry. Then they inform their families, but not necessarily to ask for their permission. Generally parents are the first to get the news, and in most cases the bride tells her parents and the groom tells his. But sometimes they do this together, sharing the news as a couple. Ideally the news does not come as a shock to the engaged couple's loved ones. If, during the courtship, the couple feels that their relationship is becoming serious, it's a good idea for each to become acquainted with the other's family members and close friends. If they live far away from family, the couple should be sure to mention their special relationship in phone conversations, letters, and/or e-mail before announcing their engagement.

Although it may seem old-fashioned, it is still courteous for the prospective groom to explain his career and life plans and his prospects to the bride's parents, as evidence of his respect for them.

Long and Short Engagements

Q: Is it better to have a long or a short engagement?

A: It depends upon the circumstances. Sometimes the shorter the time span between the engagement and the wedding day, the less stress on all parties. Some couples find that a long engagement usually means a prolonged period of planning and organizing. Indeed, in some regions this is a necessity, as ceremony and reception sites can be booked well over a year in advance. The longer the engagement, the more time you have to personalize your wedding, whether this means writing your own vows, making your own gown, or finding perfect, meaningful gifts for your attendants. It also means more time to adjust to the realities of a lifelong commitment.

Kids First

When one or both members of the engaged couple has children from a previous marriage, the children should always be the first people to hear the news, told to them by their parent alone, without the future stepparent present. Children of any age need time to adjust to the idea. You should also tell an ex-spouse, if for no other reason than to smooth the way for your children's involvement. (See "Encore Weddings," chapter II.)

Telling Other Relatives and Friends

Once parents and children have been told the news—and not before—the happy bride and groom will want to share their engagement plans with other relatives and friends. They can do so by making telephone calls, writing notes, or sending faxes or e-mails. Or they might wait and surprise everyone with an announcement at an engagement party. Regardless, there are certain people other than parents and children who should hear the news first, who would be hurt to read of the engagement in the newspaper or hear of it from someone other than the couple. These include grandparents, siblings, favorite aunts and uncles, and close friends. Always include them as special people in the know before the rest of the immediate world finds out.

WELCOME TO THE FAMILY

A betrothal is not just the joining together of two people in matrimony, it is also the joining together of two—and sometimes more—families. For the sake of the happy couple, this is the time for the parents of both to put their best faces forward and greet their new family with warmth and open hearts.

✦ *Parents meeting parents.* When parents of the bride and groom have not met each other before the wedding, tradition has it that the groom's family calls the bride's family to introduce themselves, express their happiness, and extend an invitation for a meeting. If for any reason the groom's family does not contact the parents of the bride, however, her father and mother should not stand on ceremony and wait for them to get in touch. Instead they should make the first move themselves. This is a time of joy for the couple. Both sets of parents should act with spontaneity and in the spirit of friendship, regardless of who makes the first contact. If it is impossible for them to meet, they should attempt to call or write so that an initial introduction is established.

✦ *Parents meeting divorced parents.* When the bride's parents are divorced, the groom's parents should get in touch with each of the bride's parents separately, calling first the one with whom the bride has been living or to whom she is the closest. They should arrange separate meetings with each parent so that the groom's parents can meet both the bride's parents and their spouses, if any.

When the groom's parents are divorced, the parent with whom he is closest should contact the bride's parents. Otherwise the bride's parents should initiate the introduction. If the groom's other parent and the bride's parents fail to continue the introduction process, the couple ideally steps in at this point to make sure that they do meet.

When both sets of parents are divorced, the groom's parent most inclined to begin the process of having the families meet should, in consultation with the bride and groom, contact first whichever of the bride's parents that she suggests.

Most important, under no circumstances should the bride or the groom force their own divorced parents into social situations that have the potential to make them—and others—feel uncomfortable. As much as they want to have their parents reunite as an intact family in honor of their own wedding, it is often an unrealistic expectation.

✦ *What to call the future in-laws.* You should continue to call each other's parents exactly what you have been calling them up to the moment of your engagement. If you have called them Mr. and Mrs., just continue to do so until they suggest otherwise. If they want you to call them "Mom" and "Dad," it's fine to do so if you feel comfortable. Most married couples refer to their in-laws by their first names. If, after you are married, your in-laws have not suggested a less formal address, you may then ask them what they would like you to call them.

SPREADING THE NEWS

In addition to calling and writing family members and friends, a couple often decides to submit an engagement announcement to newspapers. Because it is inappropriate to send printed engagement announcements, some couples make their announcement public through the newspaper. An engagement announcement should never be made if either member is still legally married to someone else. Nor is a public announcement appropriate when there has recently been a death in either family or when a member of the immediate family is desperately ill.

Newspaper Announcements

WHEN: Most newspaper engagement announcements appear approximately *two to three months before the wedding day,* even if wedding plans have not been firmed up. But there are really no hard-and-fast rules: an announcement may appear up to a year before the wedding date or as little as a week before. If an engagement party is planned, the announcement may appear before or after it takes place. If the couple hopes to surprise their guests at a party, the party should be held just before the news appears in the paper. If surprise is not a factor, then the party may take place soon or even weeks after the announcement is printed in the paper.

WHO: The announcement of the engagement is generally *made by the bride's parents or her immediate family,* often using a standard form provided by the newspaper. Be sure to include a telephone number so that the information can be verified by the newspaper, if necessary. The bride's parents should ask the groom's parents if they would like the announcement to appear in their hometown papers as well. If so, they can send it to those papers at the same time that they send it to their own.

BASIC WORDING: Although each newspaper may have its own format, the information included and the basic wording is as follows:

Mr. and Mrs. William Smith of Evanston, Illinois, announce the engagement of their daughter, Miss Christine Nicole Smith, to Mr. John Paul Sanders, son of Mr. and Mrs. Joseph Sanders of Monroe, Connecticut. An October wedding is planned.

Miss Smith was graduated from the University of Richmond and is a human resources assistant at Consolidated Advertising in Topeka, Kansas. Mr. Sanders was graduated from Mary Washington University and is working in the family insurance business.

In some newspapers, additional information about the bride's and groom's parents may be included, but the information as to schools and employment is usually given in the same way as in the above example. Following are some situations that require different wording:

Newspaper Announcement Nuances

WHEN THE BRIDE'S PARENTS ARE DIVORCED

The mother of the bride usually makes the announcement, but, as in the case of a deceased parent, the name of the other parent must be included:

Mrs. Donald Pico announces the engagement of her daughter, Miss Nancy Sasso . . . Miss Sasso is also the daughter of Mr. Victor Sasso of Providence, Rhode Island . . .

WHEN THE GROOM'S PARENTS ARE DIVORCED

The announcement presents the groom's parents separately, noting their places of residence, if different, but never pairing them as a couple even if they live in the same town:

> *Mr. and Mrs. Charles Cernek announce the engagement of their daughter, Miss Kathleen Mary Cernek, to Mr. Marvin Emil Henk, son of Mrs. Jeralyn Hughes Henk of Palo Alto, California, and Mr. Michael Henk of Sarasota, Florida . . .*

WHEN DIVORCED PARENTS ARE FRIENDLY

When divorced parents remain friendly, they may both wish to announce the engagement together:

> *Mrs. Walter Murphy of Palm Beach, Florida, and Mr. Timothy O'Neill of Philadelphia, Pennsylvania, announce the engagement of their daughter, Miss Linda O'Neill . . .*

When one or both parents have remarried and all parties are participating in the announcement:

> *Mr. and Mrs. Walter Murphy of Palm Beach, Florida, and Mr. and Mrs. Timothy O'Neill of Philadelphia, Pennsylvania, announce the engagement of Mrs. Murphy's and Mr. O'Neill's daughter, Miss Linda O'Neill . . .*

WHEN ONE OF THE BRIDE'S PARENTS
IS DECEASED

> *Mrs. [Mr.] Gerald Robert Havlin announces the engagement of her [his] daughter, Miss Caroline Joan Havlin, to Mr. Anthony Vellone. Miss Havlin is also the daughter of the late Gerald Robert [Carol Putnam] Havlin . . .*

When One of the Groom's Parents Is Deceased

Mr. and Mrs. William Francis Venable announce the engagement of their daughter, Miss Linda Barnes Venable, to Mr. Jonathan Huntington, son of Mrs. [Mr.] Robert Huntington and the late Robert [Eleanore Johnson] Huntington . . .

When the Bride Is a Divorcée

The parents of a young divorcée would announce her engagement as would the parents of a young widow, using her former husband's last name, if she continues to use her married name, or her maiden name, if she has changed her name back following a divorce:

Mr. and Mrs. Wilson W. Ahearn III announce the engagement of their daughter, Mrs. Caroline Howell [or Caroline Ahearn Howell] [or Caroline Elizabeth Ahearn] to . . .

When the divorcée is an older woman or independent of her parents, she may choose to announce her own engagement:

The engagement of Mrs. Patricia Hughes to Mr. Vincent Toppel is announced . . .

When the Couple Announce Their
Own Engagement

For any number of reasons, the couple may choose to announce their own engagement:

Ms. Victoria Ann Farrington and Mr. Benjamin Dodd are pleased to announce their engagement . . .

Or, as above:

The engagement of Ms. Victoria Ann Farrington to Mr. Benjamin Dodd has been announced . . .

When the Groom's Parents Announce the Engagement

Occasionally a situation arises in which the parents of the groom would like to announce the engagement. This could happen when the bride is from another country and it would be difficult for her parents to put an announcement in the paper in his hometown. Rather than announce it in their own name, the groom's parents should word the notice as follows:

The engagement of Miss Natalie Coleman, daughter of Mr. and Mrs. Clay Coleman of Munich, Germany, to Mr. John Evans, son of Mr. and Mrs. Walter Evans of Chicago, is announced . . .

❧ THE ETIQUETTE ❧ OF ENGAGEMENT PARTIES

An engagement party is a delightful way to announce the happy news of a new engagement. It's often more casual than formal, and the guest list can vary from just family to family, close friends, and friends who may not attend the wedding. Here are some guidelines to engagement parties.

- ✤ *Who hosts the engagement party?* Anyone may host an engagement party for the couple. Usually, however, it is the bride's parents who do so.

- ✤ *What type of party is proper?* It may be any type of party, but it is most often a cocktail party or a dinner.

- ✤ *Who makes the engagement announcement?* The host, usually the bride's father, makes the engagement official by proposing a toast to the couple when all the guests have assembled. At a very large party, if the announcement is not a surprise, the bride's fiancé stands with her and her mother and is introduced as the guests arrive.

+ *Who is invited?*   The majority of engagement parties are restricted to relatives and good friends of both families, but you may invite anyone you choose. The people invited to the engagement party are often those who will be your top-priority wedding guests. Occasionally the engagement party is a large open house or reception.

+ *Are gifts obligatory for engagement parties?*   Engagement gifts have never been obligatory and are not expected from casual friends and acquaintances. Still, they are becoming customary in some parts of the country, usually given to the couple by family members and close friends. Often, specifically inviting guests to an engagement party carries with it the implication that a gift is expected. If the bride and groom choose not to receive engagement gifts or don't want to burden others with an abundance of wedding-related costs, they may simply surprise all (or most) of the party guests with the announcement of their engagement. Their big news is then treated as a celebration, not as a gift-giving event.

Some guests who know of the surprise ahead of time might bring gifts. In this case, the couple sets the gifts aside and does not open them during the party. If the gifts are opened in front of all, those who did not bring a gift are made to feel uncomfortable.

If the party is a small dinner for very close friends and family, gifts may or may not be brought by guests, depending on the geographical, ethnic, and family customs. Those closest to the couple who want to give a gift should do so in private and not at the party. A good guideline for those who are attending a small party but aren't sure: Ask the hosts of the party for their guidance. The guests might then take a small gift as a token of their love and affection. If everyone brings a gift and there is time, the bride and groom may open their gifts and give thanks in person. A follow-up thank-you note is therefore not mandatory—but it is always an excellent idea.

Gifts that are sent after an announcement appears or after a party must always be acknowledged with a thank-you note.

A Broken Engagement

Q: My engagement was short-lived. My fiancé and I have decided to break our engagement. Do I have to return the ring? What about engagement and shower gifts we've already received?

A: If an engagement is broken, the bride should immediately return the ring (unless it is an heirloom of her family). There is some debate as to whether the ring should be returned if the man is the one who broke the engagement (versus the bride or the couple mutually calling it quits). It makes more sense to return it, why keep this painful reminder of the end of an engagement just to be spiteful? It's better to take the high road—and move on. The bride should also return any other presents of value her fiancé has given her, and he returns her gifts to him as well.

Wedding and shower gifts, as well as any engagement gifts, should also be returned. If it is too difficult to return them in person, they may be returned by mail, accompanied by an explanatory note:

Dear Rachel,

I am sorry to have to tell you that Ed and I have broken our engagement. Therefore, I am returning the lovely tray that you were so kind to send me.

Love,

Sara

One caveat: Should the groom pass away before the wedding takes place, the bride may keep her engagement ring, unless it is an heirloom belonging to the groom's family, in which case she should offer to return it to the family. She can keep any gifts given by relatives and friends but may prefer to return them—especially if they are constant reminders of her loss.

WHEN FAMILIES DISAPPROVE

Unfortunately there may be some people close to you who are unenthusiastic about your upcoming marriage for a number of reasons. If there are people in your life who object to your plans—whatever the reason—work hard to be gracious and forgiving. With all the tact you possess, let them know that you are not rejecting them if you disagree with their opinions or concerns, and open up several ways for them to change their minds without losing face.

When Parents Disapprove

When parents disapprove of the relationship, an engaged couple faces a real dilemma. If they decide to marry in spite of this disapproval, they should simply tell their parents when and where the wedding will take place and that they hope they can attend. Parents who care about their future relationship with their children will put aside their misgivings and attend. They gain nothing, and possibly lose a child for good, if they refuse.

Often parental disapproval stems from anxiety. If the disapproval is over an age difference, parents may worry about the health and longevity of the older person. They may think the age gap means no grandchildren. In these instances, it is wise for the bride and groom to discuss any concerns directly (and alone) with their own parents in an effort to allay any apprehensions.

If parents disapprove because of a socioeconomic divide between the bride and groom, the problem may simply resolve with time. The more affluent parents may worry that their child is being taken advantage of. If this is the one obstacle to receiving enthusiastic approval from parents, the couple can consider a premarital agreement (see chapter 3). If they prefer not to do this, then the obvious affection and commitment of the couple and a lasting marriage should eventually alleviate their parents' fears.

If it is your own parents who show disapproval, it is important to remain calm and not react with anger. Let them know that you are willing to listen to their concerns, but reiterate

---

A QUESTION FOR PEGGY

Diplomacy and Divorced Parents

Q: My parents divorced when I was young and have not had a friendly relationship since; in fact, it's been downright antagonistic. I am close to both parents, and I thought my engagement would bring my family together; instead it's brought a new set of problems. Sometimes I feel I am the parent to my parents. What can I do?

A: In these complex times, there often exists cumbersome family dynamics that a wedding can bring to light. The bride's mother, for example, may announce that she will not attend a single wedding party or the wedding itself if her ex-husband is going to be there. The groom's mother may insist that she will not participate if the groom's father's mother (her mother-in-law) is invited. Children in the custody of their other parent may refuse to attend the wedding out of fear that their custodial parent will be upset or angry with them. Ambassadorial-level diplomacy is called for in these situations, preferably coming from the member of the couple who is related to the difficult family member. Although the couple should discuss what to do, it is wise not to involve each other in family disputes at this point in their relationship—for if the difficulty is not smoothed over, it is often the outsider who is blamed for interfering.

your allegiance to your future spouse. When you adopt a calm and confident position, it is likely that your parents will take you seriously.

When Children Disapprove

If your children disapprove of the engagement, the dilemma is even greater, and family relationships can become quite strained. If time and communication cannot bridge the gap and basic civility and politeness have been abandoned, then professional counseling could be initiated to help the entire family understand each other's feelings.

❧ THE ENGAGEMENT ❧
RING

A bride-to-be does *not* need a ring to make her engagement official. And if she does have a ring, it doesn't need to be the largest diamond the groom can find. Many couples prefer to put the money that would be spent on a ring toward the practicalities of building their life together. Some couples even postpone the purchase of an engagement ring until years after their wedding, when their finances enable them to buy the special ring they've envisioned. These days the bride is often involved in selecting the engagement ring; in fact, only 30 percent of men do so alone. So it is wise for both bride and groom to bone up on the basics of the engagement ring.

Diamonds: The Four C's and More

The traditional gemstones for engagement rings, diamonds are the emblems of love and engagement. Knowing the four C's allows you to converse comfortably with jewelers when you are shopping for a diamond engagement ring.

CARAT

Carat is the weight of a diamond. One carat is one-fifth of a gram (200 milligrams). There are 142 carats to an ounce. One carat also has 100 points. This system of measuring diamond weight began in India and was based on the weight of the seeds of the carob tree, which were used to balance scales.

CLARITY

Diamonds are rated on the basis of blemishes that occur in nature, such as inner cracks, bubbles, and specks that are hard to detect with the naked eye. When a diamond is rated flawless (FL), it is given the highest clarity rating; a flawless diamond is rare. The size and placement of the blemishes determine a diamond's clarity rating, which ranges from flawless, to varying degrees of small inclusions, to the least desirable rating: "imperfect."

CUT

The way a diamond is cut determines its brilliance. In fact, cut is generally considered the most important of the four C's of diamonds. When cut, a diamond is faceted in a series of flat, angled surfaces that reflect light off one another. This is what causes the stone to sparkle.

COLOR

Another criterion for determining the value of diamonds is color. If a diamond is clear and colorless, it is rated D, the highest color ranking. The lowest rating is Z, yellow. This indicates a stone that contains traces of earthy color. Some diamonds that naturally have some tint of color are placed in a special category called "fancies."

Wearing the Ring

Q: When may a bride-to-be wear her engagement ring?

A: A bride may wear her ring as soon as she receives it—that is, unless she or the groom-to-be is still married to someone else and awaiting a divorce. Even if a divorce or annulment is imminent, it is incorrect to wear an engagement ring. If an engagement party is planned where a surprise announcement will be made, the bride may want to wait to wear the ring so as not to spoil the surprise. The ring is worn on the fourth finger (next to the little finger) of her left hand. In some countries it is worn on the fourth finger of the right hand. Regardless, it is removed before the marriage ceremony and replaced by the wedding ring, which is worn closest to the heart. The engagement ring is then placed above (closer to the fingertip) the wedding ring.

MORE C'S

A fifth C for diamonds is certification. This is the written proof of a diamond's weight, grade, and identifying characteristics from the International Gemological Institute and should come with your ring.

The sixth and seventh C for any stone and ring choice are cost and care. Cost is entirely personal. Care is an important consideration. The hardness of a diamond makes it easy to clean and the most durable of stones. Other gemstones are softer and more susceptible to damage and therefore require more care. The setting of the stone is also a care factor, particularly for brides who use their hands in their work. A raised or elaborate setting that can get caught easily or get in the way may not be as good a choice as a more protective setting. One such setting is called a bezel, where the band hugs the middle section of the stone. Another protective setting is a channel setting, where the stones are set between two strips of the band so that they are held at both top and bottom.

The last C is comfort. Whatever the shape or size of the ring you choose, it should be comfortable, allowing your finger and hand to feel unencumbered. It should not be an annoyance, nor should you even be aware that you are wearing it; otherwise you will be tempted to take it off—and then what's the point of having it?

Gemstones

Instead of a diamond, many couples prefer a gemstone—a perfectly acceptable choice—for the engagement ring. Gemstones are classified as "precious" and "semiprecious," with "precious" stones being emeralds, rubies, and sapphires. Long prized as symbols of mystical power, gemstones were also graced with symbolic meaning during Victorian times, when they became especially popular in engagement rings. Some couples select gemstones for engagement rings based on the birthstones of the bride or the groom or both. If you want your ring to symbolize something besides your engagement, you can choose the stone representing your birth months.

Karats vs. Carats

The metal used for the ring itself should always be harmonious with the other elements of the ring. Platinum is a popular choice—it is extremely durable and doesn't wear away as easily as gold. Gold becomes more durable as higher amounts of other metals are blended into it. The amount of gold is defined by karats, listed by a number, up to 24. The purest gold, and therefore the softest and most likely to bend, is 24-karat. An 18-karat gold ring is 18 parts gold and 6 parts another metal. A 14-karat gold ring, the most popular, is 14 parts gold and 10 parts another metal. Ask your jeweler's advice when choosing which metal is best for your settings and stone.

Settings

The setting of a ring is defined as the way the stone or stones are arranged within the metal of the ring itself. Two of the most popular settings are 1)

A QUESTION FOR PEGGY

Must I Wear the Family Heirloom?

Q: I was presented with a family heirloom ring as an engagement ring. It was worn by both my future mother-in-law and her mother. My problem is, I really don't like it; it's too big and ostentatious, and I had my heart set on a simpler one. Could I ask to have it reset by a jeweler? Or can I simply say thank you, but I'm just not comfortable accepting the ring?

A: If you feel uncomfortable in taking the ring, you needn't accept it. Simply decline graciously. A family has no right to demand that their future daughter-in-law wear an heirloom ring, passed along just because it exists, no matter how many generations it may have been in the family.

The Bridegroom Asks: Must I Wear a Ring?

Q: My fiancée really wants us to wear matching wedding bands. I have never liked wearing rings and would rather not, if I don't have to. Must I wear a wedding band? And if so, does it have to be matching?

A: It's not only fine for wedding bands not to match, but the bridegroom may or may not choose to wear a wedding ring at all. If it's a comfort issue, or if wearing a ring is simply not practical in your work environment, say so to your bride-to-be. If, however, not wearing a ring is simply a matter of principle, you should talk it over with your fiancée, especially if she has her heart set on exchanging rings. You may be able to compromise, such as having a ring and wearing it only on special occasions or wearing it somewhere else (around your neck, for example).

the traditional Tiffany setting, where a single diamond perches high on the band; and 2) the illusion setting, which is usually a group of smaller stones surrounding a larger one.

Two terms often used in describing stones within settings are baguette and pavé. Baguettes are smaller stones, usually rectangular with square corners, set on both sides of a larger, centered stone. Pavé diamonds are small stones that are fitted into tapered holes placed very close together, forming a continuous surface.

Stone Shapes

Just as you try on clothes to ensure a comfortable, flattering fit, so should you try on rings to find the settings and stone shapes that best fit and flatter your hand. Less traditional shapes include heart-shaped stones and "fancy cuts." The shapes described here are the most traditional.

✣ Marquise. Marquise shapes are oblong with pointed ends. This cut is named for the renowned marquise, duchess, and mistress of Louis XV, Madame de Pompadour.

✣ Round. Round shapes are the most popular, probably because their many facets allow them to reflect more light—hence their other name, "brilliant."

✣ Oval. Oval shapes are adapted from the round-cut diamond.

✣ Emerald. Emerald-cut diamonds are rectangular with levels, or steps, from base to top.

✣ Pear-shaped. Pear-shaped diamonds are round on one end and pointed on the other. The round end is worn toward the hand, the pointed end toward the fingertip.

CHAPTER TWO

Now is the time

THE BIG

for the two of you

DECISIONS

to sit down and have

a serious discussion.

The engagement is on! You and your loved ones are thrilled; the future

is bright with hope and possibility. Now is the time for the two of you to sit

down and have a serious discussion about the kind of wedding you both

envision. If you've always dreamed of floating up the aisle in a long white

gown and your mate thinks a casual clambake on the beach would suffice,

don't let that deter either of you. Keep talking.

It is also time for a reality check. Two of the biggest factors influencing

the major decisions of your wedding plans are money and convenience.

Whether you have a long or a short time to plan your wedding, start out by separating your primary decisions from less important ones. You'll find that once you've made the big decisions first, the secondary decisions will fall into place. Think of the primary decisions as the foundation for every other choice you make.

Before you start debating the merits of a large versus small wedding or a formal versus informal wedding, both of you should decide what aspects of the wedding you consider most important.

❧ THE TOP-PRIORITY DECISIONS ❧

Your initial decisions will be based on the following:

✦ The *Guest List*

✦ The *Budget*

✦ The *Date:* time of year, day of the week, and time of day

✦ The *Style* of your wedding (formal vs. informal; religious vs. civil)

✦ The availability of your wedding *Officiant*

✦ The *Locations* for both the ceremony and the reception

The Guest List

While your available budget is certainly the determining factor for your wedding, your guest list has everything to do with how the money is spent. Quite simply, any decisions about the type of wedding you will have cannot be made until you have some idea of the size of the guest list. If neither of you can imagine celebrating your nuptials without your mutually large families in attendance, the guest list will, by necessity, be a big one. If your guest list is large and your budget small, you may have to forgo a big, formal, sit-down dinner reception. Otherwise, paring your guest list down may allow it. *The easiest way to cut costs? Narrow your guest list.* (For more on guests lists, see chapter 5.)

The Mother of the Groom Asks: Should the Groom Plan, Too?

Q: *My future daughter-in-law expects my son to be involved in all aspects of their wedding planning, but I don't think it's proper. What do you say?*

A: Your future daughter-in-law is right in line with the growing trend of today's grooms being actively involved in the wedding-planning process. Many men are having their say in everything from choosing items for the gift registry to selecting music or readings for the ceremony. Some even attend wedding fashion shows and are included in wedding showers. There are several reasons for this switch: Grooms these days are apt to be older and better established and so may be paying much of the expenses. Divorce can be a factor, too. A man marrying for a second or third time tends to know what to expect; also, if his children are going to be in the ceremony (often the case), then he's certainly going to be interested in helping plan their participation. Finally, today's brides—and sometimes their mothers, too—are apt to have full-time careers. They are thrilled to have the groom's help. I'm hearing from women that they love having their fiancés involved. Certainly there are plenty of duties to share—including writing all those thank-you notes!

The Budget

If your parents are paying for the wedding or contributing to it, now is the time to discuss finances with them. Be realistic about your expenses, and be appreciative of whatever your parents can contribute. If your parents have given you a figure that is the most they can spend, it is up to you to work with that amount or combine your resources with theirs. Then tally the projected costs for your wedding and compare it against your resources. Don't be concerned that you have to cut quality to save costs. There are many smart ways of cutting corners without sacrificing quality.

If you are paying for your own wedding, you will have a good idea from the beginning what kind you can realistically afford. If your budget is limited, you will have to decide what takes priority: a big, glamorous wedding with a shorter guest list or a larger guest list and a more toned-down reception. This is the time to find compromises, by shortening the guest list, by choos-

A Proper Time to Marry

There's an old folk saying that goes "Choose not alone a proper mate, but a proper time to marry." If you don't need to contemplate practical considerations as part of choosing the month you will marry, there are folklore, myth, and tradition to guide you!

The Victorians loved attributing meaning to everything, and many paid close attention to the wedding rhymes that suggested certain results from certain wedding dates.

January—Marry when the year is new, he'll be loving, kind, and true.

February—When February birds do mate, you wed nor dread your fate.

March—If you wed when March winds blow, joy and sorrow both you'll know.

April—Marry in April if you can, joy for maiden and for man.

May—Marry in the month of May, you will surely rue the day.

June—Marry when June roses grow and over land and sea you'll go.

July—Those who in July do wed must labor for their daily bread.

August—Whoever wed in August be, many a change is sure to see.

September—Marry in September's shine so that your life is rich and fine.

October—If in October you do marry, love will come but riches tarry.

November—If you wed in bleak November, only joys will come, remember!

December—When December's snows fall fast, marry, and your love will last.

In actuality, these rhymes had a foundation that went beyond the fanciful. For example, the dire predictions for May weddings came from the custom of observing the Feast of the Dead during this month, when everyone worked hard to appease the souls of the departed. Queen Victoria took this so seriously that she permitted no royal weddings in the month of May. What made January a sure thing for a marriage to the ancient Greeks? This month was dedicated to Hera, defender of women and wife of Zeus. Anyone marrying in January received an extra blessing under Hera's power. In addition, this was the time for fertility rites, the results of which just might be passed on to the bride marrying then! September was recommended for fertility, too, because of the benefits of the full harvest moon. If love mattered most, then April was the month to marry, for it was the favored month of Venus, the Roman goddess of love.

Still undecided about when to be married? There is always the Victorian assurance that the luckiest time of all to be married was on the same day of the week that the groom was born, regardless of fertility rites, harvest moons, or when the goddess of love might be looking on. It was better yet to marry on his birthday.

ing a time of year or time of day when costs are down, by choosing an affordable reception site, by forgoing a big wedding party. The variations, as you can see, are endless. (For more on wedding expenses, see chapter 3.)

The Date

TIME OF YEAR

The time of year for your wedding is a key consideration, for several reasons. First, the most popular months for weddings are June, September, August, May, October, and July. Accordingly, the most popular wedding sites will be at a premium during those months, in terms of both availability and cost. If cost is a factor, you will do better to *select a month when rates and fees are lower.* In general, the best budget months of the year are January, February, and March. Of course, if you plan a destination wedding or honeymoon in February at a popular wintertime retreat like the Caribbean, expect to pay peak prices. Time of year is also a factor for a wedding at a hot year-round destination such as Disney World. In this case, you might want to look at those seasons when the park slows somewhat, such as the months when kids are in school.

Second, if your shared vision *involves the outdoors* in some component of your wedding, you will be limited to warm-weather months, unless you are planning a reception at a ski resort. And even a winter ski resort may be fully booked well in advance.

Third, *some religions have restrictions on weddings that take place during high holy days* such as during Lent or Passover. If you are hoping for an early spring wedding, check the calendar—and then check with your priest, minister, or rabbi.

Fourth, consider not only availability in choosing the time of year you marry, but *the effect it will have on family and close friends.* Think about any hardships your wedding may cause guests. Thanksgiving, Christmas, and the Fourth of July are prime family vacation times, when people have longtime traditions and obligations they may find hard to forgo. When school is in session, it may be difficult for families to carve out a three-day wedding weekend. Consider as well any difficulties guests who live far away will have in making their travel plans.

On the other hand, having your wedding on a secondary holiday week-end, such as Memorial Day and Labor Day, may be a smart choice: guests who have to travel will have an automatic three-day weekend and won't have to take an extra day off from work.

DAY OF THE WEEK

Most weddings are held on weekends, and for good reason: weekend days are the customary days off from work. Within the weekends, Christians don't usually wed on a Sunday, their Sabbath, and Jews don't usually wed on a Saturday, because it is their Sabbath day of prayer and rest. Historically weddings were almost always held on Sundays because the work week extended from Monday through Saturday, and who could afford to miss a day of work?

A weekday wedding can reap the benefit of lower prices and certain availability of ceremony and reception sites and vendor and supplier access. A weekday wedding, particularly in the late afternoon or evening on a Thursday, is also a logical consideration for a destination wedding. It provides an entire weekend for guests to fit in a minivacation along with the festivities.

TIME OF DAY

The most popular booking times are, in order of popularity, *Saturday after-noon, Saturday morning, Friday evening,* and *Sunday afternoon.* The time of day your wedding takes place can also make a big difference in your budget. A late afternoon or early evening wedding is generally more expensive than a morn-ing or early to mid-afternoon wedding. Reception costs are affected as well—if you plan a reception in the middle of the day or anytime from four P.M. to eight P.M., your guests will expect to be served a meal or at least some substantial food. If cost is a factor, and you are planning to be married dur-ing the wedding high season when most sites may already be booked, con-sider switching your celebrations to a less frequently booked time of day. (The later the wedding, the more formal it is likely to be.) The time of day and the wedding's formality aren't necessarily indications of how elegant a wedding will be, however. Just because you are being married in the morning doesn't mean that your semiformal or informal wedding will be any less ele-gant than one held at night.

The Style

Now is the time to start thinking about *the color scheme of the wedding.* Your wedding color choices are often influenced by the time of year, seasonal flowers, the bridesmaids' dresses, the locale, and personal preferences.

Ultimately, however, the most important choice you have to make in deciding the style of your wedding is how formal or informal you wish it to be. There are three categories of weddings—*formal, semiformal,* and *informal.* The formality is related to the location of the ceremony and reception, the size of the wedding party, the number of guests, and the time of day. While the style of a wedding in a church or synogogue may be formal or informal, a home wedding generally lends itself to informality, unless, of course, the home happens to be a mansion. In that case drag out the white gloves and candelabra! The variations on each style are endless, but there are a few basic differences in the three categories.

THE FORMAL WEDDING

✣ *Where is the ceremony held?*   The formal wedding ceremony usually takes place in a house of worship or in a large home or garden.

✣ *How many attendants?*   The bride and groom each usually have from four to ten attendants.

✣ *What is the typical attire?*   The bride and her attendants wear long gowns in formal fabrics, and the groom and his attendants wear cutaways or tailcoats. Women guests wear street-length dressy clothing for a daytime wedding and usually floor-length gowns or cocktail dresses for an evening wedding. Men guests wear dark suits and ties for a daytime wedding and tuxedos for an evening wedding. An evening formal wedding that requires white tie is the most formal of all.

✣ *What type of reception is held?*   The formal reception is usually a sit-down or semibuffet meal. Invitations are engraved, decorations can be elaborate, transportation for the wedding party is usually provided by limousines, and music, if the reception includes dancing, is often provided by an orchestra or full band.

The Semiformal Wedding

✣ *Where is the ceremony held?* The ceremony can take place in a house of worship, a chapel, a hotel, club, home, or garden.

✣ *How many attendants?* The bride and groom each usually have from two to six attendants.

✣ *What is the typical attire?* For a semiformal wedding, the bride and her attendants may wear long, ballerina, or tea-length gowns, usually made of simpler fabrics than those for a formal wedding. The groom and his attendants wear gray or black strollers with striped trousers or a formal suit for a daytime semiformal wedding and a dinner jacket with black trousers or a formal suit for an evening wedding. Women guests wear street-length tailored or semidressy dresses for a daytime wedding and cocktail dresses for an evening wedding. Men guests wear dark suits for both.

✣ *What type of reception is held?* The reception is generally a buffet or a cocktail buffet later in the afternoon with a small band or orchestra or a DJ.

The Informal Wedding

✣ *Where is the ceremony held?* The ceremony can take place in a house of worship, a chapel, or a rectory or in a home or garden presided over by a justice of the peace.

✣ *How many attendants?* The bride and groom each usually have from one to three attendants.

✣ *What is the typical attire?* At an informal wedding, the bride and her attendants wear simple white or pastel floor-length gowns or ballerina, tea-length, or street-length dresses. The groom and his attendants wear suits or sport jackets and slacks. Women guests wear what is appropriate to the location, usually street-length dresses. Men guests wear sports jackets and slacks.

✣ *What type of reception is held?* The reception can take place in a restaurant or at a home with a caterer and/or friends providing refreshments, usually a breakfast, brunch, or lunch in the morning or early afternoon and an informal buffet or simple hors d'oeuvres and wedding cake for an afternoon reception. Music may come from a single musician or background CDs or tapes.

Your Officiant

If you place great importance on who performs your ceremony and wouldn't consider getting married without having him or her officiate, check on that individual's availability before making *any* other decisions about the date of your wedding.

The Locations

THE CEREMONY

You will need to decide *whether to marry in a house of worship* or at *a secular location.*

If you plan to marry in a house of worship, try to reserve a few dates pending your final decision to be sure the church or synagogue will be available and you have confirmed your reception location.

Otherwise you will want to consider alternative possibilities, whether indoors or outdoors, in a hotel or wedding hall, at home, or at City Hall. Do you want a private ceremony with only a few close friends and family members attending? (For a further look at selecting ceremony sites, turn to chapter 9.)

THE RECEPTION

Your choice of reception site will affect the type of food you serve, beverages, service, formality level, entertainment, and reception hours. Once you have

---

A QUESTION FOR PEGGY

Is Prewedding Counseling Necessary?

Q: Must my fiancé and I go through prewedding counseling with our minister? He insists that we see him for counseling at least three times before the wedding.

A: Many clergy consider counseling a prerequisite for performing the wedding. If you really feel it's unnecessary or doesn't mesh with your religious beliefs, choose your officiant accordingly or ask your clergy if you can have informal talk sessions rather than formal religious or relationship counseling. Personally I think talking with your officiant about your relationship, your faith, and the upcoming nuptials and the change it will make in your lives can be invaluable and time well spent.

drawn up your guest list and determined a date and time for your wedding, you can focus on the kind of reception you want and your location preferences. Begin checking out sites immediately, in terms of approximate cost and availability. In some parts of the country reception sites are booked at least a year in advance. (For a further look at selecting reception sites, turn to chapter 13.)

❧ THE SECOND LEVEL ❧
OF DECISIONS

Once you have settled the who, where and when of your wedding, it is time to start shopping, interviewing, and booking vendors, suppliers, and services. Because each of these next steps generally requires a good amount of advanced time, there is no time like the present to start:

+ Shop for and make decisions about clothing and accessories—for the bride, groom, and attendants (see chapter 12).

+ Visit stores and list gifts you wish to receive with bridal registries (see chapter 7).

+ Begin reviewing reception menus (see chapter 13).

+ Interview and listen to bands or DJs, or start listing songs you would put on tapes for the reception (see chapter 15).

+ Interview and talk to florists (see chapter 14).

+ Interview and look at the portfolios of photographers and videographers (see chapter 16).

+ Order invitations, enclosures, announcements, and other printed material (see chapter 6).

The Caterer Speaks: Selection Savvy

To many couples, finding the right reception site tops the list of first big decisions. Here are some tips to consider when looking for that all-important place.

1. *Think about how much work you and your family actually want to do. Keep in mind that hotels and private clubs are experienced in handling large parties and can do much of the organizing for you. Reception halls with in-house caterers may cost more but may be worth it, considering the ease of service. Locations that offer everything under one roof—ceremony and reception area, food, decor, flowers, you name it—make planning a wedding for busy couples with a short engagement time a snap. The minuses can be the lack of choices and ways to personalize the wedding.*

2. *Sites that are bare will require more attention, in terms of food, drink, decor, help, and hookups. Everything will have to be sourced out to different vendors, and someone (you?) will be responsible for coordinating their efforts.*

3. *A wedding at a rental facility or historical site, such as a botanical garden or mansion, may require less decorating work but may also require that you use the facility's in-house catering staff and often the in-house baker for the wedding cake.*

4. *If you're considering a reception at home or at a site where a tent will be used, remember that everything—from the lighting to the flooring to decorations—will have to be delivered and assembled and then disassembled once the party's over. It can be costly to transform a tent into a ballroom.*

5. *If the idea of a destination wedding appeals to you, remember that few friends and relatives will be able to take the time off to get there and afford the additional costs. If the cost proves prohibitive for many guests, you might think about being married with the few close relatives and friends who can make the trip in attendance and then having a reception when you return home from the honeymoon.*

With all your outside resources in order, you now can turn your attention to the details that will make your wedding day personal and unique. You might do the following:

✢ Listen to and choose music for your ceremony (see chapter 15).

✢ Select readings for your ceremony (see chapter 9).

✢ Make lists of music choices for your reception.

✢ Plan special events you want to include, such as your first dance at the reception, a bouquet toss, or a party for your attendants.

✢ Select gifts for your attendants, perhaps parents, and each other (see chapter 7).

✢ Begin to chart seating arrangements for your reception (see chapter 13).

✢ Incorporate family and cultural traditions into your wedding (see chapter 10).

❧ IS A WEDDING ❧ CONSULTANT FOR YOU?

More and more couples have full-time careers and a limited amount of time to devote to wedding organization. For busy people with hectic schedules, hiring a wedding coordinator or consultant is a smart alternative to trying to do it all. Wedding consultants indeed can be of great service: they can scout sites and oversee the budget, the caterer, the band, the florist, and any number of service providers. They can snag discounts and bargains from vendors. In short, they can lift the load from your shoulders when you are feeling burdened, simply because they have encountered and solved the same problems you may be facing in hundreds of ways. Their purpose is not to take over your wedding, but to help make your dreams come true and your plans a reality. Plus, wedding consultants can save you money in the long run.

Think about what kind of help you need before making a decision. There are many different levels of service and types of consultants. A full-fledged *bridal consultant* can do anything and everything for you. A *wedding day coordinator* springs into action on the day of the wedding, making sure everything goes according to schedule. A *wedding day director* might be provided by the ceremony site to supervise all the details of the ceremony only and make sure church or synagogue rules are followed. There are consultants and coordinators who handle varying responsibilities in between. Here is a general guide on wedding consultants.

✢ *What, exactly, does a wedding consultant do?* In general, a bridal consultant can provide the following services:

Help you decide on ceremony and reception sites.

Help you select all the suppliers and vendors you will hire, such as the florist, the caterer, musicians, the photographer, the videographer.

Coordinate communication between and among vendors, suppliers, and sites, so that, for example, the florist knows when and how to obtain access to the ceremony site to decorate.

Serve as a referee, friend, budget adviser and watcher, etiquette adviser, shopper, detail manager, and organizer.

Coordinate your rehearsal with the officiant.

Supervise all the last minute details of your wedding day.

✢ *What is the typical cost of a consultant?* When an independent wedding consultant or coordinator is hired right at the beginning to oversee most of your wedding plans, she tends to work on a *fee basis,* generally 10 to 20 percent of the total wedding costs. Others charge a *flat fee,* depending on the services they provide. Once you have a budget in mind, calculate what the cost of a consultant will be and weigh that against the value of your time. Keep in mind that a successful consultant will be able to pass along enough savings to defray most of her fee—and that time can be just as important a commodity to you as money.

❧ DESTINATION WEDDINGS ☙

*Destination weddings—choosing a dream location to marry, celebrate, and even spend your honeymoon—*are becoming increasingly popular. A destination wedding is ideal for the couple who wants to get away with a few close friends and family for a combined celebration and vacation. It also is a smart solution for the couple who wants both a wonderful honeymoon and a lavish wedding but have to choose one over the other. Unless you have the wherewithal to charter a plane for a slew of guests and rent rooms for all of them (customarily these expenses are the guests' responsibility), you can't expect all of your invited guests to be able to afford such an expense. Still, by letting your guests in on your plans well in advance, you may find some who are able to swing it. The style of a destination wedding can be as formal or casual as you like; there is no set guideline. The guest list will often be shorter than that of a wedding set in a traditional location, owing to the logistics and expenses of a destination wedding; again there is no absolute rule.

If your dream is to be married at a popular travel spot, *plan early.* Find a travel agent who specializes in destination weddings and related components—finding officiants, florists, bands, photographers, and caterers. You'll want a travel agent who will spend the time to find the best airline rates and who can advise you on the difference between peak-season and off-season costs at your destination—often the price differences can be considerable. Or find a wedding consultant or resort planner on-site who has organized weddings at a chosen destination and let him or her take care of contracting the services you will need. It may be worth the fee to spare yourself the long-distance calls and difficulty in communicating in another language.

Theme Weddings

Theme weddings are becoming more and more popular. The theme of the wedding may be carried into every aspect of the celebration, from the attire to the food to the decorations.

The theme may be simply *an homage to a long-ago era*. If you are planning to wear your grandmother's Victorian wedding gown, you may want the festivities to complement the outfit. Victorian brides and their attendants often carried *tussy-mussies* (nosegay bouquets inserted in a silver, cone-shaped holder), so have your florist make some instead of traditional bouquets. Add lace to pew decorations and center-pieces. Decorate with rose petals; use candles and fans. Plan a Victorian menu.

A theme could also be *connected to your first date*. A nautical theme makes sense for a couple who met on a sailboat and who love to sail. Use nautical colors and signal flags for decorations. Have a seafood menu at a yacht club. Or your wedding could revolve around *a holiday*.

Also a possibility is a *cultural or ethnic theme*. If you have strong ties to an ethnic community or want to honor your roots and family ties, incorporate into your celebrations some of the symbols and traditions that have special meaning for you. Do your homework: plan clothing, decorations, menus, music, and events to add special meaning to your ceremony and reception. When planning, think about all the ways you can use the theme you have chosen, beginning with your invitations. Not only will you find unique ways to personalize your wedding, but you will also find new connections to your own heritage.

❖ CHOOSING WEDDING RINGS ❖

Wedding rings may be selected at the same time as the engagement ring, but often they are not. Many times they are selected and ordered during the engagement period, when the bride and groom can take the time to find what will be a meaningful, serious purchase. Even if the groom has selected the engagement ring as a surprise for his intended, both should participate in the selection of the wedding ring or rings.

✠ *Types of wedding bands.*   Wedding bands are designed in platinum or yellow or white gold and come in a variety of finishes. If the bride is going to wear her engagement ring with her wedding band, the two should preferably be of the same metal and work well together.

✠ *Narrow or wide?*   As with engagement rings, bands should be chosen with an eye to the shape of the bride's hand. If her hands are small, a narrow band looks best. Larger hands with longer fingers can wear wider and more elaborate rings. Still, for both the bride and the groom, comfort is of the utmost importance. A ring that is too wide or heavy or that gets in the way is not the right one.

✠ *Engravings.*   Wedding bands may be engraved with designs on the outside or they may be plain. The inside is usually engraved with words, initials, or simply the date. The engraved words may be a message that is a sentiment known only to the bride and groom. Before finalizing your purchase, ask the jeweler how many letters may be engraved on the inside of your wedding bands so that you can write out the inscription to be fit inside the ring.

ETIQUETTE FINE POINTS

The Groom's Ring

The bridegroom may or may not choose to wear a wedding ring. If he does, you'll then need to decide whether you want matching rings. If so, his will generally be a little wider and heavier than the bride's wedding ring. In the United States, the man's wedding ring, like the woman's, is traditionally worn on the fourth finger of the left hand.

❧ THE JOY OF COPING ❧

Not only is an engagement a time of joy and community, but planning a wedding can bring people together in the most wonderful ways. This closeness can breed friction, however, and the land mines involved in making deeply emotional decisions can detonate unexpectedly. These are highly charged times indeed, and you'll need to be on your best behavior to make sure that feelings are not hurt, that your family and close friends feel included in the planning, and that niggling old problems and past grudges don't cause wedding-planning gridlock. Most important, you'll want to find ways to take good care of yourself and your fiancé, to maximize your coping skills, and to minimize having to worry about petty matters. Here is some savvy advice on ensuring that your planning process is a smooth one.

Maintain a Solid Front

The two of you are going to have to be a solid front—a team—and, most important, each other's support amid a barrage of wedding advice as you labor over the big decisions. Although the advice is well meant, it can also be confusing and tiresome. As you sift through the advice, your fortitude will have to come from yourselves and each other.

Remember the Three C's

Always keep your focus on the three C's of wedding planning:

- ✤ Consideration
- ✤ Communication
- ✤ Compromise

How you end up handling your wedding plans can foretell how you will handle the other major decisions of your life together. This is the time to develop a way of reaching accord together in the future. But remember that along with the stress that can accompany both the big decisions and the little details, there should be a sense of adventure and fun. You are celebrating one of the most joyous milestones in your lives.

Delegate Duties

Surely others will want to help. And what bride and groom couldn't use some assistance—especially if you don't plan to use a bridal consultant? You may realize how fortunate you are to have friends and family willing to help you out. If yours is an elaborate wedding and you have a hectic personal schedule, consider delegating certain tasks and even major responsibilities to those who have generously offered to take them on. Your wedding day may be the most important time to delegate tasks. It is the time for you to focus on your ceremony and enjoy the reception afterward.

Once you have relinquished a responsibility, don't dwell on it. Don't second-guess yourself or others. Don't micromanage. When you've put someone in charge, let others know. Tell the florist your sister is in charge of flowers so that he or she contacts her and not you. Let the tent supplier know that your future spouse is in charge of tent details—and give his telephone number.

Stay Organized

It doesn't take long for chaos to reign if you don't begin with a system of organization. Whether you use the *Emily Post Wedding Planner,* set up files on your computer, or devote a separate briefcase just to wedding-related papers, you'll find everything is easier to manage when you can find it in a snap. A few tips from the most efficient brides and grooms:

‡ Create a master to-do list, preferably in time sequence.

‡ Carry fabric swatches, photos of gowns, photos of locations, and table measurements at all times.

‡ Design a contact list with the names and numbers of everyone you're working with. Those numbers might include telephone, address, fax, and e-mail.

‡ Carry a calendar with all your appointments highlighted.

‡ Create a folder for all contracts; staple copies of contracts to the appropriate page in your organizer, and don't leave home without

them in case you have to check details from one supplier when working with another.

✢ Keep important papers you will need (birth certificate, divorce papers) in one envelope or folder.

✢ Check off completed to-do's as you accomplish them. You'll feel great as you see the number of check marks grow.

Stay Calm

As you plan your wedding, don't let stress and anxiety send you into an emotional tailspin. It *is* an emotional time; you are going through a rite of passage—even if you've lived together for a few years or are an older couple with grown children. Don't let the details bog you down. When things get tough, keep reminding yourself that it is the marriage, not the wedding, that is important. To help keep things on an even keel:

1. Include, don't exclude. Even if you're doing everything yourselves, keep others—your mothers, children, or friends—in the loop. Don't let them feel left out. Ask their advice every once in a while. Don't ask their advice about things you have already decided on, however. Then you will either have to reject their advice or change your plans and give up something you really want to do.

2. Be forgiving. When things get touchy between you and your family, be the first to apologize. Remember, pride goeth before a fall. In other words, what possible difference does it make to you to apologize first? You see yourself as adding to your family with this wedding. Your family may feel they are giving you up. Give them extra attention.

3. Stop reacting. Take a deep breath. Think about what might be motivating someone to be so difficult. Is he feeling left out of your life? Is she worried about what your relationship will be with her once you're married? If you can't figure it out, take another deep breath.

Take Care Of Yourself

To keep yourselves intact and calm as all around you lose their heads, take care of yourselves:

+ Eat right—you need the energy.

+ Exercise—you need the release.

+ Get enough sleep—you can cope much better when you're rested.

+ Go on dates—the two of you need time alone together.

+ Find beauty in everything—and where you can't, find humor.

❧ PLANNING THE HONEYMOON ❧

Many couples consider making honeymoon plans a top-priority decision, particularly if they plan to marry and vacation during a peak season or travel to a popular honeymoon or travel site. In many instances couples will make their other top-level decisions around their honeymoon plans. At the very least, the newly betrothed should make some preliminary choices regarding the honeymoon date, location, transportation, accommodations, and length of stay.

Honeymoons need to be planned up front not only to ensure a place to stay and transportation reservations, but for budget considerations as well. In the frenzy of planning the wedding and reception, couples often forget to compute into their total expenses the cost of a honeymoon. The expenses of a honeymoon trip are greater than just that of transportation and lodging— the honeymoon budget must include meals, transfers, souvenirs, sight-seeing and sports-related costs, tips, taxes, and the little luxuries, like a massage or poolside charges for lounge chairs and towels. Always ask whether a gratuity is included in the final bill.

CHAPTER THREE

EXPENSES AND
LEGALITIES

Your relationship is

what is important, not the

extravagance of your

celebration.

Whatever the size or style of wedding you plan, the end result will

depend not on how much money you spend, but on how you spend it. A wed-

ding is an important milestone and should be a time of special indulgences.

But that doesn't mean mortgaging the farm to do so. There are many ways to

save without stinting.

These days a large, elaborate wedding can cost tens of thousands of

dollars. In fact, the average wedding in the United States today costs over

$20,000, although there are major regional variations. Excess does not necessarily equal success. A simpler, less elaborate wedding can be equally elegant and memorable. Remember, your relationship is what is important, not the extravagance of your celebration.

The following list of budget categories is intended only to explain the traditional division of expenses and give you a structure for planning. Keep in mind that any of these items may be omitted entirely without making your wedding any less beautiful or meaningful. Use these pages as a guide—and make your own adjustments.

There are many variations not only in ways to save, but also in how costs are divided. Traditionally the bride's family foots the bill for almost every expense, but today they are often helped out to some extent by the groom's family and even by the newlyweds themselves. Forty percent of today's couples pay their own wedding costs, particularly if the wedding is a second one. But traditions are long-standing. It is still not correct for the bride's family to ask the groom's family to pay any of the wedding costs; if, however, his family offers to pay a share, it is quite acceptable for the bride's parents to accept.

❧ WHO PAYS THE WEDDING COSTS? ❧

The answer to the question of who pays the wedding expenses is based on tradition within cultures. In Mexico and some Latin American countries, for example, the bride and groom must find as many as fifteen couples to be their sponsors, called *padrinos* and *madrinas*. These couples are responsible for a variety of the financial components of the wedding. They may pay for the bride's bouquet or for the music at the reception. In fact, there is a *padrino* for almost all wedding categories so that the costs are divided among them. The groom pays for the wedding dress; the sponsors pay for almost everything else. This custom is practiced in the United States by some families of Mexican and Latin American ancestry, particularly in the southwestern states that border Mexico. In Egypt the groom pays a bridal price to the bride and her family, but part of that price is used to pay for the costs of the wedding. Additionally the groom and his family customarily pay for the couple's apartment, appliances, kitchen furniture, lighting, and the bride's dress.

Unless this is your cultural custom, it is not correct to ask others to sponsor your wedding costs. If money is a factor in any culture, the bride and groom must accept budget restrictions with grace and good humor and scale back their plans. If their parents don't offer to make up the difference, they should accept this fact stoically.

Who Pays, Traditionally

Traditionally the bride's family assumes the burden of most wedding costs, a custom most likely translated from the ancient custom of providing a large dowry to attract a good husband. This custom was eventually replaced in Victorian times by the provision of a settlement from the bride's family to the groom's family, along with a substantial trousseau, usually a year's worth of clothing and household items. Traditionally the bride's family has been footing the bill for the majority of the wedding costs not, we presume, for the purpose of attracting a husband, but because that's the way it has been done. Until recently.

Who Pays, Nontraditionally

Today it is not uncommon for both the bride's and the groom's families to share the costs of the celebration or for the bride and the groom to pay for all or part of the expenses themselves. Modern couples are older and generally employed and independent by the time they get married, enabling them not only to plan their own weddings, but to pay for them as well.

When families are willing to share the costs, the bride and groom should consider the range of possibilities ahead of time and be certain that they are in agreement with one another before sitting down with their parents to discuss the budget. If they want financial help, they must be willing to compromise on some of their wishes for the wedding. Any conversation about money should be both dignified and candid.

If age-old tradition is ruling the financial structure of your wedding, the following lists of traditional expense responsibilities should be of assistance:

Traditional Expenses of the Bride and Her Family *	Traditional Expenses of the Groom and His Family *
Services of a bridal consultant	Bride's engagement and wedding rings
Invitations, enclosures, and announcements	Groom's gift to his bride
The bride's wedding gown and accessories	Gifts for the groom's attendants
Floral decorations for ceremony and reception, bridesmaids' flowers, bride's bouquet	Ties and gloves for the groom's attendants, if not part of their clothing rental package
Formal wedding photographs and candid pictures	The bride's bouquet (only in those regions where it is local custom for the groom to pay for it)
Videotape recording of wedding	The bride's going-away corsage
Music for church and reception	Boutonnieres for groom's attendants
Transportation of bridal party to and from the ceremony	Corsages for immediate members of both families (unless bride has included them in her florist's order)
All reception expenses	The officiant's fee or donation
Bride's gifts to her attendants	Transportation and lodging expenses for the minister or rabbi, if from another town and if invited to officiate by the groom's family
Bride's gift to groom	
Groom's wedding ring	
Rental of awning for ceremony entrance and carpet for aisle	The marriage license
Fee for services performed by sexton	Transportation for the groom and best man to the ceremony
Cost of soloists	Expenses of the honeymoon
A traffic officer, if necessary	All costs of the rehearsal dinner
Transportation of bridal party to the reception	Accommodations for groom's attendants
Transportation and lodging expenses for officiant if from another town and if invited to officiate by bride's family	Bachelor dinner, if he wishes to give one
	Transportation and lodging expenses for the groom's family
Accommodations for bride's attendants	
Bridesmaids' luncheon	

* A special note: The above items may be shared or paid for in the best ways for *you*. The lists are guidelines. These days, there are many variables, depending upon your particular circumstances.

Bridesmaids'/Honor Attendant's Expenses	Ushers'/Best Man's Expenses	Out-of-Town Guests' Expenses
Purchase of apparel and all accessories	Rental of wedding attire	Transportation to and from the wedding
Transportation to and from the city where the wedding takes place	Transportation to and from the city where the wedding takes place	Lodging expenses
A contribution to a gift from all the bridesmaids to the bride	A contribution to a gift from all the groom's attendants to the groom	Wedding gift
An individual gift to the couple (if being in the wedding is not the gift)	An individual gift to the couple (if being in the wedding is not the gift)	
Optionally, a shower or luncheon for the bride	A bachelor dinner, if given by the groom's attendants	

❧ DETERMINING A BUDGET ❧

A carefully prepared budget can spare you the nightmare of falling prey to impractical plans or running up unnecessary debts. Whether you plan an elaborate wedding with three hundred guests or a simple ceremony with thirty friends in your own home, a realistic budget will help make your preparations more stress-free. If money becomes a source of tension, simply cut the guest list and adjust your plans accordingly.

Simply put: Base your budget on what you or your parents can afford. A budget for a large wedding should include allotments for each of the expenses listed here. The budget for a simple wedding should include the items that you cannot provide yourself and intend to purchase, as well as the things you plan to do on your own or with the help of friends and family.

With imagination and good planning, a beautiful wedding can be held within any limits. Whatever you plan, stick to your budget or the worry and insecurity will carry over to your relationship and you will start your marriage in a state of anxiety and stress.

✣ *Start with a figure.*   Begin with a dollar amount of what you believe you can spend on your wedding. Do this before you sign a single contract or make a firm commitment with any vendor. If you have $5,000 to spend on your wedding and the reception site you are hoping for will cost $3,500, you are probably not leaving enough money to cover other costs—accommodations for your attendants, fees, a band or DJ, wedding attire, and so on—unless some of those items will be paid for by someone else or given as a wedding gift. If this is the case, adjust your sights and find a reception location that is not as costly. Choose a public garden or a friend's beautiful backyard. Have a morning wedding followed by a brunch or an afternoon cocktail reception instead of a seated dinner. The variations are endless. With creativity and imagination and a willingness to be flexible, your wedding plans can fit your budget and result in a wonderful day.

✣ *Work around your absolute fixed costs.*   The best way to plan is to begin with your absolute fixed costs, such as the minister's or rabbi's fees, gifts for your attendants, postage, and wedding rings. Subtract that total from your available funds and see what amount you have left to work with. This will give you a guide as to how much is left for variable costs, such as flowers, limousines, a videographer, and the rehearsal dinner and reception. If there are more categories than dollars, set your priorities. Is gourmet food more important than expensive flowers? Adjust again. Costs that are not finite tend to grow with the guest list, so you should start there to make your adjustments.

✣ *Economy versus value.*   When comparison shopping, know the difference between economy and value. Value is really knowing precisely what you want and what you are willing to pay for. In that way you can satisfy your expectations for quality and service. If you find yourself paying for extras you don't want, you're not getting good value. For example, a band that charges for a master of ceremonies when you don't want a master of ceremonies is no value to you, just as a reception package that includes printed napkins and matchbooks has less value if you don't care about these incidentals. You can achieve economy if you plan well and give yourself the time to shop around and compare costs. Know exactly what you want, and seek out great resources.

✛ *Tips on budgeting.*   There are endless ways to save on wedding expenditures without looking as though you are having a bargain basement wedding. Almost every component of your wedding has a wide range of choices and costs. Decide which components you consider important enough to splurge on; then find ways to economize with style and flair the other areas.

The best ways to economize on big-ticket items? Cut your guest list, find a smaller but no less elegant reception site, and choose a time of year, a day of the week, and time of day when prices are not at a premium. For fairly formal weddings, 50 to 60 percent of the costs generally go toward the per-person reception fees. Some caterers suggest making a budget for the reception and then cutting it back by 25 percent to cover any future overruns.

Budget Categories

The following list includes traditional costs associated with a wedding. Some are mandatory, such as marriage license fees, and some are optional, such as limousines and a videographer. Whether an optional category is mandatory to you is your decision. For example, if it is really important to you to arrive at the ceremony in a white stretch limousine, then this will become a fixed cost in your budget. A fixed cost, yes, but adjustable—if you must have a stretch limo, call more than one car service to get the best value.

Don't forget the little costs that fall into each category. These items add up quickly. Things like stockings and lingerie are considered "bride's accessories," not just shoes and jewelry. Be as thorough as you can to get the most realistic picture.

Item	Mandatory	Optional	Cost
Attendants			
Accommodations			
Bridesmaids' luncheon			
Ceremony fees			
Officiant's fee			
Church or synagogue fee			
Organist's fee			
Cantor/vocalist/instrumentalist fee(s)			
Flowers			
Ceremony			
Reception			
Bridal bouquet			
Bridal attendants' flowers			
Corsages			
Boutonnieres			
Gifts			
Bride's gifts for attendants			
Groom's gifts for attendants			
Bride's gift for groom			
Groom's gift for bride			
Honeymoon costs			
Invitations/enclosures			
Announcements			
Calligraphy			
Postage			
Ceremony program			
Legalities			
Marriage license			
Health/physical/blood test fees			

Item	Mandatory	Optional	Cost
Music for reception			
Photography			
Engagement photographs			
Photographer			
Videographer			
Reception			
Location			
Food/beverage expenses (per-person cost)			
Reception favors (per-person cost)			
Wedding cake			
Transportation/parking			
Limousines for bridal party			
Traffic officials at ceremony, reception			
Valet parking			
Travel costs for ceremony officiant, if necessary			
Trips home during planning if you live away			
Wedding attire			
Bridal gown			
Bridal accessories			
Groom's outfit			
Bride's ring			
Groom's ring			
Beauty costs (hair, nails, makeup)			
Wedding consultant fees			
Miscellaneous			
Telephone bills related to planning			
Wardrobe costs for wedding-related events			
Tips (if not included in above costs)			
Taxes (if not included in above costs)			
TOTALS	_____	_____	_____

The Value of a Wedding Consultant

One of the values of using a wedding consultant is that she or he often has access to quality services at the best prices from vendors and suppliers or may also receive frequent-user discounts from suppliers. Your consultant can comparison-shop for quality at the best prices. Be truthful and up front right away on any budget limitations so that the consultant can act capably on your behalf. Make it clear that even if you have a large budget, the sky is not the limit. Part of the consultant's job is to find the best price for whatever service or element you are seeking. But to be effective, the consultant must first know your parameters.

❧ TIPS ON TIPPING ❧

Many wedding professionals, from bridal consultants to photographers, are tipped only for extra-special service. If your florist arrived to decorate the ceremony site only to find a locked door, which caused him or her to wait an extra hour, a tip would be an added thank-you for professionalism, patience, and diligence. While you might set aside an extra 15 percent as an unexpected tip fund, you needn't always anticipate tips for the consultant, club manager or caterer, florist, photographer, or videographer. Often a caterer's gratuities are imbedded in the total costs; many hotels include a service charge for the wait staff. Always ask whether gratuities are included before signing any contract.

You should plan a gratuity budget for the following:

✢ Valet parking

✢ Coat check

✢ Powder room attendants

✢ Delivery truck drivers

✢ Limousine drivers

✢ Wait staff

✢ Bartenders

✢ Table captains

The Best Man Asks:
How Do I Deliver Ceremony Fees?

Q: As the best man, it's my responsibility to deliver the ceremony fees. What is the proper way to make these payments?

A: Fees for the officiant, the organist, the soloist, and use of a church or other house of worship are not tips but should be delivered as you would tips. Each fee is sealed in an envelope, addressed to the person, and given with your thanks—and the thanks of the groom—included.

In addition:

✤ You should tip parking lot, coat check, and powder room attendants ahead of time so that your guests have no obligation to do so. Ask a friend to make sure that there are no tip dishes or baskets sitting on the coat check counter or the powder room shelf that would make guests feel obligated to tip. A general guideline is to tip attendants a flat fee or $.50 to $1 per guest.

✤ In the case of limousine drivers and the catering staff, you can request that gratuities be included in the total bill. (Make sure there are no tip receptacles on the bar, making a guest wonder if he or she should leave a tip.) Sometimes a reception site requests that all tips be paid in cash in advance. Check your contract and take care of this detail beforehand so that no one has to settle a bill during or after the event. If gratuities are to be given after the wedding or are not included in the final bill, they still should be counted out and put in sealed envelopes beforehand so that they can be distributed easily at the end of the reception.

✤ When a tip is spontaneous and is given to a vendor who has done an extraordinary service, it can be given at the end of the reception or the next day, with a note of thanks included.

You should expect to sign a contract with every supplier, from the stationer to the florist to the limousine service to the wedding consultant. *Every single* detail should be covered in writing in the contract, including taxes, gratuities, dates, delivery schedules, payment plans, cancellation fees, and refund policies. Take the time to read everything thoroughly; if you don't understand something, ask questions until you do. Never sign a contract under pressure. If you're still unclear about some aspect of the contract, take a copy of it to a friend who has experience in contractual agreements. Be sure you are clear on how and when bills are to be paid. And make sure there are clauses in the contract that ensure proper restitution, in the event of a snafu that is clearly the vendor's responsibility. Also, keep the following in mind:

Check for Hidden Costs

Even deciphering the fine print on a contract can leave you with unanswered questions. Know exactly what you need up front so that you can ferret out hidden, unanticipated costs. You are entitled to know exactly what is included—and what is not—before agreeing to the service. If the service provider or contractor is unwilling to give you a detailed listing or breakdown of costs, consider looking elsewhere. For example, make sure that alterations to your gown are included in the service and price in the contract with a bridal salon. If they are not, ask what the general costs are. Does the salon charge extra to press your gown after alterations? Would it be less expensive for you to take the gown to a reputable and experienced dry cleaner for pressing?

Don't forget taxes and gratuities, which can add a significant amount to the total bill—especially in states that have a high sales tax. It's a good idea to make sure that taxes and tips are included in the total price. And inquire about such hidden costs as "plate charges."

❧ MARRIAGE LEGALITIES ❧

Along with the romance, fun, and excitement of a wedding come the absolutes—the legally required paperwork and to-do's without which a marriage cannot take place. In order to be married in the eyes of the law, a couple must live up to the letter of the law—and the law can vary, not just from country to country, but from state to state and even city to city. For example, you might find that Michigan requires a blood test, counseling, and witnesses for a marriage to take place (or a sixty-day waiting period for couples who ignore the counseling requirement), none of which Ohio requires. You certainly don't need to go so far as to hire an attorney to get married, but it is a good idea to check, in advance, what is required—whether you are getting married in your hometown or on an exotic island on another continent.

Where do you start? Write or call the county clerk's office or the office of the registrar in the town or county in which you are to be married. They may simply mail or fax you a list of legal requirements for acquiring a marriage license. Some states require that you register in the same state and even county where the ceremony will be performed, and some ask that you do so in person. The most important point is to start your research well in advance of the ceremony so that come your wedding day all will be legal and aboveboard.

❧ THE WHO, WHAT, WHEN, ❧ AND WHERE OF GETTING MARRIED

Legal Factors

AGE

Age is a factor in who is permitted to marry. In fact, in most states the age one may be married is much younger than the age one may legally drive, drink, vote, or apply for a credit card. A word of caution: While the following age restrictions hold true in most states, they do not hold true in all. For example, the minimum age for marriage in the state of Virginia is sixteen unless special circumstances prevail, such when a bride-to-be is underage and pregnant.

The age restrictions are, in general:

✢ If either applicant is under fourteen years of age, a marriage license cannot be issued.

✢ If either applicant is fourteen or fifteen years of age, he or she must present the written approval and consent of a justice of the state supreme court or a judge of the family court having jurisdiction over the town or city in which the application is made.

✢ If either applicant is sixteen or seventeen years of age, he or she must present the written consent of both of his or her parents.

✢ If both applicants are eighteen years of age or older, no parental or legal consent is required.

If the consent of both parents is required, there are some qualifiers. One parent alone may consent if the other parent has been missing for one year; if the parents are divorced and the consenting parent has sole custody; if the other parent has been judged incompetent; or, naturally, if the other parent is deceased.

Parents or guardians who consent to the marriage of a minor must personally appear and sign the required documentation in the presence of the town or city clerk or other authorized official. It is best to do this in the town or city where the application is made—if a notarized affidavit originated elsewhere, it must be accompanied by a certificate of authentication when it is filed in that state.

No one may legally take your word for it that you are indeed the age you say you are. In most states you may be required to submit documentary proof of age. Generally one or more of the following documents showing proof of age is required and acceptable:

✢ Birth certificate

✢ Baptismal record

✢ Passport

- Driver's license

- Life insurance policy

- Employment certificate

- School record

- Immigration record

- Naturalization record

- Court record

FAMILIAL RESTRICTIONS

A marriage may not take place in the United States between those of the following relationship, regardless of whether they are legitimate or illegitimate offspring:

- An ancestor and descendant (parent, grandparent, great-grandparent, child, grandchild, great-grandchild)

- Brother and sister (full or half-blood)

- Uncle and niece

- Aunt and nephew

In most but not all states, marriage between family members closer than first cousins is prohibited. If this is an issue, it is important to check with the town or city clerk or the marriage license bureau in the town where the marriage will take place.

CAPACITY TO CONSENT

It is the law that marriage requires two consenting people. If either person cannot or does not understand what it means to be married because of mental illness, drugs, alcohol, or other factors affecting judgment, then that person does not have the capacity to consent and the marriage is not valid. If fraud or coercion is involved, the marriage also may be invalidated.

GENDER

Generally couples must be of the opposite sex to form a valid marriage (see "A Question for Peggy: The Legality of Domestic Partnership," page 60).

REMARRIAGE

Applicants for a marriage license who were married before must provide information regarding previous marriages, including a copy of the decree of divorce or a certificate of dissolution of marriage or a death certificate. Clerks and other marriage licensing officials say the biggest problem that occurs for those who have been married before is that they neglect to bring the orginal document or a certified copy. The information the applicant needs to provide includes, but may not be restricted to, the following.

+ Month, day, and year of final divorce decree

+ County and state where divorce was granted

+ Grounds for divorce

+ Whether former spouse or spouses are living

Similar documentation may be required in the case of an annulment and that of a widow or widower. The preciseness of the legalities makes it necessary to check and double-check, because even one missing document can delay the wedding; this can be a disaster for the bride and groom who have contracted the services of countless others and then have to postpone their wedding.

The Marriage License

A marriage license authorizes you to get married; a marriage certificate is the document that proves you are married and is issued by the county office where you were married, usually within a few weeks after the ceremony. In general a marriage license may be used only in the place it is obtained, and then within a certain period of time, usually between twenty-four hours and sixty days, depending on the state; otherwise the license expires. Some states require a three-day waiting period from the time applicants apply for a license to the time the license is issued. Those states with the strictest requirements strongly advise the bride and groom to obtain their marriage license two to three weeks before their wedding day.

Health Certificates

The purpose of premarital health requirements and examinations is not to keep a person with an illness from marrying, but to ensure that the future spouse knows of the condition. Some states have no requirements for premarital examinations or blood tests in order to obtain a marriage license. In other states the law says you need to be examined and found free of communicable syphilis. In these states a marriage license is denied anyone found to have communicable syphilis until he or she has undergone sufficient treatment and ruled noninfectious. Even in states where no blood test or physical exam is required, failing to tell your prospective spouse that you have a venereal disease or a physical impairment (such as impotence or infertility) before you marry may invalidate the marriage.

The best advice? Find out the requirements in your state by calling or writing the county clerk's office or the office of the registrar as soon as you decide to marry. States that require health certificates often add further restrictions of time, so factor those restrictions into your planning along with the dates for which you can obtain confirmations for ceremony and reception sites.

In some states a counseling class is required before a medical certificate can be issued. In such classes or during required counseling, the physician involved must offer the woman a voluntary test for susceptibility to rubella (German measles); and the physician also discusses HIV/AIDS virus educational material with both the prospective bride and groom. Again, look into your state's requirements well in advance—classes can fill up quickly.

Who Can Perform a Marriage Ceremony?

Q: We're considering being married on a cruise ship and want to know whether or not a ship captain can perform the ceremony—and if not, who can?

A: Contrary to popular belief, ship captains often will not perform or are not universally authorized to perform marriage ceremonies. Increasingly, however, cruise lines are working out ways for legally recognized marriages to be performed aboardship by ship captains. A list of persons specified by law as authorized to perform a marriage ceremony is available in each state's domestic relations law. The following is a list of those who *can* perform a marriage ceremony:

Religious Ceremonies

- A member of the clergy (for example, a priest, rabbi, minister, or iman) who has been officially ordained and granted authority to perform marriage ceremonies from a governing church body in accordance with the rules and regulations of the church body
- A member of the clergy or minister who is not authorized by a governing church body but who has been chosen by a spiritual group to preside over their spiritual affairs
- A tribal chief (for Native American weddings)

Nonreligious Ceremonies
(also called civil ceremonies)

- The mayor of a city or village
- The city clerk or one of the deputy city clerks of a city of over 1 million inhabitants
- A marriage officer appointed by the town or village board or the city common council
- A justice or judge in most courts
- A village, town, or county justice
- A court clerk who has legal authority to perform marriages
- A person given temporary authority by a judge or court clerk to conduct a marriage ceremony

Religious Factors

Mastering government legalities is just one step toward ensuring the legality of your marriage. Some religions also have rules and regulations that must be adhered to—points that are best checked, immediately, with the priest, rabbi, or minister who will officiate.

In some religions, for example, "banns" must be published over a three-week period. A bann is a public statement of intent to marry that asks anyone who may object to do so. If, at the end of twenty-one days, no one has objected, the couple may marry. In other religions a set number of premarital counseling sessions must be attended before the clergyperson will marry the couple. In still other religions, if one or both members of the couple have been divorced, the divorce is not recognized and they may not be married in the church. Then there is the matter of membership. For a wedding to take place at a Quaker meetinghouse, for example, at least one-half of the couple should be a Quaker. Otherwise written support for the marriage must be obtained from two adult members of the Society.

The bottom line: Even if you are a lifelong Roman Catholic, Lutheran, or Presbyterian or a convert to Judaism or the Hindu faith who has seriously studied the tenets of the religion, inquire in advance whether the institution has any special requirements. If it is important to you to be married by a priest, rabbi, or minister or in a church, temple, or synagogue, you will need to know the requirements to make that happen.

Odds and Ends

✢ *Marriage by an American to a foreign national:* requires its own set of documents and qualifications, including certified English translation of any required documentation. You can get information on obtaining a visa for a foreign spouse from any office of the Immigration and Naturalization Service, U.S. embassies and consulates abroad, or the U.S. Department of State Visa Office.

✢ *If you are using an officiant from out of state:* know that some states require that he or she have a certificate of authorization from the state in which the wedding will take place.

The Legality of Domestic Partnership

Q: I am a lesbian, and my partner and I have been in a long-term relationship. We would like to legalize our relationship. What are our options?

A: Generally couples must be of the opposite sex to form a valid marriage. Religions have their own gender regulations, but there is a growing trend among clergy to bless same-sex unions. Most states do not allow same-sex marriages, but in Hawaii and Alaska arguments are being made in the courts that a marriage license cannot be denied based on the sex of the applicants. Vermont has passed a Civil Unions Bill giving legal status to the union of same-sex couples, assuring they receive the same benefits as those received by married couples. On the other hand, some states, including Georgia, South Dakota, Texas, and Utah, have passed laws designed to thwart same-sex marriages. Indeed, in 1996 the Defense of Marriage Act was signed into law, barring the federal government from recognizing same-sex marriages and permitting states to ignore same-sex marriages performed in other states.

Even though most states do not recognize same-sex marriages, many agencies and companies are adopting "domestic partnership" policies that accept same-sex relationships. Policies range from fair housing regulations to the granting of traditional marital benefits, such as insurance coverage, family leave, and bereavement leave.

✛ *Witnesses are required by some states:* in addition to an authorized member of the clergy or public official, to be present during the wedding ceremony. In some of these states there is no minimum age for a witness, but it is suggested that he or she be deemed competent enough to testify in a court proceeding regarding what was witnessed. In other states no witness is required other than the officiant.

ETIQUETTE FINE POINTS

Often the best man and maid of honor serve as witnesses to the marriage. They should sign the license or certificate just after the ceremony or during the reception.

❧ PREMARITAL COUNSELING ❧

Premarital counseling, whether mandated or merely recommended, is a short-term way to work through important issues ahead of time to avoid conflict over the long haul. The purpose is to raise issues that might not have been considered, to discuss potential sensitive areas, and to give words to some of the things a couple may be thinking but may not know how to express. (Note: When premarital counseling is completed, it's thoughtful of the bride and groom to write a thank-you note or a letter to their minister, priest, or rabbi to express their appreciation for the guidance they received.) Premarital counseling can help couples in the following ways:

✤ *By raising important issues.* Most couples feel that by the time they are engaged, they know pretty much everything there is to know about one another. It is very likely, however, they have not really talked through a range of issues, including their own physical and emotional needs, their respective goals and desires, and their thoughts on problem solving and compromise.

✤ *Discovering priorities.* It's a good time as well to compare notes on children, work and home priorities, coping skills in the event of sickness or a crisis, money matters, and spiritual beliefs. People of different religious backgrounds often find clergy counseling extremely helpful, especially if they are planning to have children and raise them in a religious household.

✤ *How to resolve family matters.* This is also a good time to discuss with your future mate how family matters may best be resolved. A bride or groom might be entering into a marriage with children from a previous marriage or face parental disapproval or a divided family.

✤ *Learning to share decision making.* Both members of the couple may have been on their own for a long time and aren't used to shared decision making. Counseling can help to remind them to keep an open mind when making decisions together.

The Legalities of Marrying in Another Country

Many brides and grooms dream of being married outside the United States in a romantic spot like Tahiti or Paris or St. Thomas. But before you call that little French bakery for the perfect wedding cake or put down a deposit on a Caribbean island resort, you must first check the wedding legalities of the country you wish to be married in. Each country has a different set of requirements. Some ask for residency requirements of a certain duration. Others require a specific number of witnesses. And if you're marrying in another country, don't forget to check on your legal and religious requirements at home as well. Check your passport, medical requirements, and the documentation you need to bring back home to ensure your marriage's validity in the United States.

Plenty of resources are available to help you. One surefire way to get answers is to *telephone the country's consulate or tourist office located in the United States.* The office will provide specific instructions over the phone, by mail, or by fax. In some countries, such as Mexico, the requirements vary slightly from town to town, so once you've gotten the basic information from the tourist office, you will need to call the registrar's office in the town in which you are getting married. And get all information in writing so you have all the facts.

Wedding consultants who specialize in destination weddings and *travel agents who do wedding planning* can also provide information on the documentation required and any restrictions.

❧ NAME CHANGES ❧

First off, there is no law, rule, religious dictate, or mandate that says the bride must take the groom's last name. A bride may take her husband's last name, retain her own surname, or hyphenate both her own surname and her husband's surname. When Linda Graham marries Mark Richards, she may be Linda Richards, Linda Graham, or Linda Graham-Richards. In spite of the range of acceptable choices, 90 percent of today's U.S. brides make the traditional choice of adopting their husband's names.

A bride who wishes to take her husband's last name may retain her given middle name or, more commonly, use her own surname as a middle name. Linda Beth Graham may become Linda Graham Richards, or Linda Beth Richards. The only law governing the name chosen by the bride (or by the groom, who has the option of changing his name as well) is that the name be used consistently and without intent to defraud. Any name change occurs simply by entering the new name in the appropriate space provided on the marriage license, as long as the new name consists of one of the following options:

✦ The surname of the bride (or the groom)

✦ Any former surname he or she has had

✦ A name combining into a single surname all or a segment of the premarriage surname or any former surname of each spouse

✦ A combination name separated by a hyphen, provided that each part of such combination surname is the premarriage surname, or any former surname, of each of the spouses

Why Change Your Name?

The matter of changing names is traditionally more of a consideration for the bride than it is for the groom, for it is still rare for a man to change his name upon marriage. If a woman is being married for a second time, she probably has already changed her name once. She may have kept her exhusband's surname, or she may have reverted to her maiden name. Another marriage can bring about more change. If the bride has kept her married name from her first marriage, it is likely that she will take her new husband's surname—if for no other reason than to avoid confusion for all concerned, but also out of consideration and love for her new husband (who will undoubtedly be pleased that she will be known by his name and not by another man's name).

Professional versus social.   One way to deal with a name change professionally is for the bride to continue to use the name she has been using in work or professional situations. Therefore she is known as Ms. Jane Johnson at work, while socially she is Mrs. Franklin Pierce, or Jane Johnson Pierce, if she retains her maiden name as her middle name.

Children and names.   If the bride has children from a previous marriage, their last name will very likely be that of their father, while their mother may be using her maiden name or taking the name of her new husband. How this is sorted out is up to each bride and groom, but it is important to let relevant persons and organizations know who is who. You may want to type up a note stating the proper names, phone numbers, and addresses of how you are to be notified in case of any calls or correspondence. Give copies to your child's school, pediatrician, and dentist and to any religious and sports groups.

Name Change: Official Notifications

When a bride changes her name, she must notify a vast number of people, companies, agencies, and organizations. Use your wedding organizer to list them. Some organizations require proof of the name change and will require a copy of the marriage certificate, which is issued after the marriage. When an address change is occurring as well, it is a good idea to make both changes at the same time. Those to notify include the following:

- Social Security Administration
- Motor vehicles department
- Passport agency
- Employer payroll department
- Banks
- Credit unions
- Mortgage company
- Voter registration
- Financial planner (or investment firms/stockbroker)
- Credit card companies
- Religious organizations
- Magazine subscriptions
- School alumni organizations

+ Credit accounts (local stores)

+ Frequent travel clubs

+ Doctors and dentists

Name Change: Advising Others on Nontraditional Choices

Confusion often prevails when the bride decides to retain her maiden name or use some hyphenated form of both her and her husband's name. If you decide to go the nontraditional route, you will need to graciously advise those who assume you will be taking your husband's name as your own. If you need to correct someone, do so kindly. Be patient: realize that the older generation may not understand your reasoning for making a nontraditional choice. Some commonsense ways to do so: on stationery or in the return address on thank-you-note envelopes, in newspaper wedding announcements, or on "at home" cards enclosed in wedding announcements.

Name Change: Changing Your Mind

If, at the time of the marriage, a bride (or groom) does not change her name and later changes her mind, she can file a petition for change of name with the court. However, the marriage license and certificate cannot be changed to record the surname she decides to use after she is already married and registered with a different name.

PRE- AND POSTNUPTIAL AGREEMENTS

The matter of formalizing financial and legal matters through a prenuptial contract or premarital agreement is a sensitive one for brides and grooms,

The Groom Asks: How Do I Bring Up a Prenuptial Agreement?

Q: I am getting ready to be married to a great woman. The only problem is, I have two kids of my own, and I want to make sure that they are taken care of in the event that something happens to me. How can I tactfully broach the subject of a prenuptial agreement with my fiancée?

A: As you've no doubt realized, it is often as difficult for the person requesting a premarital agreement to broach the subject as it is for the one being asked to sign it. A prenuptial contract is simply presented as a way of protecting assets you bring into the marriage in the (unlikely) event of divorce or death. A couple who communicates well has a head start in discussing a prenuptial contract. As the person requesting the prenup, your first step is to talk to your attorney to find out how the agreement would work in your case. Once you are clear on the specifics, explain to your fiancée how you feel and why you feel you want a prenup. In a loving, honest, and tactful way, tell her that it's your problem and is based upon what you have gone through before.

Discussing a prenup requires sensitivity, as it can seem that such an agreement reduces a relationship to dollars and cents or that it predetermines that a marriage is going to fail. Be clear with your fiancée that you aren't expecting your marriage to be a problem, but that because of the stress of the previous divorce, you feel you must protect yourself just in case she might decide a divorce is necessary. You might suggest that she have a similar agreement drawn up because you would want her to feel that her personal assets are protected, too. Then assure her that you want both of you to continue with focusing on building your life together while putting the agreements behind you.

many of whom consider doing so a crass form of hedging bets on the longevity of the marriage. It is certainly an issue that needs to be discussed early in the relationship—and not something you spring on your partner-to-be right before the ceremony. Otherwise serious doubts, hurt feelings, and even strong anger can result.

✣ *What is a premarital agreement?* Basically a premarital agreement is a contract between two people that defines the rights and benefits that will exist during the marriage and after, in the event of divorce. It can expand or limit a person's right to property, life insurance benefits, or support payments in the event of death or divorce. Usually it addresses the rights to property that each brings to the marriage, retirement plan assets, and how money accumulated before the marriage will be distributed in the event of death or divorce. Without a premarital agreement state laws define the rights and benefits of marriage. If the couple does not want to rely on state laws to determine their legal and fiscal fate, the premarital agreement allows them to make their own rules.

✢ *When is a prenuptial agreement used?*   Although anyone can have a premarital agreement, it is most often used when the bride or the groom or both bring assets to the marriage that they want to protect in the event of divorce or death. This is particularly true for people marrying for the second or third time who want to make sure that certain assets are passed on to their children from a previous marriage.

✢ *What is not covered in a prenup?*   What a prenuptial contract does not cover is child custody and support. The courts will disregard the contract on this point and make a decision that is considered in the best interest of the child. The courts will also disregard a premarital agreement that, in essence, leaves one person destitute.

✢ *What is a postnuptial contract?*   A postnuptial contract is one made after a couple is married and can include the same categories of consideration, usually having to do with property and money, in a prenuptial contract. This contract is usually drawn if the couple realizes that children from a previous marriage or other family members would be unprotected in the case of divorce or death.

✢ *What is meant by disclosure?*   Because one person is usually giving something up by agreeing to a prenuptial contract, both the bride and the groom must fully disclose their finances to one another in advance. Most states require that the premarital agreement include separate asset listings that describe and show the values of each person's assets. If the couple doesn't do this, each is preventing the other from knowing what he or she is losing by signing the contract—and this may constitute fraud, which makes the agreement unenforceable. Because of this, and to ensure that the agreement is written correctly and legally, it is a good idea for the bride and the groom to seek the advice of each one's respective lawyers before entering into the agreement.

✢ *What is the form of the agreement?* A prenuptial contract or premarital agreement must be in writing to be legally binding. It provides evidence of the terms of the agreement and demonstrates that both people understand and agree to the terms. It is generally legally binding as long as it is entered into voluntarily and without fraud and as long as it is reasonable and fair. It is not binding if a person is unfairly induced to sign the agreement or is coerced under excessive emotional pressure.

❧ WILLS AND FINANCES ❧

When there is no pre- or postnuptial contract, the bride and groom would be smart to put their wills and finances in order so that the disposition of their money and property is clear to each other or, should both die, to their families.

✢ *Changing beneficiaries.* Finances include such things as insurance policies and beneficiaries on retirement plan payouts. Assuming the bride and groom want to make each other the beneficiary on any existing policies they own, the couple should call an insurance broker and talk to their payroll coordinator at work to see what documentation is required to make this change.

✢ *Decisions about bank accounts.* How the couple will manage their finances is totally personal, but they should discuss their thoughts. They may decide to maintain a separate account and open a new joint account or pool their finances into a joint account. If the bride is maintaining a separate account but changing her name, she needs to take care of this paperwork when she changes other legal documents. If she is changing her name and has direct electronic deposit into her account, she needs to coordinate the account change at the same time that she changes her name at work.

Weddings have taken place for centuries without wedding insurance, but no chapter on the legalities of getting married would be complete without including it as a topic of consideration for the bride and groom. In many instances the cost of a wedding is so astronomical that the additional cost of insurance is worth every penny if it protects such a large investment.

✣ *Why buy wedding insurance?* Wedding insurance, offered exclusively by the Fireman's Fund insurance company, may be taken out by a bride and groom to cover wedding catastrophes that are beyond anyone's control. Wedding insurance can also cover any retaking of photographs, wedding attire or wedding gift replacements, and public liability.

✣ *When is it beneficial?* Wedding insurance is beneficial in certain situations: when, for example, a reception site suddenly cannot accommodate the party for reasons including fire, damage, a murder or suicide occurring at the site, or an outbreak of a contagious disease requiring a health department quarantine. Insurance will cover the cost of rebooking elsewhere.

If wedding insurance is a possibility, it is wise to consider every contingency when assessing the value and extent of the insurance you want. For example, if the reception site is suddenly not available and the wedding must be cancelled because no other site is available on such short notice, other costs may be lost, such as formal-wear rental, car hire, hotel charges for the wedding party, and flower arrangements.

CHAPTER FOUR

Wedding attendants

ATTENDANTS

are chosen as witnesses

to a couple's matrimonial

union.

Most couples these days choose to have attendants in their wedding. The nuptial celebration is one of shared happiness and joy, and including friends and loved ones in this happy milestone is one of society's most cherished customs. Wedding attendants, whether bridesmaids or ushers, are chosen as witnesses to a couple's matrimonial union in a gesture of love, friendship, and support.

There are no set rules decreeing the size and shape of your wedding party. There is no magic number of attendants allowed, no standard ratio of ushers to bridesmaids or men to women. You may have two honor attendants for the bride or the groom; or you may opt for a male attendant for the bride or a female usher, if you wish. You may choose to have no attendants at all—although you will need witnesses.

While rules don't dictate the selection and number of attendants, there are the following practicalities to consider.

✣ *Size and formality.* How big and how formal your wedding will be is likely to be the main determiners of the size of your wedding party. If you plan a small, intimate gathering, you won't want attendants outnumbering the guests. If the ceremony site itself is small, you may have room for only one or two attendants. If you're pulling out all the stops and planning a large, extravagant celebration, you may want to match it with an equally large wedding party.

✣ *Budget.* The more attendants you have, the more of a burden it puts on your expenses. The bride and groom are responsible for all bouquets, boutonnieres, and wedding party gifts. They are expected to pay for their attendants' accommodations. The more attendants you have, the larger your reception guest list, because you are responsible for feeding and entertaining not only your attendants, but your attendants' partners as well.

✣ *Religious restrictions.* Some religions have strict rules regarding official witnesses. Your honor attendants, at least, may be required to be members of your faith or may even have to attend preceremony instruction classes before they can participate. It is often a good idea to check with your officiant before asking anyone to be in your wedding.

ETIQUETTE FINE POINTS

Average Number of Attendants

The number of attendants in the average formal or semiformal wedding party includes four to six bridesmaids and at least that many ushers. The number of ushers is usually determined by the "one usher for fifty guests" guideline—a good gauge for seating guests expediently.

THE ETIQUETTE OF CHOOSING
YOUR ATTENDANTS

Sometimes choosing attendants is easy. When, however, the number of close relatives and good friends is large, it can get difficult. The possibility of inadvertently hurting someone's feelings always exists. Following are some general guidelines to use when choosing your attendants.

✢ *What are the most important considerations in selecting attendants?* Consider first the people *to whom you are closest.* Bridesmaids and ushers are traditionally chosen from among the bride's and groom's families and close friends. It is in the spirit of family unity to ask the bride's brothers to be ushers or the groom's sisters to be bridesmaids, but it is not mandatory—and sometimes it is possible only when the wedding party is large. Things get tricky when two best friends are involved and a bride chooses one over the other to be her maid of honor or the groom chooses one brother over the other to be his best man. Fortunately the times and etiquette guidelines have changed. When a decision is impossible to make, an acceptable solution is for the bride to have two maids or matrons of honor or the groom two best men. While only one attendant for the bride and one for the groom need serve as official witnesses when papers are signed, the other duties can be shared. Another solution? Some brides and grooms flip a coin to help select who one will be the maid of honor or best man.

✢ *Must there be the same number of bridesmaids and ushers?* Another change in tradition is that the bride's and groom's attendants no longer need to be evenly paired. This is always a relief to any bride and groom who have been struggling to equalize their numbers to create matched sets. You may have more bridesmaids than ushers in your wedding party or vice versa. It is all about making decisions while avoiding *hurt feelings.*

✢ *What are the* financial obligations *incurred by attendants on your behalf?* Expenses can add up, from travel expenses to clothing bills to possi-

Making Difficult Choices

Q: I have several close friends and family members, but we have decided on a small wedding and can select only a few attendants. That means we're leaving someone out. How do you suggest we tactfully explain our choices to these dear friends?

A: It is perfectly fine to be direct in explaining to relatives or friends why you have chosen others to be in your wedding party. Choosing siblings or even parents over friends needs no explanation; a choice among friends might. You may have known the person you chose longer than the other friend, for example; say so. Be forthcoming, but convey anything you say in a kind and loving manner. Explain your desire for a smaller wedding. You can even flip a coin with friends and family in attendance to give everyone a fair shake!

ble participation in parties and showers. Attendants coming from far away are expected to pay their own transportation costs. For those friends and family who would find it a serious financial strain to serve as attendants, you might thoughtfully ask them instead to participate in a different, less expensive way (see "Honor Roles," page 86). This is especially true if you are being married for the second time or are having a large second wedding. Friends who served you at your first wedding may be unable to spare the costs required to serve as attendants once more. Still, if cost is a factor for a good friend you can't imagine being married without, you can certainly offer to pay his or her bills. No one but you and your friend has to know of this special arrangement.

✢ *When is the right time to invite attendants to be in your wedding?* Attendants are invited to be in a wedding soon after the engagement is announced and when the couple has some idea as to the type and size of their celebration. It is considerate to have some basic plans in order, such as the wedding date and location, before you extend your invitation. You may ask in person, by telephone, or by letter. Let your potential attendants in on all the plans so far: the dates and times of the ceremony, reception, and rehearsal; your overall ideas for the degree of formality; and any known prewedding events that would involve them. Don't press for an immediate answer, but give those you invite a few days to review their calendars and their bank accounts. If the answer is no, graciously hasten to say that you are disappointed but understand, and you hope that they will be able to attend the wedding anyway.

✢ *What if you have a limited number of attendant spots to fill?* When you have a limited number of possible attendants and a large contin-

The Bridesmaid Asks: Does Appearance Count?

Q: *I have been asked by my good friend to be one of her bridesmaids. Admittedly I am overweight, but my mother thinks that unless I decide to lose some weight, I should decline.*

A: It goes without saying that friends' looks are not the criterion for their selection for the wedding party. A good friend's large size should play no part in any decision to ask her to be an attendant. The same is true if a friend is pregnant, disabled, short, tall, or not a physical match with the rest of the wedding party. Unless you personally feel uncomfortable taking on the role, you may accept with love and happiness. Your friend has extended a warm welcome to you to be part of her celebration; that should do nothing but make you feel comfortable, confident, and honored to be sharing her special day.

For brides who have friends or relatives who decline because they aren't comfortable in the role of attendant, be sensitive and understanding. As long as they know that being overweight or pregnant or whatever doesn't make a difference to you, you must respect their decision to decline. If they think that accepting will make them feel miserable, let them be.

gent of close friends and family, don't panic. There are other honors you can bestow, such as reading a passage at the ceremony, serving as guestbook attendant, or working with the photographer to organize candid pictures and formal portraits.

✤ *What are the obligations of asking attendants to participate in a destination wedding?* If you are planning a destination wedding, whether to Disney World or a Caribbean island, it is especially important that you make that clear to possible attendants in your initial invitation. You could say, for example, "We're getting married in Bermuda! If you can get yourself there, we'll pick up the tab of your accommodations, as we've rented several villas where everyone will stay. We hope you can come on Wednesday and stay until Sunday, so you can have a little vacation at the same time." While the bride and groom are financially responsible for the wedding party accommodations—and some will foot the bill for travel costs as well—the other costs fall to the attendants themselves. That's why they need to know the basic costs ahead of time before they can make a decision.

DISPATCHES AND UPDATES

Once you have affirmative answers from all your attendants, you should keep them informed of your ongoing plans. Details can be shared by telephone, letter, or e-mail. Keeping your attendants informed helps everyone stay organized and allows them to become more familiar with the rest of the wedding party—an especially nice touch if they've never met. The information could include the following:

+ List of names, addresses, and phone numbers of the wedding party

+ Dates and times of parties and showers they will be invited to (they are not obligated to come, but it is nice for them to know when the events are occurring)

+ Rehearsal time and place

+ Rehearsal dinner arrangements

+ Where they will stay

+ What their wardrobe needs might be—from wedding attire to clothes for other activities (such as shorts for a picnic)

+ Reminders to bridesmaids and ushers to break in their shoes

+ Any plans for breakfast, lunch, or tea before the wedding

+ Where they will dress

+ The time and place for any prewedding photos

+ Transportation arrangements to the ceremony and reception

A Little Luxury

Treat attendants (and moms and little sisters, too!) to a little luxury a few days before the wedding. Hire a facialist or licensed aesthetician to give everyone an herbal facial and a manicure and pedicure. Or make appointments for all to get massages. Or have a hairdresser on hand to help pin up hair, tuck in flowers, and add finishing touches the morning of the wedding. Turn part of the house into a "women only" retreat for some fun, relaxing time together. If the wedding is to occur later in the day, a light lunch of tea sandwiches and fruit is the perfect accompaniment.

ATTENDANT DUTIES AND RESPONSIBILITIES

While the bridal party is there to help and support the bride and groom during the wedding events, the traditional roles followed by attendants are no longer rigidly followed. It had long been the tradition, for example, that the maid or matron of honor helped the bride dress and change outfits and coordinated bridesmaids' activities. On rare occasions a bride will choose to have both a maid and a matron of honor. Traditionally in this case, the "maid" takes precedence, holding the bouquet and serving as a witness.

Still, whether a bridesmaid or a groomsman, an attendant has certain responsibilities, which are usually determined by the bride and groom. Some of these responsibilities are derived from tradition; others are based on practicalities. Following are descriptions of the traditional and modern duties of wedding party attendants.

Honor Attendants: Duties and Responsibilities

An "honor attendant" is another, more modern term for the matron or maid of honor and the best man. Honor attendants have two primary roles in the wedding. The first responsibility is to be a best friend—to be fully supportive of their respective charges on the day of the wedding, from the moment they wake up to the time the newlyweds leave for their honeymoon. The second responsibility is to make sure bridesmaids and ushers are where they should be and that they are organized and set to do their own jobs.

Today, if the bride chooses a male friend to be her honor attendant, she would obviously alter some of the following duties, such as help with changing clothes. There would nonetheless still be plenty of ways for him to assist her. The bride and he might choose to adapt some of the duties to suit them both. One bride's male honor attendant chose to hand the bride's bouquet to her grandmother seated in the front pew. The grandmother was thrilled to hold the bouquet during the ceremony, and the male attendant felt more comfortable having her perform the duty. *Adaptations and personal touches are fine, as long as they are applied thoughtfully.*

Similarly, the best man traditionally serves as the groom's right hand, helping him dress. A female "best" or honor attendant for the groom, or groom's honor attendant, would not perform these duties.

Honor attendants may fulfill any or all of the following:

THE BRIDE'S MAID OR MATRON OF HONOR: DUTIES CHECKLIST

✢ Helps the bride select bridesmaids' attire

✢ Helps address invitations and place cards

✢ Attends as many prenuptial events as possible

✢ Organizes bridesmaids' gift to the bride; usually gives individual gift to the couple

✢ Makes sure that all the bridesmaids, the flower girl, and ring bearer are at fittings, the rehearsal, and the ceremony on time

✢ Is expected to attend the rehearsal and is included at the rehearsal dinner

✢ Walks in processional and recessional

✢ Holds the groom's wedding ring

✢ Helps with the bride's gown

✝ Arranges the bride's veil and train before the processional and recessional

✝ Makes sure the bride's gown is "picture perfect" throughout the day

✝ Holds the bride's bouquet during the ceremony

✝ Witnesses the signing of the marriage certificate

✝ Stands in the receiving line

✝ Keeps the bride on schedule

✝ Helps the bride change into her going-away clothes

✝ Takes care of the bride's gown and accessories after the reception

✝ Pays for own wedding attire and transportation to wedding

The Groom's Best Man: Duties Checklist

✝ Organizes a prewedding party for the groom, if there is one

✝ Coordinates the ushers' gift to the groom; usually gives individual gift to the couple

✝ Is expected to attend the rehearsal and is included at the rehearsal dinner

✝ Gets the groom dressed and to the ceremony on time

✝ Makes sure the groom's wedding-related expenses are prepared (clergy fee, for example)

✝ Makes sure the groom has the marriage license with him

✝ Delivers any payment to officiant, sexton, and ceremony musician(s), as prearranged

✝ Enters the sanctuary with the groom

✝ Takes care of and holds the bride's wedding ring

✝ Makes sure all ushers are properly attired and in place on time

✝ Walks in recessional

- ✢ Witnesses the signing of the marriage certificate

- ✢ Drives the bride and groom to reception if no driver hired

- ✢ Helps welcome guests at reception

- ✢ Offers first toast to bride and groom at reception

- ✢ Dances with the bride, maid of honor, mothers, and single female guests

- ✢ Helps the groom get ready for the honeymoon

- ✢ Gathers up and takes care of the groom's wedding clothes after he changes

- ✢ Has a car ready for the bride and groom to leave the reception or perhaps drives them to their next destination

- ✢ Pays for own wedding attire and transportation to the wedding

Bridesmaids: Duties and Responsibilities

Assuming that the maid of honor is able to take care of her responsibilities, the main charges to the bridesmaids are to help the maid of honor in any way they can and to take care of their dress and accessories fittings. They may help with a shower for the bride, although this is totally optional, and may look after the flower girl and ring bearer before and during the ceremony. Other duties they might perform include the following:

THE BRIDESMAIDS: DUTIES CHECKLIST

- ✢ Attend as many prenuptial events as possible

- ✢ Possibly host or co-host a party or shower (not mandatory)

- ✢ Assist bride with errands

- ✢ Contribute to bridesmaids' gift to the bride; usually give an individual gift to the couple

- ✢ Are expected to attend the rehearsal and are included at the rehearsal dinner

The Best Man

The tradition of having a best man at a wedding is thought to have originated with the **Germanic Goths** of northern Europe in **A.D. 200.** If there was a shortage of women to marry in his own community, the bridegroom would have to find a bride in a neighboring village—and that would often mean taking her by force. So he would be accompanied by his strongest or best friend, who helped him capture and carry off a bride.

✦ Arrive at dressing site promptly

✦ Walk in processional and recessional

✦ Possibly participate in receiving line

✦ Dance with ushers and single male guests

✦ Help gather guests for the first dance, cake cutting, and bouquet toss; participate in bouquet toss, if single

✦ Look after the couple's elderly relatives or friends

✦ Pay for their dresses and transportation to the wedding

Ushers: Duties and Responsibilities

Ushers serve as the official greeters of all guests at the ceremony and as such should be in place one hour before the ceremony begins. Very often a head usher is appointed to oversee the ushers, which relieves the best man of both having to attend to the groom and keep watch over the ushers.

THE HEAD USHER: DUTIES CHECKLIST

✦ Is expected to attend the rehearsal and is included at the rehearsal dinner

✦ Receives any lists of guests who are to be seated in a specific pew and is aware of the importance and sequence of seating special guests, such as the mothers and grandmothers of the bride and groom

When an Attendant Backs Out

Q: One of my attendants had to back out of my wedding because of her job. I'm getting married in less than three weeks; should I try to find a replacement?

A: It used to be that an attendant could back out of a wedding commitment only in the event of ill health or a death in the family. Today the press of careers is as urgent for women as it is for men, and a critical business trip or other work-related issue can force either an usher or a bridesmaid to back out altogether. If this happens early in your planning and before you have announced the names of all your attendants, you may easily ask someone else. It is generally incorrect, however, to ask someone else to fill in at the last minute, although there are exceptions, such as asking a close friend who would be honored to fill in.

+ Makes sure that programs, if used, are handed to guests when they are seated

+ Makes sure that the people who are designated to receive special flowers or corsages do, if the flowers have not been delivered to the recipients beforehand

+ Checks that all ushers are dressed properly and wearing their boutonnieres on the left side, stem down

+ Makes sure that the ushers know how to usher: how to greet guests, how to offer an arm to a single woman guest, and how to precede a couple to their seats

+ Makes sure the seating in the church is balanced, so that one side—whether the bride's side or the groom's—has no more people than the other; instructs the ushers to ask guests whether they would mind sitting on the other side

+ Helps gather the wedding party for photographs either before or after the ceremony and ensures that transportation arrangements have been made for all members of the wedding party to and from the ceremony

THE USHERS: DUTIES CHECKLIST

+ Participate in a party for the groom, if there is one

+ Contribute to the ushers' gift to the groom; usually give an individual gift to the couple

+ Are expected to attend the rehearsal and are included at the rehearsal dinner

+ Review any special seating situations with the head usher before the ceremony begins

+ Greet guests as they arrive

+ Seat the eldest woman first if a group of guests arrives simultaneously

+ Ask guests whether they are to be seated on the bride's side (left, from the back) or the groom's side (right, from the back)

+ Offer their right arm to female guests (with the guest's escort walking behind) or ask couples to follow behind (leading a couple to their seat)

+ Walk to the left side of a male guest

+ Hand each guest a program when they are seated

+ Put the aisle runner in place after guests are seated, before the processional begins

+ Know the order for seating: special guests, grandmothers of the bride and groom, groom's mother, and bride's mother last

+ Remove pew ribbons, one row at a time, after the ceremony

+ Close windows and check pews for programs or articles left behind after the ceremony

+ Are prepared to direct guests to the reception site (having extra maps available, if used)

+ Dance with bridesmaids and other guests at the reception

+ Look after elderly relatives or friends

+ Participate in garter ceremony, if there is one, and encourage other single men to participate, too

+ Coordinate return of rented apparel with head usher or best man

+ Pay for their own wedding attire and transportation to the wedding

Junior Bridesmaids: Duties and Responsibilities

Junior bridesmaids are girls between eight and fourteen who are too old to be flower girls and too young to be bridesmaids. Having junior bridesmaids in your wedding is completely optional. Their duties and responsibilities are as follows:

✣ They are expected pay for their own dresses.

✣ They are expected to attend the rehearsal and may be included at the rehearsal dinner, depending on their ages.

✣ Their single duty is to walk in the processional, as instructed.

✣ They are not expected to give showers, although they may be invited to attend.

✣ They do not stand in the receiving line unless asked.

Flower Girl: Duties and Responsibilities

The flower girl is often a young relative of the bride, between the ages of three and seven years. Having a flower girl in your wedding is completely optional. The flower girl's duties and responsibilities are as follows:

✣ Her dress and accessories should be paid for by her family.

✣ She attends the rehearsal, although she usually does not go to the rehearsal dinner.

✣ In the processional she walks alone, directly before the bride and her father.

✣ The flower girl often scatters petals from a basket she holds, although this is sometimes too overwhelming a responsibility for a young child to manage in front of a large group of people. It's usually easier for her to carry either a small basket of flowers or a tiny nosegay of flowers similar to those carried by the bridesmaids.

✣ In the recessional she walks with the ring bearer, directly behind the couple.

✣ The bride may hire a baby-sitter or ask one of the bridesmaids to look after the flower girl, to be in charge of checking her appearance, making sure she is present for formal pictures, helping her manage her food at the reception, and escorting her to the ladies' room.

Ring Bearer: Duties and Responsibilities

A small boy between three and seven is chosen for this honor. Having a ring bearer in your wedding is completely optional. The young ring bearer is traditionally dressed in short pants with an Eton-style jacket, preferably white but occasionally navy. These days, the older boys are often dressed in blazers or even suits; either choice is usually a navy blue. Small editions of the ushers' costumes are not worn except as is traditional in some cultures. The ring bearer's duties and responsibilities include the following:

✢ His attire is paid for by his family.

✢ He attends the rehearsal; he usually does not go to the rehearsal dinner.

✢ He immediately precedes the flower girl in the processional.

✢ The ring bearer either carries the actual rings or a facsimile of the rings (often a practical idea), on a white velvet or satin cushion. If the rings are actually the ones that are to be used, they should be fastened to the cushion with a very thin thread or placed over a firmly fixed hatpin. The best man takes the rings from the cushion at the right moment.

✢ He walks with the flower girl in the recessional, directly behind the bride and groom.

✢ The bride may hire a baby-sitter or ask one of the ushers to look after the ring bearer, to be in charge of checking his appearance, making sure he is present for formal pictures, helping him manage his food at the reception, and escorting him to the men's room.

Train Bearers and Pages: Duties and Responsibilities

Train bearers and pages may be included in the wedding party, although they usually participate only in very elaborate, formal weddings. The presence of too many very young children in the wedding party may detract from the solemnity of the ceremony. Unless the bride's gown is so elaborate that the maid of honor can't manage it or unless the pageantry of the processional and recessional calls for the addition of train bearers and pages, the flower girl and ring bearer suffice as the youngest participants.

Honor Roles

In some parts of the country, particularly in the South, it is often the custom to have relatives and friends who have a special relationship with the couple help out in some way at the ceremony or reception. Those who fill these "honor roles" are often identified by matching corsages in wedding colors and may be asked to help out with such duties as pouring coffee or tea, serving cake at a house wedding, greeting guests, handing out ceremony programs, if used, or distributing rose petals or bubbles. They may be in charge of the guestbook or serve as liturgical assistants, such as readers, lectors, soloists, cantors, deacons, or altar assistants.

Eliciting the help of these special relatives and friends bestows honor on them and gives them a way to participate without having to invest in the cost of wedding party attire. Be sure to include them in a few wedding photographs with the bride and groom, and be sure to thank them in some special way, such as with a small gift.

When choosing honor roles, consider those friends and family members you can count on, who share a willingness to help.

CHAPTER FIVE

FAMILY, FRIENDS, AND A CAREFULLY PLANNED GUEST LIST

The guest list, carefully counted and coordinated within the budget.

It happens to almost every bride and groom: the guest list, carefully counted and coordinated within the budget, slowly but surely inflates. Don't think it can't happen to you. Indeed, as cousins you've never heard of come out of the woodwork and your mother's work friends inquire about the date, guest lists can grow at an alarming rate.

Most brides and grooms, in planning their nuptials, must work around financial considerations. The biggest factor in the cost of a wedding? The guest list. That's because the reception costs generally are the most expensive aspect of weddings today.

Guest list grousing can turn the most compatible families into feuding factions and leave brides and grooms feeling that elopement is a reasonable resolution. Insisting that all involved whittle down their lists often makes the person who is paying feel guilty and petty. The bride and groom become anxious, parents complain, and tensions rise.

Tact and diplomacy, two of the cornerstones of etiquette, can save the day. Make sure you never lose sight of your first shared vision of your wedding—and give yourselves a budget reality check.

❦ GUEST LIST SURVIVAL GUIDE ❦

1. *Realize that you have choices to make.* Do you want to plan your guest list and reception around a budget or make a guest list first and plan the reception around that? Either way you will likely find that your list requires some fine-tuning.

2. *Remember: It's **your** wedding.* Don't automatically agree that cousins you've never met or Mom's office colleagues take precedence over your own good friends. Think and talk it through—calmly. You might end up inviting the cousins, but you'll be more understanding and less resentful if you agree it's the way to go.

3. *Don't opt for the easy solution.* Inviting a large number of guests to the ceremony but only a small number to the reception is no solution at all. It can be insulting to send a formal ceremony invitation to many and a reception invitation to a favored few. (Some exceptions: inviting children, or your entire congregation, to the ceremony only.) For example, an open invitation to the ceremony issued to church or synagogue members by the priest, rabbi, or minister, with your permission, carries no gift obligation for those who attend, nor does it carry any obligation to the bride and groom to invite them to the reception. The reverse—inviting a small number of guests to an intimate or private ceremony and a larger number to

the reception—can be perfectly acceptable, too. The key: Think carefully through any variables in numbers of ceremony and reception guests.

❧ NUTS AND BOLTS: ❧

THE GUEST LIST

✢ *What constitutes a guest list?* A guest list consists of a magical number of family and friends that 1) suits the size of your ceremony and reception sites, 2) corresponds with the level of intimacy desired for the wedding, and 3) can be accommodated within your wedding budget—an important reality.

✢ *How many guests can each family invite?* Traditionally each family is allotted half of the desired total guest count, a figure determined largely by the person hosting the wedding. A way of starting to decide whom to invite is to combine four lists, thus formulating the master list. Start with lists from the bride, the groom, the bride's parents, and the groom's parents. It is necessary that everyone make up their lists realistically. As acceptances and regrets become known, the "weights" of the lists may vary.

✢ *Don't forget these guests:*

The spouse, fiancé, or live-in partner of each invited guest—even if you've never met (necessary)

The person who performs the ceremony and his or her spouse (necessary)

The parents of ring bearers and flower girls (necessary)

The parents of the bridesmaids (not necessary, but a nice gesture when feasible, especially when the bride knows them well)

Counselors, advisers, or mentors to the bride or groom who are not close friends but have been an important part of their lives (not absolutely necessary, but often meaningful)

✣ *Other factors that will affect your numbers:* Do you plan to include children? To invite single friends to bring guests? Neither inclusion is necessary, but both necessitate "proper etiquette," meaning consideration and sensitivity. Are you planning a destination wedding, which may make it difficult for people to attend? Is this an encore wedding? If so, you may prefer to limit the guest list at your ceremony and reception to just close family and friends and enjoy a later general get-together instead.

✣ *What do we do if a good number of our guests send their regrets?* Be prepared. Ask each family to compile a rough standby list of supplementary guests, to be invited if room allows, along with their "definite invite" list. People on a B list can then be invited, given at least four weeks' notice, if guests on the A list send regrets. Your list may read something like this:

First tier: immediate families (parents, siblings, grandparents, the couple's own children)

Second tier: extended family members (aunts, uncles, cousins, nieces, nephews)

Third tier: family friends (parents' close friends, longtime friends and neighbors, childhood friends and their parents, if close to you)

Fourth tier: bride and groom's friends, in further tiers of closeness to you (childhood friends, high school and college friends, work friends, new friends)

Fifth tier: parents' colleagues (associates, employers, employees)

Of course, this guide should be based upon what makes sense in your case. Any planning must be adapted to your situation. If you and your fiancé are established professionally, perhaps marrying for a second or third time, you will probably be paying for all or most of the wedding yourselves. Perhaps your wedding will take place far from your hometown or where your parents live. Under any of these circumstances it could make sense to switch tiers three and four, as just defined.

The Wedding Consultant Speaks

Tips on Inviting Guests to a Destination Wedding

If you are planning a destination wedding to a site where guests will have to travel a good distance, the sooner you can share your plans with them, the better. While costs are considerable for any travel, they can be astronomical if the venue is an exotic island or out-of-the-way hamlet. The sooner your guests can start making their travel arrangements, the less it will cost them. A long lead time also allows them to arrange for time off from work and perhaps even plan a family vacation around the wedding. This does not mean you should send out invitations a year in advance. A telephone call, a note, or a "save the date" notice is all your guests need to begin planning; the written invitation can follow. While a destination wedding guest list is often smaller than one at a traditional location—simply because of the logistics and expenses of a destination wedding—there is no guideline as to how many people you may invite.

TRIMMING AN OVER-AMBITIOUS GUEST LIST

Your invitation guest list can be pared down in a number of thoughtful ways, including the following:

✤ *Make across-the-board, clear-cut distinctions.* To avoid hurt feelings when a guest list is limited, subdivide the groupings across the board. For example, if numbers are limited, you could invite all aunts and uncles and forgo cousins. Then stick to categories equilaterally, treating each list as a whole.

✤ *Leaving out work associates—all or some.* When space is absolutely at a premium, some couples delete work associates entirely. This can reduce the list considerably while at the same time keeping the wedding a more personal one, with only family members and close, long-time friends attending. Or perhaps you invite only your boss and your respective assistants or just your immediate department. Your other co-workers will clearly understand that you had to make a cutoff.

The Etiquette of a Standby Guest List

Q: My future mother-in-law says it's appropriate to have a standby guest list ready when guests from the main list decline. Is this proper?

A: Some couples are understandably hesitant to have standby wish lists. But these lists do provide a practical solution to controlling the numbers—and budget. If you and your fiancé (and parents) apply *discretion*, making sure that guests do not even know that you have A and B lists, feelings won't be hurt. Guests won't feel slighted as long as the later invitations are mailed promptly. To devise a standby guest list, ask everyone involved in choosing the main guest list for the names and addresses of "wait list" guests; then you and your partner can prioritize them. Plan for enough time for responses from the master list guests to be received—no less than four weeks—to invite guests who are on the B, or standby, list. Making this choice early in your planning process will facilitate sending the second group of invitations. Incorporate the name into the master list in your organizer.

✣ *Beware of parental paybacks.* This is not the time for parents to insist on reciprocity for all the gifts they've given and weddings they've attended in the past, nor does your wedding need to be the occasion for them to fulfill their own social obligations.

✣ *Remember: Shower guests are wedding guests.* Any guest who is invited to a shower must also be invited to the wedding, with a few exceptions, such as co-workers who give an office shower. Keep that in mind when drawing up your guest lists for wedding showers.

✣ *Talk to friends who live far away.* If you know that distance will prevent certain people from attending, call them to see if they think they can make the wedding. If not, factor this in.

✣ *Stick to your first-tier and second-tier guest lists.* Try to redraw your lines equilaterally, bumping entire groupings of people—second cousins, work associates with whom you've never socialized, friends from the health club—to a B list (see earlier).

❧ ORGANIZING ❧ A CAREFULLY PLANNED MASTER GUEST LIST

A beautifully organized and orchestrated wedding, most brides will tell you, is the happy result of single-minded attention to lists. By incorporating your personal list, your parents' list, and your groom's parents' list into one alphabetical master list—and putting that list into your wedding planner and a computer file—you will have one of the most important documents of your wedding planning readily on hand. You will refer to this list endlessly as the weeks go by—to address invitations, delineate who needs maps and directions, check off acceptances and regrets, and record gifts received and thank-you notes written. You will also use this list to count heads. The master guest list is the *foundation of your wedding plans* and as such should be carefully thought out and maintained. A savvy guest list includes the following:

✢ Each guest's full name, address, telephone number, and relationship to bride or groom. These days e-mail addresses have become an important way to send and receive information; it may be, in fact, the best, quickest way to update guests on plans.

✢ A space to indicate (with a check mark or an X) whether or not a guest has RSVP'd, and how many members of the family or party will attend. Writing down the name of a single guest's date or fiancé will help you remember his or her name, as well as enabling you to extend your welcome with a personalized place at the reception.

✢ A description of any gift received and the date a thank-you note was sent.

✢ If you have the room, you might want a space to indicate if the guest is coming from out of town, so that you can mail him or her information on lodging and directions and any parties being thrown for out-of-town guests.

❦ ALL ABOUT CHILDREN ❦

One of the most hotly debated issues in planning a wedding is whether or not to invite children. Some people feel that having children at a wedding can be an intrusion or a distraction for guests intent on participating in and honoring a very grown-up ritual. Others can't imagine a wedding celebration without children. One undeniable factor is the additional financial burden inviting a number of kids can incur. If you are determined to include children on your guest list but your budget is tight, there are compromises you

Entertaining the Kids

If you are planning to invite more than just a few children to your wedding celebrations, finding ways to keep them occupied can be great fun. You could have your floral designer create a piñata filled with inexpensive toys. Or you could set up a designated children's table with coloring books and favors. If children are seated with parents, you could still provide each with a coloring book and small box of crayons. Make sure, too, that your menu includes some kid-friendly foods, like chicken bites, little raviolis, or minipizzas. Another consideration is to hire a baby-sitter or two to help out. Some reception sites even provide a separate room where children can color, watch a video, or just gather. In that case the kids should be supervised, and baby-sitters are a must.

can make (see following). Here are some general guidelines for inviting—and not inviting—children to wedding celebrations.

✢ *How to let guests know whether or not children are invited:*   Simple. If children are invited, their names are on the envelopes of your invitations. If children are not invited, the proper way to communicate this is to write only the parents' names on the outer and inner envelopes on your invitations. It is *inappropriate* to write "No Children" on the invitations.

✢ *How to restrict the number of children:*   One of the most common problems is that of restricting the number of children attending the reception. In large families with dozens of cousins, nieces, and nephews, the costs of inviting them all may be prohibitive. Yet some relatives feel so strongly about including their children that they will consider refusing the invitation altogether if the children are left out.

No easy answer exists. You can, however, *tactfully* discourage the youngsters' attendance in one of several ways. You can *discuss it with friends and relatives.* You may talk to them in person or by telephone, explaining the problem and asking them to help by spreading the word. Enclose a note to those friends and relatives who may be the most understanding about your situation, explaining that costs and space prevent your asking all children. You can also *offer to hire a baby-*

sitter during the hours of the wedding celebration to watch the children of out-of-town guests, either at a relative's home or at the hotel where the guests are staying. Or you could *draw the line* by including only the children of close family members and/or children of the wedding party, or by establishing an age limit—inviting children ten and older, for example—to the wedding. Either way you should make an effort to make no exceptions, since doing so may cause more hurt feelings than holding the line.

❧ HELP! WHAT DO I DO ABOUT . . . ❦

1. *Including Partners*

Partners of invited guests must be included in a wedding invitation, whether or not they are married, engaged, or living together and whether or not anyone in the wedding party knows them. Suggesting that single guests who aren't attached to a significant other bring a date is a thoughtful gesture, but one that is certainly *not required* and often not realistic. A single invitation addressed to both members of a married couple, or a couple who live together, is sent to their shared address, while invitations to an engaged or long-standing couple who don't live together are sent separately, to each address. Envelopes addressed to a single friend may include "And Guest," indicating that he or she may bring an escort or friend. If it is possible to obtain the name of the guest, the name would be included on the invitation to the friend, or a second invitation may even be sent directly to the date at his or her home address instead.

Note: Occasionally a single guest will become engaged or reunite with a separated spouse after the invitations have been mailed. In that case it is perfectly correct for the bride or groom to extend a verbal invitation to the guest's friend or spouse.

2. *Guests Who Ask to Bring a Guest*

The answer is straightforward: It is impolite of a guest to ask if he can bring a date—but it is not impolite of you to refuse. You may certainly answer no. However, if you do discover that they are engaged or living together, the thing to do is invite your friend's partner, whether verbally or by invitation.

3. Sending Invitations to Out-of-Town Guests Who Can't Possibly Attend

Apply careful thought. Many people prefer not to send invitations to those friends and acquaintances who they feel cannot possibly attend the celebrations. They believe that doing so makes it look as if they are merely inviting those friends in order to receive a gift. In most cases these friends should receive a wedding announcement instead, which carries no obligation whatsoever.

There is the flip side to this dilemma. Some good friends who live far away might actually be hurt if you do not send invitations, even if your intent was to spare them from feeling obliged to send a gift for a wedding so far away. These friends, upon hearing news of your engagement, may actually have been making plans to travel to your wedding. In general, *always invite truly good friends*—even if they live far away.

❧ OUT-OF-TOWN GUESTS ❧

It is certainly not the bride and groom's obligation to plan constant entertainment for out-of-town guests who are not part of the wedding party. But it *is* a nice touch to offer activities, gatherings, and other forms of hospitality to those who have come from far away to celebrate your nuptials.

Events for Out-of-Towners

Once your engagement is announced, you will likely be approached by friends and relatives offering to help out in some way. One ideal way for a group of friends and family to pitch in is to entertain out-of-town guests. In many cases the costs and preparations are shared by a grouping of friends and family. It's up to you to provide the hosts of these parties with a list of names and addresses so they can send invitations, if necessary, and plan the party accordingly. If out-of-town guests are staying in private homes, their hosts should also be invited to the events and parties. And don't forget to send thank-you gifts or flowers to the party hosts, in addition to your words

The Personal Touch

✾✿✾

Planning Activities for Out-of-Town Guests

If there is open time in the wedding celebrations schedule, you may want to provide your out-of-town guests with a list of local activities, sports centers, museums, and other attractions, along with addresses and phone numbers. Here's where you can get creative: your town may have a singular attraction that may be a must-see for any person new to the area. You might even provide tickets or passes. Don't make an activity mandatory, however—simply provide irresistible options. You might ask a friend to gather local information for you to arrange in an attractive "welcome pack" that will await guests at the hotel.

of appreciation. There are several different opportunities to entertain out-of-town guests. These parties may occur:

✢ *During the rehearsal dinner.* Friends and relatives may offer to host a cocktail party, barbecue, or other gathering for guests while the wedding party is at the rehearsal and rehearsal dinner. Note: Some couples, instead, include out-of-town guests at the rehearsal dinner. While this is in no way obligatory, if circumstances (especially space, budgets, and the hosts' invitations) enable their inclusion in the rehearsal dinner, it's a viable option.

✢ *On the day of an evening wedding.* Other friends might host a brunch or luncheon for guests on the day of a late afternoon or evening wedding.

✢ *At a postwedding brunch.* Out-of-town guests at an evening wedding generally stay the night. For them a breakfast or brunch makes for a nice send-off.

Lodging for Out-of-Town Guests

In general, out-of-town guests are expected to pay for their own lodging. It is a courtesy—and certainly not obligatory—for the bride and groom to take responsibility for finding or recommending lodging for out-of-town guests. But if yours is a large wedding and you expect the attendance of a good number of out-of-town guests, it's a smart idea to *prereserve a block of rooms in a hotel;* some hotels will even offer discount room rates if a minimum number is booked in a block. Some friends may offer to *put up out-of-town guests at their homes.* If so, it is up to you to make the best match so that all involved are comfortable with the arrangement. Then either you or the hosts can send the out-of-town guests the name, address, and telephone number of their host and hostess and directions to their home and let them know what to expect (whether their hosts have a pet, a swimming pool, children, and the like). Make sure the hosts are clear on the guests' arrival and departure dates and times. Remember to give a thank-you gift to those who are providing lodging.

❧ GUEST ETIQUETTE ❧

Guests invited to participate in a wedding celebration have as much of an obligation to exhibit good manners and thoughtful behavior as their hosts have to make them feel welcome and comfortable. Here are some guidelines to proper guest etiquette:

- ✢ *RSVP: Respond to the invitation immediately.* The most important obligation a guest has upon receiving a wedding invitation is to respond immediately to said invitation, *particularly* if he or she can't attend. This allows the bride and groom to promptly send out another invitation in its place, if desired. At the very least, the hosts have realistic numbers of guests to relay to the caterer and others— as long as guests abide by the RSVP.

- ✢ *Send a gift.* Guests invited to the ceremony and reception have an obligation to send a gift, whether they are attending or not. There are a few exceptions. Those who receive an announcement after the wedding has taken place have no obligation to send a gift, although it is always nice to acknowledge the receipt of the announcement by sending a card or note expressing best wishes to the couple. A request for a contribution to a charity in lieu of gifts, particularly in the case of an older couple or a remarriage, should be respected and adhered to by guests.

✦ *Be on your best behavior, please.*   Just as there are guidelines to help the bride and groom and their families organize the most wonderful wedding possible, there are guidelines for guests who sometimes, in their enthusiasm, pose thorny problems. Guests have the responsibility to behave with decorum, and this responsibility extends to immediate family members as well. No matter what level of rancor has been reached between some members of the family, a wedding is not the place to wage war. Best behavior is the code, so guests should practice civility during any and all proceedings in which they are participating.

❧ THE GOOD GUEST'S PLEDGE ❧

Some behavior may seem harmless and trivial in casual circumstances, but within the context of a special occasion it can appear ill-mannered and unruly. The good guest is almost invisible, busy enjoying him- or herself, communing with fellow guests, and, most of all, basking in the generous hospitality of the hosts. The good guest is thoughtful and solicitous, paying respect to his hosts, the wedding party, and the other guests. The bad guest, on the other hand, sticks out like a sore thumb and can be counted on to behave poorly, forcing the hosts to graciously grin and bear it when possible. Ultimately it's up to the guest to do the right thing. Here is the Good Guest's Pledge—a promise to behave at his or her most thoughtful and respectful best during the wedding celebrations.

During the Ceremony

✦ I will respect the sanctity of the occasion and not talk during the wedding ceremony or interrupt the service by taking pictures with a flash camera. This is also not the time to mingle or loudly greet friends and acquaintances.

✧ I will participate in as much of the ceremony as my own religion and that of the ceremony permits. If a mass or communion is offered and I choose not to participate, I will remain quietly in my seat. Otherwise I'll stand when others stand and sit when others sit. I am not required to kneel or to recite prayers that are contrary to my own beliefs.

✧ I will not show up at the ceremony and reception with a surprise guest, whether a date, children, or extras in general.

During the Reception

✧ I will not grab the microphone to croon a few favorite numbers or broadcast stories or jokes, no matter how impressive my singing voice or how humorous I can be. The bride and groom have taken great care to orchestrate a few hours of entertainment that do not include an amateur hour.

✧ I won't monopolize the bride and groom in the receiving line. Guests in the receiving line should introduce themselves to the first person in the line and then keep their comments to the bare minimum: "What a lovely wedding!" "I'm so happy for you." Then they should move quickly on. The same brevity of comment is appreci-

The Bride's Mother Asks: Can We Do Without the Sound of Forks Upon Glass?

Q: *I feel like an old fuddy-duddy bringing this up, but I have a real problem with guests banging their utensils on glasses in order to get the bride and groom to kiss. What are your thoughts?*

A: The custom in some regions of the country for guests to clink their forks or spoons against their glasses indicating that the bride and groom should kiss should be kept to a minimum. It is annoying to those who are trying to speak; it is annoying to the bride and groom who are trying to greet guests or simply enjoy the food; it is annoying, *period.*

ated during the reception, for the bride and groom have many people with whom to speak.

✣ I will never alter place cards or switch tables at a wedding reception. Instead it is my responsibility to be as cordial as I can be wherever the bride and groom have designated that I sit. I won't stand on ceremony and wait to be introduced to tablemates and others. I will introduce myself and add a little explanation: "I'm Lorrin's aunt from Hawaii," or "Jen and I were roommates in college."

✣ It is kind but not required for men at a table to ask single women to dance at some point during the reception and for anyone at the table to offer to assist an older or infirm guest with a buffet meal.

After the Reception

✣ I will not take the centerpiece upon departing, scoop up matchbooks, or request that any uneaten portion of my meal be put in a doggie bag to take home. The centerpieces should be left in place unless the bride and groom have actually encouraged guests to take them; and asking for leftover food is not in keeping with the elegance or dignity of the event. The bride and groom may have made arrangements to have flowers delivered to shut-ins, to hospitals or nursing homes, or to guests unable to attend the festivities because of health or family issues. The flowers, in other words, belong to the bride and groom to dispose of as they wish.

CHAPTER SIX

Your invitation is

INVITATION

a keepsake for the

ETIQUETTE

bride and groom to

cherish forever.

Your invitation is the first important indication to your guests of the style and tone of your wedding, as it reflects the degree of formality of the celebration. It is also a keepsake for the bride and groom to cherish forever, and as such your choices should be based on personal preferences. The couple who enjoys a long engagement has the luxury of having more time to look through the choices available to them before making a final selection.

Even with a long engagement, choosing, printing, and mailing invitations must be planned well enough in advance to allow time for the invitations to be mailed and guests to respond. The rule of thumb is to allow at least six to eight weeks for printing formal invitations and their related enclosures. Try to plot out the time so that you will be addressing your invitations no later than two months before the wedding and mailing them out six to eight weeks before the wedding date.

Of course, customs have loosened as busy couples find themselves pressed for time. For the bride and groom who decide suddenly to marry, tradition is often thrown to the wind. A couple may telephone, fax, or overnight-mail their requests for the honor of the presence of their family and close friends.

❧ INVITATION STYLES ❧

These days the range of invitations is infinite. You'll want to shop around before making a final decision. You can get catalogs from the many wedding stationery companies that advertise in the pages of bridal magazines. Local stationers and printers also have a wealth of sample books and catalogs on hand.

The general categories can be broken down into *third-person formal invitations, semiformal invitations,* or, in the case of a small, intimate wedding, *handwritten notes* on beautiful stationery.

The elements to consider when choosing invitations are *paper shades, paper weight, typefaces, size,* and *wording.* Visit several vendors and check costs for these as well as for coordinating *inserts and envelopes.* Then compare prices and the length of time required for printing. While some stationers require several weeks for an order to be placed and returned to them, printers who do the work themselves can often guarantee a faster turnaround time. If the delivery time is considerable, ask if you can receive your envelopes early so that you can get a jump on the often time-consuming task of addressing them.

Don't forget to keep samples of what you order so that you can coordinate the design scheme of other printed accessories—whether inserts, place cards, or personalized napkins—with that of the invitation.

Formal Invitations

✢ *Color.*   The correct paper shades for the most formal and traditional wedding invitation are ivory, soft cream, and white.

✢ *Paper.*   The heaviest-weight paper in these shades may cost a bit more, but its appearance and feel are substantial and bespeak formality. You may want your paper flat or prefer a raised plate mark or margin. It is correct to use either a large double sheet, which is folded a second time, or a smaller single sheet.

✢ *Typeface.*   After choosing paper shade and weight, you should select a typeface. For formal invitations, shaded and antique roman faces are traditional choices. Remember, simple styles are in better taste than ornate and flowery styles—and are easier to read as well. No other ornament should be added to a formal invitation, with the exception of a coat of arms (if the bride's father's family has one). A coat of arms or a crest may be used without color at the top center of the invitation.

✢ *Nontraditional alternatives.*   Printed invitations that do not follow the traditional, third-person wording style can be quite beautiful. These invitations may be engraved or thermographed in as formal a style as traditional ones. If the wedding is to be a simple and nontraditional celebration, the invitations may be printed on paper with a design or border, often in a color carrying out the color scheme of the wedding.

Printing Options

Formal and semiformal invitations may be printed in several ways. Of course, whatever you use is a matter of personal preference and budget, but in general the more formal the wedding, the more formal the printing style.

✢ *Engraving.*   Engraved invitations are the most traditional printing style for formal invitations, if only because the engraving method has been around the longest time. Engraving results in raised print that is pressed through so that it can be felt on the back of the paper. It is also the most expensive form of printing.

‡ *Thermography.* Thermography results in raised print that is shinier than engraved print and does not press through the back of the paper. Thermography is less expensive than engraving.

‡ *Lithography.* Lithography imprints lettering with ink but results in neither raised nor pressed-through lettering. It is less costly than either engraving or thermography.

‡ *Laser.* Invitations can be produced on a laser printer, either at a professional print shop or at home. The result is similar to that produced by lithography. Blank invitation forms are available at better stationers. A word of caution: Great care must be taken to ensure that the forms are fed through the desktop printer straight and evenly. You should also choose a typeface that is formal, crisp, and easy to read, duplicating other professionally produced print. Laser printing is the most inexpensive form of printing, but when it is used for a formal wedding it also can look inexpensive. Make sure to print out a few practice invitations to get the look you want before it's too late to have invitations printed professionally.

‡ *Handwritten.* A personal invitation may be handwritten on lovely stationery when it is an invitation to a very small wedding or when the bride and groom want to personalize their invitations, no matter how formal the ceremony may be.

The most formal invitations have the name of the recipient written by hand on an otherwise printed card. You may want to employ the services of a *calligrapher* for this form of invitation, unless you or someone close to you has beautiful penmanship. It is also possible to use a desktop laser printer to "write" in the name of the recipient, but to ensure a handwritten result it is imperative that a type font that duplicates a calligraphy style is used. Make sure too that the invitation (which must be a single sheet, not a fold-over style) can be fed evenly through the printer.

Doctor and Mrs. Reid W. Coleman
request the honour of the presence of
Mr. and Mrs. Christopher Wicke
at the marriage of their daughter
Laura Jeanne
to
Mr. Patrick Desmond Whelan
Saturday, the twelfth of May
Two thousand and one
at half-past eleven o'clock
St. John's Church
Rehoboth, Massachusetts

❧ INVITATION WORDING ❧

✢ *Traditional wording.* For the bride and groom who cherish long-standing traditions, conventional wording and spelling will govern their invitation choices. Some specific rules for *formal* wedding invitations are as follows:

1. The invitation to a wedding ceremony in a house of worship reads *"Mr. and Mrs. Henry Stuart Evans request the honour"* (using the traditional "u" spelling) *"of your presence . . ."* *"Favour,"* as in *"the favour of a reply,"* too uses the traditional spelling.

2. The invitation to a reception reads: *"Mr. and Mrs. Henry Stuart Evans request the pleasure of your company . . . "*

3. When a Roman Catholic mass is part of the wedding ceremony, invitations may include *"and your participation in the offering of the Nuptial Mass"* beneath the groom's name.

4. No punctuation is used except after abbreviations, such as "Mr." or "Mrs." or when phrases requiring separation occur in the same line, as in the date.

5. Numbers in the date are spelled out, as in *"the twenty-seventh of August,"* but long numbers in the street address may be written in numerals: *"1490 Kenwood Parkway."*

6. Half hours are written as *"half after four o'clock"*—not *"half past four"* or *"four-thirty."*

7. Although "Mr." is abbreviated and "Junior" may be, the title "Doctor" is more properly written in full.

8. If the invitation includes the handwritten name of the recipient, the full name must be written out. The use of an initial—*"Mr. and Mrs. Scott E. Jenkins"*—is not correct.

9. The invitation to the wedding ceremony alone does not include an RSVP.

10. On the reception invitation, *"R.S.V.P.,"* *"R.s.v.p.,"* *"RSVP,"* and *"The favour of a reply is requested"* are equally correct. If the address to which the reply is to be sent is different from the one appearing on the invitation itself, you may use *"Kindly send reply to,"* followed by the correct address.

11. Traditionally the date of the wedding on a formal invitation does not include the year, but today it is considered correct to include it, spelled out: *"Nineteen hundred and ninety-nine."* (The year has traditionally been a part of wedding announcements.)

The most common, traditional wording used today for a formal wedding given by the bride's parents reads:

> Mr. and Mrs. Henry Stuart Evans
> request the honour of your presence
> at the marriage of their daughter
> Katherine Leigh
> to
> Mr. Brian Charles Jamison
> Saturday, the twelfth of June
> two thousand and one
> at half after four o'clock
> Village Lutheran Church
> Briarcliff Manor

✣ *Less Formal Wording.* When less formality is desired, alternatives to traditional third-person wording can be used. These invitations may be engraved or printed by a stationer in just as formal a style as traditional invitations:

> Our joy will be more complete
> if you will share in the marriage of our daughter
> Carole Renée
> to
> Mr. Domenick Masullo
> on Saturday, the fifth of June
> two thousand and one
> at half after four o'clock
> 7 Old Elm Avenue
> Salem, Massachusetts
> We invite you to worship with us, witness their vows and
> join us for a reception following the ceremony
> If you are unable to attend, we ask your presence in thought and prayer
> Mr. and Mrs. Earl Rinde [or Lorraine and Earl Rinde]
> R.S.V.P.

When the invitation is to come from both sets of parents, it might be worded as follows:

Sharon and Elliot Karp
and
Hilari and Kenneth Cohen
would be honoured
to have you share in the joy
of the marriage of their children
Leah Rachel
and
Jonathan
This celebration of love will be held on
Sunday, the ninth of September
two thousand
at five o'clock
Temple Shalom
Englewood, New Jersey
A reception will follow the ceremony
at the Palisades Lodge
Palisades Parkway

Kindly send reply to
Mr. and Mrs. Elliot Karp
[address]

Less formally, the bride and groom may design and print or handwrite their own invitations on a simple card:

> *Anne Bell McKune and Michael Smithson*
> *invite you to celebrate*
> *their marriage*
> *on*
> *Saturday, June the 5th*
> *Two thousand and one*
> *at four o'clock*
> *2 Fox Run*
> *Danville, Kentucky*
>
> *R.S.V.P.*

Personal invitations to very small weddings are often issued in the form of a personal note. It is a most flattering invitation and typically would read:

> *Dear Aunt Ruth,*
> *Sean and I are to be married at Christ's Church on June tenth at four o'clock. We hope you and Uncle Don will come to the church, and afterward to the reception at Greentree Country Club.*
> *With much love from us both,*
> *Laura Jeanne*

Other personal forms of invitation for weddings that make no pretense of being traditional may be as original as the couple and/or the bride's parents wish, as long as the invitations are dignified and sincerely reflect the sentiments of the bride and groom and their families. Among the loveliest and most meaningful is the following example, written as a letter from the bride's parents.

> *Our daughter, Lisa, will be married to Frank Adams O'Gorman, on Saturday, the fifth of February, two thousand, at half after seven o'clock in the evening. Their vows will be spoken at St. John's Lutheran Church, Mamaroneck, New York.*
> *We invite you to worship with us, witness their vows, and be our guest at the reception and buffet which follow at the Beach and Tennis Club, New Rochelle.*
> *If you are unable to attend, we ask your presence in thought and prayer.*
> *Helen and Davis Wilson*

✣ *Wording for Special Cases.*   The wording in an invitation may undergo subtle changes for different circumstances. For example, if a formal invitation is to the ceremony only, the traditional wording should not include an RSVP. When a reception follows, a separate reception invitation or response card is inserted in the mailing envelope with the invitation to the ceremony. Circumstances dictate what kind of invitation is mailed, whether one to the ceremony only, one to both the reception and the ceremony, or one to the reception only.

❧ SAMPLE INVITATIONS ❧

TO THE CEREMONY AND RECEPTION

When all the guests invited to the wedding are also invited to the reception, the invitation to both may be combined:

Mr. and Mrs. Kenneth McGuigan
request the honour of your presence
at the marriage of their daughter
Joanne Marie
to
Mr. Stephen Dempsey
Saturday, the ninth of April
two thousand
at half after five o'clock
Church of the Resurrection
Evanston
and afterward at the reception
Lake Michigan Shore Club
The favour of a reply is requested
23 Soundview Avenue
River Forest, Illinois 60601

To the Reception Only

When the wedding ceremony is private and a large reception follows, the invitation to the ceremony is extended orally or by personal note, and the wording of the reception invitation is as follows:

Mr. and Mrs. Douglas Charles Campbell
request the pleasure of your company
at the wedding reception
for their daughter
Deirdre Mary
and
Mr. Jeffrey Keller
Saturday the twenty-fourth of June
two thousand and one
at seven o'clock
Horseshoe Harbour Yacht Club
Larchmont
R.S.V.P.

Reception Cards

A reception card, an invitation to the reception, is often sent when the ceremony and reception are held at different locations. The reception card is enclosed with the wedding invitation.

The reception card is also used when the guest list for the ceremony is larger than that for the reception. Here, the reception cards would be enclosed with wedding invitations only for those being invited to the wedding and reception. This is the most commonly used form:

Reception
immediately following the ceremony
Knolls Country Club
Lake Forest

The favour of a reply is requested
Lakeside Drive, Lake Forest, Illinois 61300

INVITATIONS TO A BELATED RECEPTION

When a reception is not held at the time of the wedding, the couple or their parents may have one later, possibly when the newlyweds return from their honeymoon. Although the party is held to celebrate the wedding, the wording must be changed slightly:

Mr. and Mrs. Wayne Matteis
request the pleasure of your company
at a reception
in honor of
Mr. and Mrs. Scott Nelson
[etc.]

AT SOMEONE'S HOME

Even though the wedding and reception are to be held at a friend's house, the invitations should be written in the name of the bride's parents or sponsors or in the name of the bride and groom:

Linda Lanier-Keosaian and Gregory Keosaian
request the honour of your presence
at the marriage of her daughter
Peternelle Van Arsdale
to
Mr. Bryan Keith Oettl
Saturday, the twelfth of October
two thousand
at half past three o'clock
at the residence of Mr. and Mrs. Robert Cozza
Kansas City, Missouri
R.S.V.P.

A growing number of wedding invitations issued today do not follow the traditional, formal style illustrated in the previous sections but instead reflect the often complicated makeup of modern families. A bride may have two divorced and remarried sets of parents giving her away. A groom may have the blessing of one divorced parent but not the other. Birth mothers of adopted children may be involved. For brides and grooms in these situations, there is no need to panic. Etiquette accommodates most any circumstance with elegance. These sample invitations are just a few that cover a variety of complex situations gracefully:

When the Bride Has One Living Parent

When either the bride's mother or father is deceased, the invitation is issued only in the name of the living parent:

Mr. [Mrs.] Daniel Watson Driskill
requests the honour of your presence
at the marriage of her [his] daughter
Susan Patricia

to

Mr. Drew Randolph Donney
[etc.]

However, there are circumstances when the bride very much wants to include the name of the deceased parent. This is acceptable, as long as the invitation does not appear to be issued by the deceased. In other words, don't word the invitation so that it reads *" . . . the late William Tierney requests the honour of . . ."*

Diane June Tierney
daughter of Mary Ann Tierney and the late William Tierney
and
James Thomas Duffy
son of Mr. and Mrs. Keon David Duffy
request the honour of your presence
at their marriage
Saturday, the fifth of October
[etc.]

WHEN THE BRIDE'S MOTHER IS DIVORCED

A divorcée giving her daughter's wedding by herself sends out her daughter's invitations using her first and last names:

Mrs. Ann Syverson
requests the honour of your presence
at the marriage of her daughter
[etc.]

WHEN DIVORCED PARENTS GIVE THE WEDDING TOGETHER

In the event that relations between the bride's divorced parents (one or both of whom may have remarried) are so friendly that they share the wedding expenses and act as co-hosts, both sets of names should appear on the invitation. The bride's mother's name appears first:

Mr. and Mrs. Shelby Goldring
and
Mr. Michael Levy
request the honour of your presence
at the marriage of their daughter
Rachel Lynn Levy
[etc.]

If, however, the bride's parents are not sharing expenses, yet the bride wishes both parents' names to appear, a different situation exists. If the bride's mother is not contributing to the cost of the wedding, the bride's father's name appears first on the invitation, and he and his wife host the reception. The bride's mother is then included only as an honored guest at the reception.

WHEN THE BRIDE HAS A STEPFATHER

When the bride's mother has been widowed or is divorced and remarried and she and her husband are hosting the wedding, the invitations are worded as follows:

Mr. and Mrs. Kevin Michael O'Callaghan

request the honour of your presence

at the marriage of her daughter [or, Mrs. O'Callaghan's daughter]

Kelly Elizabeth Quimby

to

[etc.]

If the bride's own father has no part in her life and her stepfather has brought her up, legally adopted or not, the invitation reads:

Mr. and Mrs. Kevin Michael O'Callaghan

request the honour of your presence

at the marriage of their daughter

Kelly Elizabeth Quimby

to

[etc.]

WHEN THE BRIDE IS AN ORPHAN

"Miss," Ms.," or "Mrs." are rarely used before the bride's name. The following case is an exception:

Mr. and Mrs. Paul John Carey
request the honour of your presence
at the marriage of
their niece
Miss Rosemary Gelbach
to
Mr. Karl Andrew Rauch
[etc.]

WHEN THE BRIDE AND GROOM ISSUE THEIR OWN INVITATIONS

A bride and groom who send out their own invitations would also use a title ("Miss," "Mrs."):

The honour of your presence
is requested
at the marriage of
Miss Andrea Mignone
to
Mr. Robert White
[etc.]

[OR]

Miss Andrea Mignone
and
Mr. Robert White
request the honour of your presence
at their marriage
[etc.]

Or less formally:

> Beth Holland and Christopher Saladino
> invite you to attend
> their marriage
> on
> Saturday, October the twenty-ninth
> two thousand
> at half past three o'clock
> The Hopewell School
> Richmond, Virginia
> A reception on the grounds will follow the ceremony
> R.S.V.P.
> Ms. Beth Holland
> 87 Grace Street
> Richmond, Virginia 23223

Mature couples or couples who have been living together may prefer to send out wedding invitations in their own names and not use social titles:

> Mary Ann Schmidt
> and
> George James MacLellan
> invite you to share with them
> the joy of their marriage
> Saturday, the tenth of July
> two thousand and one
> at half after four o'clock
> First Congregational Church
> Baton Rouge, Louisiana
> R.S.V.P.

When Other Relatives Issue Invitations

If the bride has siblings or other relatives who are giving the wedding, then the invitations should be sent in their names:

Mr. Robert Mazzone
requests the honour of your presence
at the marriage of his sister
Elizabeth Ann
[etc.]

When a bride and groom's grown children are giving their wedding, the invitation may be issued in their names, with the bride's children listed before the groom's. When several children are involved, their names are given in the order of their age, from the oldest to the youngest in each family. When the bride's married son and the single daughter and married son of the groom are giving the wedding together, the invitation should read:

Mr. and Mrs. Brendan Shine
Miss Christine Shine
Mr. and Mrs. William Barrett, Junior
request the honour of your presence
at the marriage of their parents
Madolyn Whitefield Shine
and
William Wyndham Barrett
Sunday, the tenth of September
two thousand
at half past three o'clock
at the Belle Haven Club
Greenwich, Connecticut
R.S.V.P.

WHEN THE BRIDE IS A YOUNG WIDOW OR DIVORCÉE

Invitations to a young widow's second wedding may be sent by her parents using the same wording used in the invitations to her first marriage. The only difference is that if she continues to use her married name, it should be included:

Doctor and Mrs. Daniel Thomas McCann
request the honour of your presence
at the marriage of their daughter
Sheliah O'Neill
[etc.]

A divorcée's second wedding invitation may read the same way. The bride's name would be the one she is using—either her first name, maiden name, and ex-husband's last name or, if she has dropped her ex-husband's name, her own middle and maiden name.

A more mature woman whose parents are deceased or a divorcée who has been independent since her divorce would, along with her groom, generally send out her own invitations.

A widow or divorcée's invitation would read:

The honour of your presence
is requested
at the marriage of
Mrs. Susan Green Millman
and
Mr. Elliot Franklin Aiken
[etc.]

If the bride prefers, she may drop the title and have her name simply read *"Susan Green Millman."*

When the Bridegroom's Family Gives the Wedding

When the bride's family lives far away and she is alone, the groom's parents may give the wedding and issue the invitations. This is also true if the bride's family disapproves of the wedding and refuses to take part in it.

Mr. and Mrs. Wendell William Orr
request the honour of your presence
at the marriage of
Miss Latoya Kienisha Anderson

to

their son
Joshua Allen Orr
[etc.]

If any announcements of the marriage are sent out to friends and colleagues who weren't invited to the wedding day celebrations, they should be sent by the bride's family, if possible. If that is not possible, then the groom's family should include the names of the bride's parents.

Including the Groom's Family in the Invitation

Increasingly, there are occasions when the groom's family shares in or pays the major part of the wedding expenses. In such a case it is only fair that their names appear on the invitations. The bride's parents' names would be first, and the wording would be as follows:

Mr. an Mrs. David Zimmerli
and
Captain and Mrs. John Gonzalez
request the honour of your presence
at the marriage of
Cynthia Ann Zimmerli
and
John Howard Gonzalez, Junior
[etc.]

When both the bride's and groom's parents have been divorced and have remarried, and all are participating in giving the wedding and hosting the reception, it is not unusual for all their names to appear on the invitation. In this instance the bride's mother and her husband would appear first, the bride's father and his wife second, the groom's mother and her husband third, and the groom's father and his wife fourth:

Mr. and Mrs. Michael Hannigan

Mr. and Mrs. Lawrence Anvik

Doctor and Mrs. Russell Healy

Mr. and Mrs. Jeffrey Jacobs

request the honour of your presence

at the marriage of

Lindsay Catherine Anvik

to

Andrew Lloyd Jacobs

[etc.]

A form followed in some foreign countries provides for a double invitation with the bride's family's invitation on the left and the groom's family's invitation on the right:

Mr. and Mrs. Arturo Mendel	*Mr. and Mrs. Roberto Perez*
request the honour of your presence	*request the honour of your presence*
at the marriage of their daughter	*at the marriage of their son*
Angelina Ruth	*Eduardo Robert*
to	*to*
Mr. Eduardo Perez	*Miss Angelina Mendel*
[etc.]	*[etc.]*

When the Bride Has a Professional Name

If the bride is well-known by a professional name and has many professional friends to whom she wishes to send invitations or announcements, she may include on the invitations her professional name in parentheses engraved or printed below her real name:

Margaret Marie

(Meg Drake)

to

Mr. Carl Louis Valentine

[etc.]

When Military Titles Are Used

When the groom is a member of the armed services or is on active duty in the reserve forces, he uses his military title.

For officers whose rank is captain in the army or lieutenant, senior grade, or higher in the navy, the title should appear on the same line as the name:

Colonel Graham O'Gorman

United States Army

Those with lower ranks should have their name and title engraved in this form:

John McMahon

Ensign, United States Navy

In the case of reserve officers on active duty, the second line would read *"Army of the United States"* or *"United States Naval Reserve."*

First and second lieutenants in the army both use "Lieutenant" without the numeral.

A noncommissioned officer or enlisted man may, if he wishes, include his rank and his branch of the service below his name.

Henry Delucia
Corporal, Signal Corps, United States Army

[OR]

Marc Josephson
Seaman Apprentice, United States Naval Reserve

High-ranking officers of the regular armed forces should continue to use their titles, followed by their branch of service, even after retirement, with "retired" following the branch of service:

General George Harmon
United States Army, retired

When the father of the bride is a member of the armed forces, either on active duty, a high-ranking retired officer, or one who retired after many years of service, he uses his title in the regular way:

Colonel and Mrs. James Booth
request the honour of your presence
[etc.]

When the bride is on active duty, both her rank and the branch of military are included in the invitation. The name of the bride appears on one line with her rank and the branch of the military on a separate line:

marriage of their daughter
Joanne
Lieutenant, United States Navy

WHEN OTHER TITLES ARE USED

Medical doctors, dentists, veterinarians, clergymen, judges, and all others customarily called by their titles should have those titles included on their own wedding invitations and on the invitations to their daughters' or sons' weddings.

Holders of academic degrees do not use "Doctor" unless they are always referred to in that way.

Women use their titles only when the invitations are issued by themselves and their grooms:

The honour of your presence

is requested

at the marriage of

Doctor Laurie Neu

and

Mr. Norbert Rudell

[etc.]

Otherwise she is *"their daughter, Laurie."*

The bride's mother uses the title "Doctor" on her daughter's invitation if she feels strongly about it: *"Doctor Lynn Josephson and Mr. Marc Josephson request..."* Otherwise the invitation would read, *"Mr. and Mrs. Marc Josephson request..."*

SAME-GENDER UNIONS

A formal invitation to a gay or lesbian commitment ceremony may be issued by the couple themselves or by one or both sets of parents:

The honour of your presence

is requested

at the marriage of

Susan Beth Gibson

and

Georgia Lee O'Dell

[etc.]

[OR]

Mr. and Mrs. Franklin Johnson
Mr. and Mrs. Jason Bolivia
request the honour of your presence
at the marriage of their sons
Victor Kenneth Johnson
and
Marc William Ballet
[etc.]

A gay or lesbian couple formally joining together may decide to use a different phrase than "marriage" on their invitation, depending on their feelings and the type of ceremony in which they are participating. Choices include *"Commitment Ceremony," "Affirmation Ceremony," "Celebration of Commitment," "Rite of Blessing," "Relationship Covenant,"* and *"Union Ceremony."*

DOUBLE WEDDINGS

Double weddings almost always involve the marriages of two sisters, and the form, with the elder sister's name first, is as follows:

Mr. and Mrs. Roderick Thorn
request the honour of your presence
at the marriage of their daughters
Jessica Ann
to
Mr. Bradley Peterson
and
Amanda Lynn
to
Mr. Richard Suarino
Saturday, the twenty-second of October
at four o'clock
Good Shepherd Church

In the event that two close friends decide to have a double wedding, the invitation reads:

Mr. and Mrs. Richard McMillan

and

Mrs. Karen Clark

request the honour of your presence

at the marriage of their daughters

Kerry Ann McMillian

to

Mr. Stephen Bonner

and

Amanda Louise Clark

to

Mr. Kenneth Kienzle

[etc.]

⊛ WEDDING ANNOUNCEMENTS ⊛

Sharing the happy news after the wedding in the form of printed or handwritten announcements is never obligatory, but it is a nice idea.

✣ *Who receives wedding announcements?*   Printed or handwritten wedding announcements sent through the mail can serve a useful purpose. These are generally sent to those friends and family who were left off the guest list because the celebration was too small to accommodate them, or to acquaintances or business associates who, while not particularly close to the family, might still wish to hear news of the marriage.

✣ *Are recipients obligated to send a gift?*   Announcements carry no obligation for the recipient to return a gift to the bride and groom, so many families send them rather than invitations to friends who are not expected to attend or to send a present. They are never sent to anyone who has received an invitation to the ceremony or reception.

✣ *When are announcements mailed out?* Ideally announcements are mailed the day after the wedding but may be mailed up to several months later.

✣ *What is the traditional wording for announcements?* Announcements were traditionally sent in the name of the bride's parents, with wording as follows (still perfectly correct):

Mr. and Mrs. James Welch
have the honour of
announcing the marriage of their daughter
Amy Sue
to
Mr. Jonathan Scott Jamison
Saturday, the twelfth of June
two thousand
Mansfield, Pennsylvania

VARIATIONS

Several other variations are equally correct. You may use *"have the honour to announce,"* or merely *"announce."* The year is always included. The most formal wording is *"one thousand nine hundred and ninety-nine,"* but *"nineteen hundred and ninety-nine"* is not incorrect.

Today, however, when the attitude toward marriage is that it is a "joining" rather than a "giving" of a woman to a man, there is no reason that announcements should not go out in both families' names. Although this privilege has always been accorded the bride's family, the parents of the groom are also presumably proud and happy to share the announcement. The wording is as follows:

Mr. and Mrs. James Welch

and

Mr. and Mrs. Dewey Jamison

announce the marriage of

Amy Sue Welch

and

Jonathan Scott Jamison

on . . .

The variations in circumstances, names, and titles follow the rules under wedding invitations. In general the wording used for the wedding invitation is the basis for the wording of the wedding announcement.

❧ ALL ABOUT ENVELOPES ❧

One or Two Envelopes?

When formal, third-person invitations are written, they are traditionally inserted into two envelopes, an *inner envelope* and an *outer envelope.* The outer envelope is the one that is addressed and stamped, while the inner envelope bears only the names of the people to whom the mailing envelope is addressed. For example, a married couple's inner envelope is addressed to *"Mr. and Mrs. Anderson"* with neither first names nor address.

This convention serves a useful purpose—it permits the bride and groom to be very specific as to whom is invited. If, for example, a close friend is invited and the bride and groom want her to bring a guest (whose name they don't know), the outer envelope is addressed to the friend and the inner envelope reads *"Miss Smith and Guest."* Not only would it be awkward to address the outer envelope this way, but there is no other way, short of a personal note or telephone call, to let Miss Smith know that a guest is welcome. An inner envelope that reads only *"Miss Smith"* clearly indicates that Miss Smith is not supposed to bring a guest.

Of course, this kind of communication may be unnecessary for the type of guest list you have, and you may want to dispense with the custom of the inner envelope altogether; it is correct to do so.

If you do plan to use inner envelopes, you may write the names of intimate relatives and lifelong friends in informal and familial terms. For example, it is perfectly fine to write, *"Aunt Deirdre and Uncle Tom,"* or, *"Grand-mother."*

Addressing Envelopes

✣ *To a married couple:* Wedding invitations are always addressed to both members of a married couple, even though the bride may know only one or knows that only one will attend.

✣ *To an unmarried couple living together:* Invitations to an unmarried couple who reside at the same address should be addressed to *"Ms. Nancy Fellows and Mr. Scott Dunn,"* with each name appearing on a separate line.

✣ *Including children:* Children over thirteen years of age should, if possible, receive separate invitations. Young brothers and sisters may be sent a joint invitation addressed to *"The Misses Smith"* or *"The Messrs. Jones"* on the outer envelope, with *"Andy, Doug and Brian"* written on the inner envelope to make perfectly clear that all are invited. If there are both boys and girls, the outer envelope address may read:

The Messrs. Jones
The Misses Jones

If children are not receiving a separate invitation, their names may be written on a line below their parents' names on the inner envelope and do not have to be listed on the outer envelope at all. However, if no inner envelope is used, their names must be written on the outer envelope, or their parents won't know that they are included in the invitation. When possible, be specific and list names. Still, it is often difficult to know all of the names and relationships within a family. If, for example, relationships are so complicated or children so numerous that it seems simpler to address the envelope

"Mr. and Mrs. Vito Sessa and Family" you may do so—but *only* in the following circumstances:

1. When it is clear that you are inviting just the people living under that roof, not the aunt and uncle next door.

2. When the children are young; adult relatives who reside in the household should receive their own invitation.

3. When every person living under the same roof is included in the invitation.

✢ *Return address:* The U.S. Postal Service requests that all first-class mail bear a return address. This information also lets invited guests know where to send replies and gifts if an RSVP address does not appear on the invitation. The postal service prefers that the return address be printed or handwritten on the upper-left-hand corner of the envelope. It is nonetheless acceptable to clearly emboss the return address by stamping it on the envelope's flap (although sometimes the embossing is difficult to read).

Using Abbreviations

Just as abbreviations are not used in the wording of the invitation, so are they not used in addressing the envelopes. A person's middle name may or may not be used. If it is, it must be written out in full, as should "Street" and "Avenue." The name of the state is traditionally not abbreviated, but because the post office prefers the use of two-letter state abbreviations and no comma between the city and the state, it is fine to do so.

❧ INSERTIONS ❦

In addition to the invitation, several enclosures may be placed in the inner envelope (or in the outer envelope, if you omit an inner one).

Admission Cards

Admission cards are necessary only when a wedding is held in a popular cathedral or church that attracts sightseers. To ensure privacy in these circumstances, each guest is asked to present his or her card at the entrance. It is generally engraved or printed in the same style as the invitation and reads:

PLEASE PRESENT THIS CARD

AT

ST. PATRICK'S CATHEDRAL

SATURDAY, THE TWELFTH OF JUNE

Pew Cards

Small cards with *"Pew Number _____"* engraved on them may be enclosed with the invitations going to those family members and close friends who are to be seated in reserved pews. Recipients simply take the pew cards to the ceremony and show them to ushers, who escort them to their seats.

Similar cards are sometimes engraved *"Within the Ribbon."* This indicates that reserved pews or seats with white ribbons across the ends have been set aside for special guests. When ushers escort recipients of these cards to their seats, the ribbon is lifted and then replaced after the guests are seated. Guests receiving pew cards can sit anywhere within these seats.

Pew cards are sometimes sent separately after acceptances or regrets are received, when the bride knows how many reserved pews are needed.

At Home Cards

If the bride and groom wish to let friends know what their new address will be, they may insert an "at home" card in with the invitation or wedding announcement. These cards traditionally read:

Bullying the Bride

Q: I am getting married in a few weeks, and I am steamed about something. Friends of mine returned their invitation with their children's names written in as attending. I am not having children at my wedding, which was made perfectly clear on the invitation. What do I do?

A: There are those parents who go right ahead and write their children's names on the response card, even though the kids clearly weren't asked to attend. Some do this intentionally, believing they can bully the bride into having them; others truly believe it is understood that the children are included. Whoever is hosting the wedding may call immediately and explain in kind terms that the children are indeed not invited. If this results in an angry "Then I'm not coming, either," so be it. The breach of etiquette is theirs, not yours.

AT HOME [OR, WILL BE AT HOME]

AFTER JULY SECOND

3842 GRAND AVENUE

HOUSTON, TEXAS 77001

(898) 555-4321

The problem with the example above is that many people receiving these cards often put them away, intending to enter them in an address book or file at some point in the future. When they come across the card weeks, even months, later, they may find they can't recall just who will be "at home at 3842 Grand Avenue after July second." Therefore, even though you are not married at the time the invitation is sent, it is perfectly all right to have an at home card printed with the couple's names:

MR. AND MRS. BRUCE MOORE

WILL BE AT HOME

[Etc.]

An at home card also gives the woman who plans to keep her own name the opportunity to let friends know. In this case, the at home card would read:

PETERNELLE VAN ARSDALE AND BRYAN OETTEL

WILL BE AT HOME

[Etc.]

Reception Cards

When a separate reception card is used, it is placed in front of the invitation to the wedding ceremony (for suggested wording of reception cards, see "Reception Cards," pages 113–14).

Response Cards

It used to be that the only correct response to a formal invitation was an equally formal reply, handwritten by the invited guest. This reply is still correct, but because fewer and fewer people these days will take the time to pen a formal reply, in the last decade or so response cards have replaced the handwritten reply in popularity. The response card is inserted with the invitation and is engraved or printed in the same style as the invitation on card stock, in the following form:

M_____

ACCEPTS_____

REGRETS_____

THE FAVOUR OF YOUR REPLY IS REQUESTED BY JULY 26

The *"M"* precedes the space where the guest writes his or her title and name, as in *"Miss Phyllis Reynolds"* or *"Mr. and Mrs. Joseph DeRuvo."*

A *printed, stamped envelope* is included so that all the guest has to do is write in his, her, or their names: "Mr. and Mrs. Stephen Nelmes," check *"accepts"* or *"regrets,"* place the card in the envelope, and mail it. When one guest is able to accept and the other is not, it is necessary to make this clear on the response card.

Generally a response card should not include the phrase *number of persons.* The names on the outer and inner envelopes are those of the only persons invited, which means that other members of the family whose names do not appear on the envelopes are not invited. When *"number of persons"* is printed, recipients may confuse this to mean that other members of the family are indeed invited to attend, resulting in a wedding that overflows with too many guests.

When one invitation is received by a couple whose children are included, *every name* must be written in on the response card.

If one invitation is sent to a friend with *"and guest"* written on the envelope, the friend should write in the name of the guest so that his or her name can be written on a place card. If the friend is not bringing a guest, only the friend's name should be written on the response card.

Handwritten Formal Reply

When a formal invitation does not include a response card insert, a guest may certainly send a formal handwritten reply. The formal reply should be written on plain or bordered letter paper or notepaper in blue or black ink. The lines should be evenly and symmetrically spaced on one page. The formal reply, which follows exactly the form of the invitation, should read if accepting:

MR. AND MRS. MARK ROSS

ACCEPT WITH PLEASURE

MR. AND MRS. MCCULLOUGH'S

KIND INVITATION FOR

SATURDAY, THE TWENTY-SECOND OF MAY

[OR]

MR. AND MRS. MARK ROSS

ACCEPT WITH PLEASURE

THE KIND INVITATION OF

MR. AND MRS. FRANK MCCULLOUGH

TO THE MARRIAGE OF THEIR DAUGHTER

KRISTIN LYNN

TO

MR. BRENT BROWN

SATURDAY, THE TWENTY-SECOND OF MAY

Regrets are sent in the same manner:

MR. AND MRS. CHARLES COLETTI

REGRET THAT THEY ARE UNABLE TO ACCEPT

MR. AND MRS. ALIBERTO'S

KIND INVITATION FOR

SUNDAY, THE FOURTEENTH OF MARCH

When one invited guest is able to attend and the other is not, the form reads:

MRS. LAWRENCE HIRES

ACCEPTS WITH PLEASURE

MR. AND MRS. BENSON'S

KIND INVITATION FOR

SATURDAY, THE FIFTH OF FEBRUARY

BUT REGRETS THAT

MR. HIRES

WILL BE UNABLE TO ATTEND

Tissues

The delicate tissues that are sometimes included in a wedding invitation are optional today. Their prior usage had a real function: to keep the oils from the ink on engraved invitations from smudging as it slowly dried. Improved printing and engraving techniques have made tissues unnecessary for decades, but their use continues as a bow to tradition. While the tradition is fine, it is perfectly correct to exclude the tissues if a couple chooses to do so.

Maps

You can insert maps and directions to the wedding sites in a number of ways. You may enclose them with the invitation or you may mail them after you have received an affirmative response to your invitation. Sometimes maps are provided by the ceremony and/or reception sites. If they are not, you will have to order them or design them yourself. Be sure your directions are clear and accurate and that they are written in as concise and abbreviated a manner as possible to avoid adding extra bulk to the invitation.

Rain Card

When a ceremony and/or reception are planned for outdoors, you must have an indoor contingency plan of action in the event of inclement weather. A rain card is a small card that gives the alternate location for the wedding and/or the reception. It might read, "In case of rain, the ceremony and reception will take place at 33 Elm Street, Traverse City."

❧ STUFFING THE ENVELOPES ❧

1. When two envelopes are used, the invitation (folded edge first for a folded invitation, left edge for a single card) and all enclosures are put in the inner envelope, facing the back.

2. The inner envelope is then placed, unsealed, in the outer envelope, with the flap away from the person inserting it.

3. When there are insertions, they are placed in front of the invitation, so that they face the flap (and the person inserting them).

4. In the case of a folded invitation, insertions are placed in the same direction but within the fold.

Travel Information for Guests

If you have the time and the inclination, gather as much travel and lodging information as you can for your out-of-town invited guests. This information can be sent by e-mail after you receive a response or can be included with the invitation, perhaps laser-printed on a card or a single sheet of small stationery. Helpful information to include: the names of airlines that fly into nearby airports, hotels, motels, inns, and bed-and-breakfast lodging, ground transportation services, and car rental rates. If events are planned for out-of-town guests, this information should be sent as soon as a response is received, along with travel directions. That way your guests can best plan their arrival and departure times. Along with the travel information, the schedule of events can be e-mailed or printed right from your own desktop computer and coordinated in color and paper, if possible, with the other printed pieces.

A CHANGE IN PLANS

Even the best-laid plans can go awry. Here are some of the more typical situations that warrant some sort of communication that plans are changed.

When the Wedding Is Cancelled After Invitations Are Mailed

If the decision to cancel the wedding is a last-minute one, guests must be notified by telephone. If there is time, printed cards may be sent:

MR. AND MRS. OLIVER GRANT

ANNOUNCE THAT THE MARRIAGE OF

THEIR DAUGHTER

DEBRA

TO

MR. CHRISTOPHER BRONNER

WILL NOT TAKE PLACE

When the Wedding Date Is Changed

When it is necessary to change the date of the wedding and the new date is decided upon after the invitations have been printed but before they are mailed, it is not necessary for the bride to order new invitations. Instead she may enclose a printed card, if there is time to print one, saying, "The date of the wedding has been changed from March sixth to April twelfth." If there is not time for the card, she may neatly cross out the old date on the invitation and insert the new one by pen.

If the invitations have already been mailed, she may mail a card or a personal note or, if the guest list is small, telephone the information.

When the wedding is postponed, not cancelled, and there is time to have an announcement printed, it would read:

Mr. and Mrs. Roy Westgate

regret that

the invitations to

their daughter's wedding

on Saturday, December fourth

must be recalled

[OR]

Mr. and Mrs. Scott Pierce

announce that

the marriage of their daughter

Janet Ann

to

Mr. Peter Norton

has been postponed

If the new date is known, it is added: *"has been postponed to February third."* If there is no time to have a card printed, the information must be communicated by telephone, fax, or e-mail, by mail, or by personal note.

Here are some invitation issues that warrant particularly careful attention.

✢ *Order extras.* Even the most carefully held pen can experience a slipup, so it is the wise bride who orders at least a dozen extra invitations and envelopes. At the very least, order extra envelopes. It is far less costly to print extras that you may not need than to go back to the printer to order more. Remember to order an extra for yourselves, to include as a keepsake in your album or organizer, as well as extras for your family and in-laws, who may want to do the same.

✢ *Think about where you want responses sent.* Do think about where you want responses sent. Usually gifts are sent to the return address on the envelope or to the address printed by the RSVP. If the bride lives in New York City but her wedding will be held where her parents live in Chicago, it is far handier to have gifts sent to her New York City home than to her mother, who will have to pack them up and ship them to New York. Then there is the question of who is keeping track of responses. If it is the bride, then by all means her address should be used. If it is her mother, then the question of which is easier to ship back and forth—responses or gifts—is the determining factor.

✢ *Allow plenty of time.* This is both an invitation do and an invitation don't. Don't run out of time. Do allow plenty of time to carefully address, assemble, and mail your invitations, especially if you are using a calligrapher to do the writing. If other obligations leave you pressed for time, ask to have envelopes sent to you well in advance of the invitations so that you can start addressing early.

✢ *Get organized.* Develop a system of organization that makes the process of addressing and mailing your invitations pleasurable, not painful. Prepare in advance by writing in your wedding organizer the names and addresses of everyone on your guest list. Perhaps family and future in-laws could be persuaded to send you a complete list with full names and addresses (including names of any children or unmarried partners) to be invited. Other brides find a computer database or file cards helpful. Otherwise you'll spend all your time looking up addresses in the phone book and other sources.

Use proven time-management systems and handle each piece only once, if possible. Arrange each element that goes into an invitation in a stack, in the order it will be picked up, assembled, and inserted.

As replies are received, make helpful notes to yourself, such as "friend of Andy's parents" or "Susie's date" so that you'll know who's who when finalizing your table arrangements and greeting guests in the receiving line.

✣ *Check postage.* It would be extremely annoying to mail all your invitations only to have them returned because of insufficient postage. Before you buy stamps and apply them, take an assembled invitation to the post office and have it weighed. It's likely that the inserts, or even an unusually shaped envelope, will necessitate extra postage. Remember that maps and other directional inserts sent to out-of-town-guests will make a heavier invitation than those sent to local guests and may require a postage adjustment. In that case be sure to assemble two sets, have both weighed—and pay close attention when affixing postage so that the appropriate stamps go on the right envelopes.

✣ *Double-check spelling.* Ask for the business cards of the contacts at your ceremony and reception sites before you order your invitations. You'll want to get the spelling and titles of the sites absolutely correct. Guests directed to *"St. John's Church"* could easily miss the wedding ceremony at the *"Evangelical Lutheran Church of St. John."*

✣ *Use the correct names of guests of invited guests.* It is so much warmer and more welcoming, on invitations and place cards, to use the correct names of those who will be guests of your friends. Whether you also send these guests their own invitation or include their name on your friend's invitation is up to you, but the guest feels personally invited when his or her name is actually written on the envelope. This also enables you to write a place card using the person's name instead of "and guest" on your friend's place card or a card that reads "Miss Johnston's Guest."

✢ *Use correct titles.* It is most flattering when invitations are addressed correctly. This means using correct titles as well as spelling names right. Some professional titles that are also used socially and that would be used when addressing an invitation include *"The Honorable"* (judge, governor, mayor, United States senator, member of Congress, cabinet member, ambassador); and *"The Reverend," "The Most Reverend,"* or *"The Right Reverend."* When in doubt, ask before addressing.

✤ INVITATION DON'TS ✤

Certain information should never be included on or placed inside a wedding invitation:

✢ *Registry or gift information.* Although a wedding invitation demands a gift in return, it is in extremely poor taste to insert a "helpful" list of places where the bride and groom are registered or a checklist of the things they want or don't want. This information should be shared with parents and attendants who can be resources for guests who want to know.

✢ *The inclusion of "No Gifts."* Often a second-time bride or groom or an older couple feels that they have everything they need and prefer that their guests not give them a gift. Regardless, the joy and happiness a wedding represents include the giving of gifts to celebrate that happiness, and the printing of *"No Gifts, Please"* on the invitation is not acceptable. Again, family members and attendants can share this information with guests or can provide the name of a favorite charity to which guests may contribute in lieu of giving a nuptial gift.

✢ *The inclusion of "No Children."* Never print "No Children" or "Adults Only" on an invitation. The way an invitation is addressed, whether on the outer or inner envelope, indicates exactly who is— and by omission who is not—invited to the wedding.

✢ *Bulletin board invitations.* It is not a good idea to post an invitation on a bulletin board at work. It implies that anyone reading it is welcome to attend, and each person may feel he or she is also welcome to bring a spouse, a date, or children—which would surely skew the count for the reception. Instead it is better for each person to receive his or her own invitation at home, not at work, particularly if some colleagues are invited and others are not.

✣ *Dictating dress.*   It is incorrect to put *"black tie"* or *"white tie"* on the invitation to the ceremony. If it seems essential to include this directive, it can be added only to the invitation to the reception and is placed in the lower-right-hand corner. Avoid writing *"black tie invited"* or *"black tie preferred."*

✣ *Labels.*   Do not use labels to address wedding invitation envelopes, even when inviting hundreds of guests. Instead plan ahead and take the time to handwrite (or hire a calligrapher to do so) every envelope, so that it is in keeping with the personal tone of the wedding.

✣ *Choice of entrée.*   It is best not to put entrée choices on the response card or the envelope. If you are offering menu choices, work out the arrangements with the club, restaurant, or caterer to provide French service—where each wait-staff member carries a tray with both or all entrées already plated and offers each guest his or her choice—or have the wait staff ask each guest his or her preference at the table before serving. The wait staff could also offer a little of each entrée to each guest.

✣ *Alcohol information.*   It is unnecessary to put *"alcohol-free"* or *"wine and beer only"* on the invitation. Surely this information will not be the deciding factor as to whether or not guests attend. You are inviting them to a wedding, not a cocktail party.

✣ *Don't underestimate your time.*   Count on the printing of your invitations and their related inserts to take six to eight weeks. Keep in mind that in the case of a large, formal wedding, invitations should be mailed six to eight weeks in advance. Take into account the fact that it can take an extraordinarily long time to address, assemble, and mail invitations. Don't underestimate the time this takes. Allow several extra weeks in your schedule to prepare your invitations for mailing.

✣ *Don't mix typefaces.*   Once you have selected a typeface for your invitation, stick with it for all related printed insertions and other printed material. The typeface you choose is part of your overall theme, and even though you may love both a shaded roman and a flowery script, you should avoid mixing them.

✣ *Don't offend your B list.* When a bride and groom draw up a bigger list of guests than they can accommodate, they must pare it down. They can do so in a number of ways: they can include first cousins, for example, but not second; they can invite only the friends from work with whom they've socialized before. The second cousins and the other work pals should not be forgotten, however, and can be invited if several guests on the A list send regrets. A word of caution: Do not invite your "second tier" of guests less than three weeks before the wedding. Inviting people at the last minute makes it obvious that they are on your B list—a notion that will make them feel more unwelcome than if you had not invited them at all.

❧ MISCELLANEOUS ❧ STATIONERY ITEMS

Ceremony Programs

Programs can be smart additions to your ceremony and are especially helpful to guests of other religions who may not be familiar with your service. This is particularly true when the wedding is a mix of religions and cultures and not all guests necessarily understand the liturgy or ritual. Programs are not Broadway playbills, however, nor are they a forum for profiling the bride, the groom, their attendants, or their families. Therefore avoid biographical write-ups. Under no circumstances should programs be advertisements for wedding service providers, such as florists or consultants. They may, however, be embellished with art, poetry, or fine calligraphy or can simply list the order of the service in a fold-over bulletin. (These bulletins can often be ordered from the diocese, synod, or home center of the church or synagogue; or they can be printed on a desktop publishing system.) Ushers hand programs to guests as they seat them, or children can hand them out as guests arrive. Programs can also be placed in pews or on chairs or in baskets by the door. Flower girls can offer them to arriving guests if they are at the ceremony site early and are not arriving with the rest of the bridal party.

Program elements can include

+ Processional
+ Service music
+ Translations
+ The order of the service
+ Explanation of symbolic meaning of service components
+ Text for group prayers or readings
+ Poem or thought of thanks and love
+ The names of soloists (particularly if they are contributing their talents as a gift to the couple), the officiant(s), and the attendants, altar assistants, organist, and readers.

Place Cards

While the use and placement of place cards is reviewed in chapter 13, they are mentioned here because they are a stationery item that is often ordered with the other paper and printed items. Place cards should be written or calligraphied in one hand. Because they will be presented all together on one table, they should have a uniform look. Place cards may be decorated, have a gold or colored border, or be simple white or colored card stock fold-over place cards. Place card forms are available at better stationers. Place cards created and printed by computer (using an 8½-by-11-inch sheet to run through a laser printer) are acceptable as long as the typeface chosen looks handwritten and as long as the individual place cards are separated carefully with no rough edges left to indicate that they were from a computer-designed tear-off form.

Printed Accessories and Favors

Some couples like to have personalized cocktail napkins, matchbooks, or other memorabilia at their receptions. If this is your choice, it is a good idea to see if they can be done by the printer who is printing your invitations, announcements, and other inserts. Sometimes you can get a better price when ordering everything from one source.

Personal Stationery

Don't forget to order stationery for your thank-you notes. Fold-over note cards are perfect for this purpose and can be printed with your monogram or name on the front. Remember, the groom can also write thank-you notes. You might want to order "his" and "hers" stationery to use before you are married and at the same time order stationery with your married name, monogram, or initials to use after you are married. A monogram of just the initial of your last name, or "Mr. and Mrs." stationery can be used by both of you.

❧ NEWSPAPER WEDDING NOTICE ❧

Most newspapers request wedding information at least three weeks before the big day. The wedding announcement generally appears the day following the ceremony. Since newspapers often receive more wedding announcements than they can print, the sooner yours is sent and the clearer and more concise the information, the better your chance of having it published. Each paper generally uses as much of the information as it wishes and rewrites it to match the paper's style. It is a good idea to call the paper ahead of time and request a form, but in general you should provide the following:

The bride's full name

The bride's parents' name and town of residence

Bride's parents' occupations

Bride's maternal and paternal grandparents

Bride's school and college

Bride's occupation

Groom's full name and town of residence

Groom's parents' name and town of residence

Groom's parents' occupations

The Bride's Mother Asks About Place Cards

Q: My daughter and I have decided to use place cards in order to minimize confusion when it comes time to serve dinner at her reception. Is there a way to approach this task in order to assure that there is a place for everyone and everyone can find their place?

A: One way to envision who sits where is to write your place cards as responses are received and place them in stacks, by table. This will assure a card for each guest. Then you can review each stack to make sure that you haven't, by accident, seated together people who are antagonistic toward each other. Actually "seeing" names on place cards helps you imagine the makeup of a table even better than a printed list.

Groom's maternal and paternal grandparents

Groom's school and college

Groom's occupation

Date of wedding

Location of wedding and reception

Names of bride's attendants and relationship to bride or groom, if any

Names of groom's attendants and relationship to bride or groom, if any

Description of bridal gown and bouquet (optional)

Description of attendants' gown (optional)

Name of minister, priest, or rabbi

Name of soloist, if any

Where couple will honeymoon

Where couple will reside (town) after wedding

Photograph. If a photograph of the bride is to be included, the photo needs to be taken in time to be provided with the announcement information. If a photograph of the bride and groom together is to be included, the announcement is usually printed a week or two after the wedding so that a portrait can be taken on the day of the wedding.

CHAPTER SEVEN

It is a tangible

GIFTS OF LOVE

representation of love

and support.

The showering of gifts on the newly betrothed is a tradition that seems

to become only more deeply ingrained with time. And no wonder: wedding

gift giving is big business. Still, the idea behind wedding gifts is a fine one.

It is a tangible representation of love and support, a generous offering to

help young marrieds get a head start in their lives together.

Customs regarding gifts vary by culture and ethnic groups; in some

cultures a wedding gift is presented at a shower, for example, or money is

presented as a wedding gift. In other cultures the groom's family presents lavish gifts of jewelry to the bride at her engagement party, draping necklaces around her neck and bracelets on her wrist. The gift suggestions in this chapter are based on traditional customs, however. Use them as a base from which to begin. If you are uncertain of custom when invited to the wedding of friends of a different cultural or ethnic background, simply inquire of other guests-to-be or of any acquaintances from that culture or ethnic group.

ALL ABOUT BRIDAL REGISTRIES

Gift registries are showing up in the most unusual places these days. While the tradition of registering at department and gift stores for china, silver, and crystal continues to be as popular as ever, more and more couples are also selecting other types of gifts—particularly in second- and third-time couplings, where multiple sets of china and crystal have already been amassed. In response, creative retailers are offering registries for nontraditional wedding gifts. A national chain hardware store started it first, opening a gift registry in 1991, largely to draw women customers to the stores. The idea took off, with many prenuptial couples choosing practical items like lawn mowers, kitchen fixtures—even camping equipment—in addition to or instead of the more customary china or glassware. Today couples can register at garden and home centers, national chains, specialty stores, and recreational sports stores.

Store Gift Registries

Registering at stores simply means completing a list of things you would like to have, in the quantity you would like to have them. The procedure for registering generally is as follows:

‡ The store provides the *registry form,* which includes your name, wedding date, a listing of gifts, and the address to which gifts are to be sent. A store well versed in registering gifts can do even more: salespeople will help you choose patterns; figure the correct number of

items ordered on your list in relation to your guest list; and give you a printout updating the latest purchases.

✢ Many stores with gift registries now have *Web sites,* where each couple's gift suggestions are listed along with a posting of items already purchased. Guests can often simply order the gifts on-line.

✢ A store registry generally keeps *all pertinent information on file* for up to several months after the wedding date.

Choosing Gifts

The following is advice and guidelines on selecting and registering for gifts:

✢ *Consider your needs.* Decide what you truly want—basic appliances, for instance, or fancy silver—when selecting gifts in a registry. If your lifestyle is casual, you may not be interested in formal crystal, china, and silver, all traditional wedding gifts. Even so, there is nothing wrong with planning for the day when you will appreciate a formal setting, and registering for patterns is a time-honored bridal tradition.

✢ *Register as soon as you can.* You should have your registries completed by the time invitations are sent.

✢ *Register for items in a variety of price ranges.* Keep in mind that guests have a wide range of budgets.

✢ *Register in national chain stores.* This works nicely for out-of-town guests, who can order easily from the companies' Web sites or 800 numbers and have the gifts delivered by mail. Couples also can register for gifts on one of the growing number of retail chains' Web sites—allowing friends to easily place an order while sitting at their computers.

✢ *Don't register for the same things at different stores.* A national store or catalog service will remove items that have been bought for you from your list so that you don't get duplicates of those items, or they will indicate that these items are no longer available. One store does not coordinate with a different retailer, however, so if you register for eight woven placemats at store A, don't also register for them at store B. Otherwise you're likely to end up with more placemats than you'll ever need.

✤ *Don't insist that guests use the registry.*   Avoid thinking that guests must use registries. Gifts are selected by your friends and family. Remember, it's their choice as to whether to use your gift registry. Some presents are carefully chosen surprises—sometimes the most favorite gifts of all.

ETIQUETTE FINE POINTS

Getting the Word Out

How do you get the word out that you've registered at a particular store? The old-fashioned way: word of mouth. Tradition still holds that the practice of including lists of gift registries with wedding invitations is considered tacky and inappropriate. A simple phone call to you, or to your close friend or relative, will provide guests with all the registry information they need. A way to facilitate sharing information: Once you have registered, give your mothers and your maid of honor a list of the stores, mail-order catalogs, Internet addresses, and other places where you are registered, to share with guests when they ask for gift ideas.

❧ WEDDING CELEBRATION GIFTS ❧

Engagement Party Gifts

Traditionally, engagement presents are given only by close relatives and intimate friends upon the announcement of your engagement and are almost always intended especially for the bride. When the engagement party is a small dinner, cocktail party, or luncheon, and a guest wants to give a gift, he or she takes it to the party. If everyone brings a gift, the bride-to-be may open them as part of the festivities. When the party is a large reception or cocktail party, gifts are not generally taken; if they are, they should not be opened during the party, to avoid embarrassing those guests who (correctly) did not bring gifts.

Wedding Shower Gifts

Unless culture and custom rule that shower gifts should be the equivalent of wedding presents, gifts given to the bride or engaged couple at a shower should not be elaborate. Traditionally, shower gifts were handmade for the occasion, and such gifts are still treasured. Shower gifts should be appropriate to the shower, if the shower has a theme. At a bath or kitchen shower, for example, guests comply by bringing gifts related to the theme. Sometimes guests contribute to a joint gift for bride or the couple.

‡ *If a guest can't attend, must he or she send a gift?*   If an invited guest can't attend the shower, it is not obligatory to send a gift. Sometimes close friends or relatives wish to, however, which is fine. If a nonattending invitee does send a gift, he or she should send it directly to the shower hostess and not from the store directly to the bride. The gift should be accompanied by a card to let the guest of honor know the name of the donor.

‡ *When are shower gifts opened?*   Shower gifts are opened at the party, and each donor is thanked personally then and there.

‡ *When are thank-you notes mandatory?*   The bride may write thank-you notes later if she wishes, and it is much appreciated if she does, but it is not absolutely mandatory—unless the donor was not there or did not receive thanks from the bride in person.

‡ *Is it appropriate to have a gift shower for an encore bride?*   It is perfectly acceptable to have a shower for a second marriage or for an older couple who have been independent for a number of years. For couples who may already have all of the basic necessities, food showers, garden showers, and ticket (to some entertainment) showers may be more appropriate than traditional kitchen or linen showers. In general the guest list is made up of new friends of the bride or couple or very close friends and relatives. Other than the closest of friends, it is better not to invite guests who attended a shower for the first marriage.

The Maid of Honor Asks:
Any Ideas for Smart Shower Gifts?

Q: I am my best friend's maid of honor and as such am invited to two showers. I know I'm not required to give a gift at both showers, but I would like to present a token of my affection for the bride—maybe even something she could really use on her wedding day. Any thoughts?

A: The maid of honor is not expected to take a gift to each shower and party she is invited to, but she can bring a small token. A great gift idea, especially coming from the maid of honor, who is supposed to be the bride's most important helper: a little emergency kit for the day of the wedding. In it she could place an extra pair of panty hose, a mirror, hairspray, hairpins, a small comb, nail file and nail polish, all sizes of safety pins, a small sewing kit, white masking tape, a package of tissues, bottled water, breath mints, scissors, superadhesive glue, and packages of hand wipes.

✦ ALL ABOUT WEDDING GIFTS ✦

It is truly a remarkable phenomenon to be an engaged couple suddenly deluged with crisply wrapped packages, shiny new appliances, sparkling china, and colorful linens, all accompanied by heartfelt notes conveying love and best wishes. Indulgences, all—much like having a lifetime of Christmases, birthdays, and graduations delivered into your lap in one fell swoop. Feel privileged—because you are. Here, then, are some guidelines for *both* giving and receiving wedding gifts.

✢ *Are guests obligated to send wedding gifts?* It was once considered absolutely obligatory for anyone invited to a wedding to send a gift, whether they attended the wedding or not. This is still true when the recipients are friends whom you see from time to time or who live nearby. In the days when that rule was made, people did not move around as much as they do today, and invitations were sent only to those within a reasonable distance. Because invitations still carry a gift-in-return obligation, it is more proper to send a wedding

The Wishing Well

Sometimes the invitation to a wedding shower asks each guest to bring a gift for a wishing well in addition to the shower gift. The wishing well gift is a small, inexpensive item, such as a measuring spoon or cup set, herbs or spices, or bars of scented soap. These presents may be wrapped or not, accompanied by a card or not, and put into a replica of a well. A gift for the wishing well should not be expensive, since the shower guest has invested in a shower gift and most likely a wedding gift, too.

announcement to mere acquaintances or distant friends you haven't seen in years, for an announcement carries no gift obligation. If you do send an invitation to people who are not close to you and they do not attend the festivities, you should not expect a gift in return.

✤ *Is there a special formula for calculating how much a guest should spend on a gift?* Any formula wherein a wedding gift should cost at least as much as the bride and groom are spending on entertaining each person at the reception is a myth. Such extravagance is impractical, uncalled for, and ostentatious—and therefore in poor taste. Fortunately most guests know that they have no such obligation. The cost of a gift should be based on the guest's affection for and relationship with the bride, groom, or their families. No one should feel pressed to spend more than can be afforded. That doesn't mean, however, that guests have the green light to be stingy in purchasing a gift. Each guest should simply give what he or she can afford, along with love and best wishes.

Gift Delivery

✤ *Where should gifts be sent?* Sometimes gifts are delivered in person. Generally wedding gifts are delivered to the bride's home or to the home of her parents before the wedding, addressed to the bride. When gifts are sent after the wedding, they are sent to the couple at

A QUESTION FOR PEGGY

Gifts for Those Who Are Marrying Again

Q: I am invited to a friend's second wedding. I went to the first wedding and gave an elaborate gift. Do I have to give a gift the second time around?

A: Although family members—and some very close friends—usually give a gift to a bride being married for the second time, friends who gave gifts the first time around need not do so. If it is the first marriage for the groom, it is fine for his family and friends to give the couple gifts.

If a couple is being married again and prefer that guests forgo gifts, it is considered incorrect to include that information on the invitation; the word that gifts are not expected should be spread verbally. The couple's families, attendants, and close friends can help get the word out for them.

their new address, if known, or to their parents' home. When a couple is living together before their wedding, gifts are either sent to them at their home address or to the bride's parents if they are hosting the wedding. The circumstances are the guide.

✤ *When are gifts sent?* Gifts may be sent as soon as a guest receives an invitation. They may be mailed by the donor or sent directly from the store where they were purchased.

In some localities and among certain ethnic groups it is customary for guests to bring their gifts to the wedding reception rather than deliver them ahead of time. In some cases checks are handed to either the bride or the groom in the receiving line or sometime before the end of the reception. Gift packages should be put on a table set up for them. The newlyweds are not expected to open these gifts during the reception, but they should delegate the tasks of making sure they're safe at the reception and of packing them up and transporting them from the reception to a safe place.

✤ *How can the couple keep track of the gifts as the come in?* Develop a system for recording every single delivered gift. As soon as the invitations are mailed, you should set up a system for keeping track of gifts as they arrive. You can use your wedding organizer, a computer database system, or a handwritten log—whatever is easiest for you. Record the article, the date it was received, the name and address of the donor, and the store the gift came from, if necessary. Some couples like to attach a small number to each gift, for cross-referencing on their master list. Include a column to indicate the date you sent a thank-you note. If you are numbering gifts for display or insurance purposes, add a column for that. Your system might look something like this:

No.	Date Rec'd	Gift	Sent by	Address	Where Bought	Thank-You Sent
1	6/21	silver platter	Mr./Mrs. Allan Anderson	2 Hill St. Peekskill, NY 10960	Tiffany	6/22
2	6/22	8 linen placemats	Aunt Ruth	24 Millstone Lane, Southampton, NY 11968	Hillberts, Southampton	6/24

Displaying Gifts

✢ *May we display our gifts? If so, where?*   Displaying gifts is a tradition that some couples choose to follow today. It's entirely up to you: if you want to show your gifts, or if your reception will be held at your home, your gifts may be displayed in a room easily accessible to others. If you want only close friends and relatives to see your gifts, place them in a back room. Often tables are set up and may be covered in plain white (or the color of your choice) cloths or sheets. Sheets can hang down to the floor so that the boxes for presents can be tucked underneath.

✢ *Where are gifts generally not displayed?*   Gifts are rarely displayed at the club, hotel, or hall where the reception is held. Instead relatives and friends are invited to the home in the days before the wedding to see the gifts.

✢ *How can gifts of varying size and worth be displayed tactfully?*   You won't want to step on any toes in displaying the gifts guests have given to you. Take care in placing the gifts so that comparisons aren't made. A piece of silver plate should not be placed next to pricier pieces of sterling, for example.

✢ *Should cards be displayed with gifts?*   There is no rule about whether the cards sent with the gifts should be displayed or not. Showing them saves answering the question "Who sent that?" over and over again, but some couples feel that it is a private matter, while others believe it is okay to let others know who sent what.

✢ *Should checks be displayed?*   Ordinarily it is in bad taste to display gifts of money. But to be fair to a generous relative or friend who sent a wedding check, it is quite proper to display it—but with the amount concealed. If you have more than one check, simply lay them out on a flat surface, one above the other, so that the signatures alone are disclosed. The amount of the one at the top should be covered with a strip of paper. Then place a sheet of glass over the whole thing to prevent snoopy guests from taking a peek. You may also write on plain white gift enclosure cards, "Check from Mr. and Mrs. Harold Brown," and display just the cards.

✢ *How can gifts be kept safe during the wedding celebrations?* When wedding gifts are numerous and valuable, it's wise to hire a security guard to watch the house while everyone is at the wedding and reception.

Be sure to check with your insurance company about additional coverage or a rider on your homeowner's policy to cover the value of the gifts. Your itemized list of gifts received serves as a record.

Exchanging and Returning Gifts

✢ *What can be done with duplicate presents?* You may discreetly exchange duplicate presents. If friends who have given a gift realize that you have more than one, they should encourage you to exchange theirs for something else.

✢ *Can unwanted gifts be exchanged?* If a gift is not a duplicate but rather is something you neither like nor need, you may exchange it as well—unless it is from a close friend who would be hurt if he or she found out. If the gift is from someone you rarely see, simply write a thank-you note for the gift they sent, even though you've exchanged it for something else. You should not, however, exchange the presents chosen for you by your own families unless you are specifically told to do so. Nor should you discard a gift that was made especially for you.

✢ *Do I have to let the giver know I exchanged her gift?* When you write a thank-you note for a duplicate gift that you have exchanged, simply thank the giver for the present, with enthusiasm. You don't have to explain that you exchanged the gift for something else.

✣ *What do I do if a gift arrives broken?* If a gift that was sent directly from the donor arrives broken, immediately check the wrapping to see if it was insured. If so, notify the person who sent it at once so that he or she can collect the insurance and replace it. If it is not insured, you may not want to mention that it arrived broken; otherwise the person who gave it may feel obligated to replace it. When a broken gift arrives directly from a store, simply take it back without mentioning a thing to the donor. Any reputable store will replace merchandise that arrives damaged.

✣ *Is it proper to return a gift to the donor?* The only time that gifts are returned is when a marriage is either cancelled or immediately annulled. When wedding plans are cancelled, gifts that have already been received must be returned. If there is simply an indefinite postponement, but the couple does intend to be married, the gifts that have arrived are put away carefully until such time as the ceremony takes place. If, after a period of six weeks to two months, it becomes doubtful that the wedding will take place at all, the couple must send the gifts back to donors to return.

❧ GIFTS AMONG THE ❧
WEDDING PARTY

To and from the Attendants

It's customary for the bride and groom to give each of their attendants gifts as a thank-you for their participation in their wedding. It is also customary for the bride's and groom's attendants to give a gift in return. Because they bear considerable costs to be a part of the wedding party, each of the attendants is certainly not required to give an individual wedding gift to the couple. A gift is often given jointly instead. Still, if an attendant is already stretched beyond his or her means, he or she is not mandated to give another gift. The attendant or usher should feel comfortable deciding what is appropriate: a small, meaningful token, a traditional gift, or none at all.

From Groom to Ushers

The groom's gifts for his ushers are either put at their places at a bachelor dinner, presented at the rehearsal dinner, or given just before leaving the rehearsal when no dinner is planned. Any kind of small, personal item—a nice pen, a leather wallet, or cuff links—is suitable and may be engraved or monogrammed. The groom's gift to his best man may be the same gift he gives to the ushers or a slightly more elaborate one.

From Bride to Bridesmaids

The bride's gifts to her bridesmaids may be given at a bridesmaids' luncheon shortly before the wedding, at the rehearsal dinner, or just after the rehearsal when no dinner is planned. A piece of jewelry that they can wear to the wedding, such as earrings or a necklace, is a perfect gift. The bride's gift to her maid or matron of honor may be the same gift she gives to her bridesmaids or a more elaborate one. If you plan to give an engraved gift, such as a silver picture frame, you may have the wedding date and your initials engraved to commemorate the occasion.

Attendants' Gifts to Bride or Groom or Both

It is often customary for bridal attendants to give a joint gift to the bride, for the groomsmen to give a joint gift to the groom, or for both sets of attendants to give a large gift to the couple. This is in addition to any shower and other gifts they may wish to give along the way. These gifts can be personal or household items.

Gifts for Each Other

Upon their engagement, the bride-to-be may decide to give her fiancé a small engagement present, such as a watch, a personal organizer, or a book. These items may be engraved with the date of the engagement. Often the groom will give his bride a present apart from the wedding and engagement rings. The bride may also wish to give her groom a wedding present separate from the wedding ring. It might be jewelry engraved with the date of the wedding or a beautiful book. They could also buy themselves gifts for their new life together—matching mountain bikes, for example, or a hammock for the backyard.

Gifts for Parents

Although it's not necessary to give your parents a gift, it's a nice way to thank them for everything they have done. One touching token of love is a rose placed near the spot you will stand after the processional. After the bride's father or escort is seated, the bride and groom each take a rose and present it to their parents, with a kiss.

Gifts for Your Children

If either of you has been married before and has young children, give them an extraspecial gift to make them feel they are a big part of your wedding festivities. Try to give them something they've been asking for, especially if the nuptials have left them feeling anxious and uncertain. Another lovely gift is to present children with a family medallion during the ceremony (see chapter 9 for more on this idea).

❧ ALL ABOUT ❧
THANK-YOU NOTES

Whatever the gift, whether a place setting or a gift of time or talent, it must be acknowledged. Thanks take many forms, but all share one common guideline—they should be prompt. This is particularly true when gifts have been sent in the mail or delivered by a store; it lets the sender know his or her gift has arrived safely. The bottom line is that *a separate, handwritten thank-you note must be sent for each wedding present you receive.*

Wedding Favors

Q: Many of my married friends offered favors at their wedding. I think it's an unnecessary expense—the reception, to my way of thinking, is gift enough. What do you think?

A: Gifts from the bride and groom to their wedding guests, referred to as wedding favors, are necessary only when part of a cultural tradition. European brides and grooms, for example, have long given their guests favors, as have some brides and grooms in the American South.

Favors are a special gesture from the newlyweds to guests for being a part of the occasion. Traditional favors include a piece of groom's cake boxed and wrapped or a miniature box of chocolates. Favors can also be tiny pots of flowers, miniature bottles of champagne or wine, or keepsakes made by the bride.

Unfortunately the concept of presenting favors to wedding guests has become big business, and many brides and grooms are pressured to feel that they must offer them. It cannot be said enough times that while favors are a nice thought, unless they are part of your tradition, they are completely unnecessary and simply another drain on your budget.

✦ *When should a thank-you be written?* If humanly possible, you should write each note of thanks on the day the present arrives. Otherwise the list will soon get ahead of you, and the first weeks of your marriage will be spent writing thank-you notes. A note of thanks should also be sent to those who send congratulatory telegrams on the day of the wedding. There is *no excuse* for not having all thank-you notes written within three months of the wedding—at the most—especially now that the groom is expected to share in this task.

✦ *What is included in the thank-you note?* Every thank-you note, no matter how short, should include a reference to the present itself. You don't have to lie about your feelings for the gift; simply express your appreciation for the thought and effort.

✦ *What kind of stationery is required?* No special stationery is required for writing thank-you notes. You can use paper printed or engraved with your maiden name initials, your married initials, or a monogram of your last name. If you've taken your husband's name and you are using initials, however, you should wait until after your wedding to send initialized notes. Use plain paper or notes printed with your maiden name until your new name is "official." The paper can be bordered, white or colored, ecru or ivory. In fact, plain, foldover notes are just fine. It is no excuse, therefore, to delay writing your notes simply because personalized note cards have not arrived from the printer.

Preprinted Thank-You Cards

Q: Is it proper for me to send out thank-you notes on preprinted thank-you cards? I've got so many to write, I can't possibly write a personal message to everyone!

A: In a single word: no. Your personal message is the only way to send your thanks. If you prefer a card that reads "Thank You" or has a poem or message on it, choose one that is simple and dignified and then add your own note, mentioning the gift by name and why you are so happy to have received it. Since you must write your own note anyway, you might simply decide against buying cards that probably cost more than a box of plain notepaper.

Some brides and grooms order preprinted thank-you cards from the photographer, who inserts their portrait in little corners designed for this purpose. The recipient of the note then receives not only a personal thank-you, but a souvenir photo as well. Unfortunately the wait for these types of cards can be up to two or more months, much too long a time for keeping current with writing notes. You can get around this problem by having a portrait taken a month or so before the wedding—whether during the photograph sittings for newspaper shots or formal portrait shots—so that the cards and photographs can be ready and waiting for you when you return from your honeymoon. Also, you can get the photographer to supply you with blank cards before the photograph is ready. You'll be able to write your notes as gifts arrive, adding the photographs (and dates on the notes) a little later.

What's in a Note?

Notes are written by one person, so they should be signed by one person. If the bride writes, she should mention the groom's thanks in the note and vice versa.

> Dear Mr. and Mrs. McKune,
>
> How did you ever find those perfect candlesticks? They are wonderful, and John and I want to thank you a thousand times! We have just rented a great apartment with a fireplace, and your candlesticks will be just right on the mantel.
>
> Thank you so much!
> With love from both of us,
> Christine

Dear Aunt Ruth,

Catherine and I truly love the quilt you made for us. It is perfect on the bed, and we take friends right into the bedroom to see it, practically before they get their coats off because we are so excited about it. The colors are perfect and the quilt is beautiful, but the best part is feeling the love you put into making it for us. Come visit us (and your quilt!) soon. We miss you already and still treasure the time we spent with you right before the wedding.

Love,
Richard

✤ *Thanks for gifts of money:* When gifts of money are given, the thank-you note should, if possible, indicate how the money will be spent. It is optional as to whether or not to mention the amount of the check. Since it is fine for you to state the amount, do so, just as you would mention the specific item in a thank-you note for a place setting of china or a bread maker.

Dear Aunt Kate and Uncle Reid,

Wow! You have no idea how wonderful it was to open your card and find that incredible check for $100. We used it to help us buy the Ernest Garthwaite painting we've been saving for for the living room, and when we look at it, we'll think of you. Thank you for rearranging your schedules so you could be with us at the wedding, too. Laura and I didn't think we could get married without you there to share the day with us, and we know what trouble you went through to be there. It meant the world to us.

Laura sends her love with mine,
Jeremy

Dear Mr. and Mrs. Brown,

You know how much Ted and I love camping, and we want you to know that your $75 check has gone right into our tent fund. We can't thank you enough for such a generous gift, and who knows? You might wake up some morning and look out your kitchen window to find us camped out right in your backyard on our way to the mountains.

Thank you again!
Love,
Cindy

The Guest Asks: Why No Thank-You?

Q: *I sent out a wedding gift quite a long time ago and have never received a response. Is it proper for me to ask whether the gift arrived or not?*

A: When the donor of a gift to the bride and groom receives no thank-you note after three months have gone by, he should feel no hesitation in calling or writing to ask whether the present ever arrived. The question may serve to clarify the situation for both parties. Wording is important; the donor should sound concerned rather than critical. If the newlyweds have not received the gift, the donor can then trace it, if it was insured, or replace it. If, on the other hand, the couple has not sent thanks because of simple thoughtlessness, hopefully they'll learn a lesson and write their other notes more promptly.

Some guests prefer, instead, to ask a family member to check with the couple about the receipt of an unacknowledged gift. Other guests choose to check by yet another method: if their gift had been sent directly from a store, they can simply ask the retailer to have the package traced, tracking whether the couple signed for it. It's rare, but a package can get lost.

✦ *Thanks for acts of kindness.* There will likely be many people who help out with any variety of elements at your wedding, from attendants who orchestrated the details on the big day to a neighbor who stamped your envelopes. These acts of kindness are often the best gifts of all and should be acknowledged with a note of thanks.

Dear Mrs. Hausler,

I'm sure the invitations to the wedding would not have been mailed on time if you hadn't come to the rescue and helped. I really appreciated it and loved spending time with you and hearing about your and Mr. Hausler's wedding. It was one of my favorite wedding moments. Thank you so much.

Love,
Helen

Dear Nancy,

Well, we're back from Lake Tahoe and I can't wait to tell you all about it. In the meantime, I wanted to say thank you. I honestly couldn't have made it without you. I know you will just say, "That's what friends are for," but your support, not to mention everything you took care of and did, was bigger than that. Once we were in the plane and on the way, what I thought about most was how lucky I am, and have been for fifteen years, to have you for a friend. Thank you for helping me organize the list and address envelopes, for finding such wonderful "old, new, borrowed, and blue," for dashing out for pink lipstick at the zero hour, for holding my hand, for being so nice to Aunt Ginny, for making the list for the photographer, for staying up with me till two baking cookies when I couldn't sleep, for dragging my train around, for keeping me calm, and for just being there. I'll never forget.

 Love,
 Lisa

Dear Mrs. McCaffery,

 I never saw you, but I knew you were there. There's no other way everything would have been ready so perfectly for the wedding. Thank you so much for taking care of letting the florist in, for putting the new candles on the altar, and for making sure the acolytes were doing their job. The church has always been lucky to have you quietly taking care of so many details, but I was the lucky one last month. Steve and I look forward to seeing you soon, and thank you again—

 With affection,
 Joanne McGuigan

✛ *Thanks and gifts to hosts.* When friends, neighbors, or relatives offer to take in out-of-town guests or host a party or shower during the wedding festivities, you should of course thank them. It is also a nice idea to give them a thank-you gift. It needn't be elaborate—an arrangement of flowers delivered before or after the wedding or event is a perfectly appropriate token of your appreciation. You could also buy them tickets to an upcoming concert if they like music or take them out to lunch or dinner if time permits.

 Your card with flowers or a small gift can read simply *"With thanks and love," "What a wonderful shower,"* or *"Thank you so much for giving shelter and respite to Frank and Judy."* Later you can send a heartfelt thank-you note that mentions their kindness at length.

Dear Mr. and Mrs. Werner,

My bridesmaids had so much fun staying at your house that they could hardly tear themselves away to get ready for the wedding! I don't know how to begin to tell you how much it meant to all of us that you took them in, and then that you took such good care of them, too. I know Mom has told you how grateful we were, but I wanted to add my thanks to hers and Dad's for your, as always, incredible generosity.

Rob and I can't wait to see you and will ask Mom to let you know the next time we're visiting to see if we can find some time to get together. In the meantime, please accept our thanks for everything you did, from practically running your own inn to shuttling everybody back and forth to being two of our favorite guests at the wedding.

Love,

Cassie

MONOGRAMMING AND ENGRAVING

If the bride and groom want to have linens monogrammed or silver engraved, they should include the initials they want to have used on their registry information.

Marking Linen

The traditional way to monogram linens would be for Katherine Leigh Adams, who marries Brian Charles Jamison, to use linens initialed with her married initials, *KJ* or *KJA*, or her future husband's last initial, *J*. Often the single initial embellished with a scroll or pretty design is more effective than three initials, and the cost may be less. A popular way to monogram linens today is to use the first initial of both the bride and groom, with their last initial enlarged between them: *KJB*. The bride who is keeping her own name may have her last initial and that of her husband divided by a dot or design: *A·J*.

Towels are marked at the center of one end so that the monogram shows when they are folded lengthwise in thirds and hung over a rack.

Long rectangular tablecloths are marked at the center of each long side, midway between the table edge and center of the cloth. Small square cloths are marked in one corner midway between center and corner, so that the monogram shows on the table. Dinner napkins are marked diagonally in one corner or centered on a rectangular fold.

Sheets are monogrammed so that when the top is folded down, the letters can be read by a person standing at the foot of the bed. Pillowcases are marked approximately two inches above the hem.

Marking Silver

If silver flatware is monogrammed, a triangle of block letters—last-name initial below and first-name initials of the bride and groom above—works well on modern patterns.

If a single initial is used, it is the last-name initial of the groom.

Monograms on flat silver have always been placed so that the top of the letter is toward the end of the handle. In other words, when the piece is on the table, the monogram is upside down as seen by the diner at that place. If you prefer, you can have initials engraved the other way so that they can be read more easily.

CHAPTER EIGHT

Permitting joy to

WEDDING

surround everything

CELEBRATIONS

having to do

with a wedding.

A well-planned wedding party or prewedding event can be as fun, joyous, and celebratory as the wedding itself. It wasn't always so: in some cultures prewedding get-togethers were anything but happy. Arranged marriages, a matter of course in many countries, seldom led to joyous celebrations. In the Middle East women would gather and sing mournful songs until the day of the wedding, regretting and lamenting the loss of the bride and the life she was about to enter.

Today things are different, and free choice indicates a happy choice, permitting joy to surround everything having to do with a wedding. While no events other than the wedding itself are necessary for the marriage to be celebrated, those that occur should be festive occasions that heighten the excitement of the impending big day.

❧ WEDDING SHOWERS ❧

A wedding shower is a gathering of good friends in honor of a forthcoming marriage. It is a celebration distinguished by the "showering" of gifts on the guest of honor, the bride, or, increasingly, both the bride and groom. Following are some general guidelines for a traditional wedding shower.

- ✤ *What form must it take?* Showers vary. A shower may be a morning coffee, a luncheon, a tea, a cocktail party, or a buffet dinner.

- ✤ *When is a shower held?* Ideally wedding showers should be held from two weeks to two months prior to the wedding. A shower that takes place too close to the wedding date may be more of an inconvenience than a party for the bride, who is likely to be inundated with chores in the last busy days. A shower held too early may occur before the bride knows what she needs and before her wedding plans are firm. There are many other varying circumstances, particularly due to complicated logistics, school calendars, and work schedules. Exceptions to the timing may be necessary, particularly for encore couples with obligations and families to care for.

    A shower may be held on any day of the week that is convenient for the guest of honor, the hostess, and the majority of guests.

- ✤ *Who hosts the shower?* Contrary to some misconceptions, bridesmaids are *not required* to host a shower, although they certainly may do so. One of an attendant's duties is to "host a shower"—*if* she chooses to do so. Friends of the bride and groom, friends of parents, and members of the wedding party other than immediate family may host a shower, as may an office staff or other colleagues. Traditionally the bride's or groom's immediate family members do not host a shower (doing so can appear self-serving), but these days it is happening more and more. Under certain circumstances—say, when a bride-to-be lives far away from her family or is visiting her future family prior to the wedding—the groom's sisters or mother may correctly host the shower. In such a case the traditional rules of etiquette are bent—and a bride far from home is given a warm welcome.

✢ *Who is invited?* A shower guest list is generally made up of close friends, attendants, and family members. Normally anyone invited to a shower should be invited to the wedding. One exception would be when co-workers wish to throw an office shower for the bride, even though all are not being invited to the main event. The shower in this case is their way of wishing the couple well. The days of the strictly all-female wedding showers are fading fast. More and more, grooms-to-be and their male friends are included on the shower guest list. Attendants and mothers are generally included on lists for wedding showers but are not required to bring gifts to each party. They can, if they wish, bring small, inexpensive presents or go in together on a joint gift. One thing you should avoid is inviting the same guests to multiple showers. Being invited to many parties puts a serious strain on guests' budgets. In fact, *showers for the bride and/or couple should not number more than two,* with different guests being invited to each.

✢ *How many people can be invited?* Since the hostess is the person footing the bills and providing the space, it is she who decides on the number of guests. If the shower is not a surprise, she most likely gets input from the bride on the guest list. Keep in mind that a huge shower that includes almost everyone invited to the wedding is in poor taste. The idea of an intimate party is lost, and the shower becomes little more than a demand for gifts, which can often be more of an imposition on those invited than a reason to celebrate.

✢ *Can an encore bride have a wedding shower?* If the bride has been married before, she may be given a shower, but it's better to cut back on inviting friends and relatives who were invited to a shower for her first wedding. If the bride is marrying for the first time but her groom has been married before, she certainly may have a shower.

The First Shower

The first wedding shower was said to have taken place in eighteenth-century Netherlands, when a bride's father did not care for her choice of a husband, a poor miller. Accordingly he refused to give her a dowry, thereby eliminating her chance of marrying her beloved. The groom was not to be deterred, however, and he shared his plight with the townspeople. Because he had always been generous to hungry families in the community, giving them flour at no charge, they joined forces and shared their wares and riches with the couple, showering the bride with enough of a dowry to make the marriage possible. The father was so impressed by the neighbors' "shower" that he consented to the marriage.

✥ *What types of invitations are required for a shower?* Invitations to wedding showers are often written on commercial fill-in shower cards, which are available in a variety of styles. Or they are written on personal notes or informal cards. In some cases invitations are telephoned or issued in person, as might occur when a hostess asks her co-workers to a shower for one of their colleagues.

The Etiquette of Shower Gifts

A shower is the one prewedding event where gifts are expected. In fact, giving gifts is largely the purpose of a shower. In general shower gifts should be relatively inexpensive. Guests can, however, pool their resources and go in on one large, expensive gift for the couple instead of several smaller ones. Following is a guide to the etiquette involved in giving and receiving gifts at a wedding shower.

✥ Any *theme or related gifts* should be noted on every invitation.

✥ The invitation should not include a *registry list.* Guests who wish to know where the couple is registered should call the hostess and ask.

Theme Showers

A shower needs no theme other than to celebrate the upcoming marriage of a couple. Sometimes, however, a hostess narrows or custom-designs the focus of a shower (often after discussions with the bride regarding the wedding couple's needs) to a certain theme. Guests are then expected to bring gifts related to that theme, and the hostess may even provide theme-related food and decorations. Ideas for themes are limitless. Some choices are as follows:

Kitchen Shower

Suggested gifts: glasses, knives, linens, utensils.

Spa Shower

Suggested gifts: massage certificates, aromatherapy oils, candles, robes.

Honeymoon Shower

Suggested gifts: travel clock, sewing kit, first-aid kit, travel book.

Leisure-Time Shower

Suggested gifts: movie tickets, board games, videos and CDs, cocktail glasses and napkins.

Gourmet Cook Shower

Suggested gifts: gourmet foods and wines, utensils, cookbooks.

The Great Outdoors Shower

Suggested gifts: badminton net, flower seeds and gardening tools, picnic basket, Japanese lanterns, croquet set.

Happy Holidays Shower

Suggested gifts: decorations for every holiday of the year.

Recipe Shower

Suggested gifts: favorite recipes. Guests are given recipe cards to record their favorites, and these cards are collected as they arrive and put into a recipe box provided by the hostess. At some recipe showers guests may even prepare one of their recipes.

Labor of Love Shower

Suggested gifts: promises, not gifts, are brought to this shower, where friends pledge to paint, wallpaper, garden, or donate their talents in any number of ways.

✣ If the event is a *kitchen or bathroom shower,* the couple's color preferences may be noted on the invitation. It is never correct, however, for the hostess to write on the invitations a list of specific gifts that the couple needs; she would do that in person or over the phone.

✣ In the case of a *lingerie shower,* it is helpful to include the bride's sizes.

✣ Gifts are generally opened *after refreshments have been served.* The guests gather around while the bride (or the bride and groom together if it is a joint shower) opens the packages one by one and thanks each giver.

✣ Someone—often one of the bridesmaids—is designated *official "note taker."* The note taker sits beside the bride and makes a list of the gifts and who gave them, making sure the gift cards are kept with their respective gifts.

✣ Often gifts are *passed around the room* so that everyone can see them— and so that the giver can be showered with praise for her good taste and thoughtfulness.

✣ The bride is not required to send *thank-you notes for shower gifts,* as long as *the giver is present at the shower and is thanked directly, in person.* If time permits, however, it's always a nice touch to follow up a verbal thank-you with a written one. (In some communities it is customary for the bride to send thank-you notes regardless of whether or not she personally thanked the giver.) *Remember, the bride must always send a thank-you to those she was unable to thank at the party and to anyone who might have sent a gift but was not able to attend the shower.*

✣ If the *shower is a surprise,* it's a delightful idea for the bride to send an arrangement of flowers to her hostess with a personal note of thanks, after the shower. She should also call the hostess to say thank you the day after the shower.

✣ When the *shower is not a surprise,* the bride should give the hostess a thank-you gift as a way of showing her appreciation. She can give her a personal gift or send flowers beforehand so that they can be used by the hostess as a shower decoration. The bride then follows up with a thank-you telephone call and a note of appreciation.

The Groom's Cousin Asks:
Can I Host a Shower for an Absentee Bride?

Q: My cousin is marrying a wonderful woman who lives a long way from here. Her work prevents her from coming to town for a shower before the wedding. We have lots of friends and relatives who can't make the wedding but who would love to honor the couple. Can I give the bride and groom a wedding shower without their being present?

A: Certainly you can! Throw the bride and groom a proxy shower, the name for a shower given for a bride who cannot attend or who lives far away. Although a proxy shower is an acceptable way of celebrating, it can pose problems for the hostess who is responsible for sending the gifts to the bride. One solution is to have the hostess ask guests to bring their gifts unwrapped so that everyone can see them. She then provides a variety of wrapping paper and ribbons for the guests to wrap their gifts, so that she can pack them into large cartons and mail them to the bride. At most proxy showers a telephone call is made to the bride or the couple so that they can briefly join in the fun, long distance. Thank-you notes should be written once the gifts have been received by the couple.

❧ BRIDESMAIDS' LUNCHEON ❧

In many communities it's traditional for the bridesmaids to host a "farewell" luncheon or maybe a tea or dinner for the bride, either in addition to a shower or instead of a shower. Here are some general guidelines regarding bridesmaids' luncheons.

✢ *When does the luncheon take place?* This luncheon usually takes place very close to the wedding, particularly if bridesmaids live in different communities and will be arriving only for the wedding celebrations.

✢ *Can someone else host?* In some communities the bride and her mother host a luncheon or tea for the bridesmaids as a respite in the midst of a busy time—and as a thank-you to the attendants for their presence and support.

✢ *What type of celebration does it involve?* A bridesmaids' luncheon is a little different from any other lunch party. The table may be more elaborately decorated and the linens are often white or the bride's chosen wedding colors. The bridesmaids' luncheon is the perfect time for the bride to give her bridesmaids their individual gifts, thanking them personally for being a part of her wedding. For the bride and attendants who work during the day, a more convenient get-together may be after work, at a small cocktail party or intimate dinner. Another venue could be a day spa, where they all could share a prewedding pampering.

BACHELOR AND BACHELORETTE PARTIES

The bachelor party of legend and lore is a sodden farewell to old bachelor days, an event where the groom and his ushers traditionally share an evening of debauchery the night before the wedding. It may be a simple gathering of good friends over beer and barbecue; it may be a night at a restaurant, where reminiscences are shared over he-man steaks, wine, and cigars. The reality these days is that bachelor parties and dinners are much more low-key affairs than they used to be, in part because ushers and friends may be scattered far and wide. Work can also prevent a wedding party from gathering for a bachelor's night out.

If a dinner is held, it is usually *hosted by the ushers* and held in the private dining room of a restaurant or in a club. Aside from *toasting the bride* and *reminiscing,* the bridegroom's farewell dinner is like any other dinner among friends, although it might include the groom's father, brothers, and the bride's brothers. Instead of a dinner party, the groom and his buddies might spend the day on a boat, at the beach, on the golf course, playing baseball or football, or enjoying a picnic.

A bachelor party is certainly not off-limits for a *second-time groom.* His status as a bachelor alone fits the bill.

In the same way that the bachelor party is generally gender-specific, the *bachelorette party* is given by a bride's women friends. It is different from the bridesmaids' luncheon in that it is often held at night and may include toasts and a dinner, similar to the bachelor party. The guest list may also include other friends in addition to the attendants.

❧ AND THE PARTY NEVER ENDS . . . ❦

If the traditional wedding parties are not enough celebrating for you, here are some ideas for filler events, whether held to thank a group of people, to honor out-of-town guests, or simply to keep the party going through the wedding weekend.

The Appreciation Party

Instead of trying to schedule a series of luncheons and bachelor and bachelorette parties, a couple might host one big appreciation party instead. Invited are attendants and anyone else who has given generously of their time and ideas to help make the wedding wonderful. The appreciation party is often a casual affair, a barbecue or picnic, especially if the rehearsal dinner is to be formal. It is usually held just before the wedding, when everyone has gathered, and is another prime opportunity for the bride and groom to give their attendants gifts of appreciation. An appreciation party can also be held after the couple returns from their honeymoon, if their attendants and special friends live close enough to attend.

The Prewedding Luncheon

For a late afternoon wedding, a small luncheon for the bridal party may be given by friends or neighbors. This takes the burden off the busy mother of the bride to host yet another entertainment on her daughter's wedding day. It may be as simple or as elaborate as the host and hostess wish, but laidback and relaxing may be just the ticket to put an excited and nervous bridal party at ease. The bride and groom are absolutely not required to attend, however; it depends on their schedule and energy level.

Parties for Out-of-Town Guests

A lovely gift for the couple from relatives or friends is a party for out-of-town guests and early-arriving wedding attendants. This too relieves the bride's parents of extra work before the wedding and gives guests a chance to spend time together in an informal atmosphere. Invitations should be sent well in advance so that guests can plan their travel itinerary accordingly. Often the party is entertained by multiple hosts, who share the expenses and work in order to have a bigger, more elaborate fete. These parties may be held at home or in a club or restaurant. Guests may be the attendants, the couple's families, their close friends, and friends of their parents.

❧ THE WEDDING REHEARSAL ❧

Although the traditional marriage service is a familiar one to most, it is easy to forget the sheer volume of details that goes into its planning. Add to that the excitement and nervousness all involved may be feeling on the big day. It is essential, therefore, that the wedding party participants be fully involved in the wedding rehearsal. It is even more important for those involved to pay close attention when a service is unfamiliar or nontraditional. Here are some guidelines to consider for the traditional wedding rehearsal.

✛ *Who attends?*   A tradition in years past held that it was bad luck for the bride to take part in the rehearsal, so her part was taken by a stand-in. The modern bride no longer goes by that superstition and recognizes the need to rehearse and feel comfortable with the ceremony. Other than the *bride*, the only other people required to attend the rehearsal are the *groom*, the *attendants*, and the *bride's parents*. Since the groom's parents have no active part in the ceremony, they needn't be present—but usually enjoy being there.

Also present will be the *officiant* and the *organist or musician* playing the processional and recessional. The *wedding consultant,* if one is being used should also be on hand to help instruct the ushers, line up the wedding party correctly, and help with the spacing and pace of all persons as they practice walking up the aisle. If *young children* are participating in the ceremony, their presence is required only if the rehearsal is not held too late at night. If they come, they are generally accompanied by their parents.

✢ *When is the rehearsal held?*   The rehearsal is scheduled with the officiant at a time when all attendants will be present. For a Saturday wedding it is usually held on Friday afternoon or early evening. The closer to the wedding the rehearsal takes place, the better the chances that all will go smoothly.

✢ *What should participants wear?*   People taking part in a church wedding rehearsal or attending as observers should remember that they are in a house of worship and dress accordingly. This means no shorts or jeans and, in some houses of worship, no bare arms or legs. When the wedding is taking place at a secular location, clothing might be more informal, unless the rehearsal is to be followed immediately by a dinner requiring dressier attire.

✢ *What happens during the rehearsal?*   The *actual service* is not read at the rehearsal. The officiant simply tells the couple the order in which the words of the service come and what their responses will be. The couple do not say *responses or vows.* The officiant might ask the bride and groom to recite one verse, however, so they can find the right tone and volume.

ETIQUETTE FINE POINTS

A Simulated Train

If the bride's gown has a long train, she will need a simulated train for the rehearsal. She can create one by pinning a sheet or a length of fabric to her outfit so that she can practice walking with it. This also gives her maid of honor an opportunity to practice keeping the train in place during the ceremony and the recessional.

An *aisle runner,* if there is one, is discussed with the ushers. The timing and signals of placing the runner are determined and discussed so that the officiant knows when the bride's mother has been seated, that the bride has arrived, and when the service should begin.

The organist is also present at the rehearsal and plays *the processional* so that pace and spacing can be practiced.

The *order of the procession* is established, and the attendants walk up the aisle two or three times until all goes smoothly.

Everyone *lines up at the chancel* to make sure that all fit comfortably and that the order looks symmetrical. The maid of honor learns *when to take the bride's bouquet* and *how to rearrange the bride's train* without fussing or attracting attention to herself.

The best man and the maid of honor learn *when to give the rings* to the officiant and how to remove the rings if they are affixed to a pillow carried by the ring bearer.

The officiant will explain *when a veil, if worn, should be turned back,* and a decision is made on who will do so.

The ushers are given instruction by the officiant or the wedding consultant on their roles in *escorting guests.* The ushers are the first people guests see, and they should be confident about what they are doing and look as though they have done it for years. They should be shown *how to offer an arm* and *how to remove pew ribbons,* noting which pews have been set aside for special seating. The ushers will learn how to escort guests in and out of the ceremony site in an orderly fashion.

How attendants will leave the chancel is arranged at the rehearsal, whether in pairs or singly. They should all practice the *recessional* at least once, just to ensure that the attendants know how they will exit. Note: The pace of the recessional is set by the bride and groom on the day of the wedding, and the others should follow at a natural, nonstilted walk.

The rehearsal dinner has become a popular tradition of the wedding party weekend—and is nearly as festive as the wedding reception. It's a time to celebrate and savor the upcoming nuptials in a relaxed atmosphere, without the pomp and ceremony reserved for the wedding day. Here are some guidelines to consider when planning a rehearsal dinner.

✢ *When is the rehearsal dinner held?* The rehearsal dinner generally takes place the night before the wedding, regardless of when the rehearsal is held.

✢ *Who hosts?* It has become custom, but not obligatory, for the groom's family to host the rehearsal party. If they do so, they may elicit the help of the bride or her mother in selecting a location—especially if they are from another town and unfamiliar with what is available. In this case preliminary plans are made by telephone or confirmation letter, and the final arrangements are made when the groom's family arrives for the wedding celebrations.

    If the groom's family does not or cannot give the rehearsal dinner, one may be arranged by the bride's family. It may take the form of a picnic, a simple buffet, or a formal dinner. The only guide: The rehearsal party should never be more formal than the wedding reception, particularly if the party is given by the groom's parents.

✢ *Who is invited?* The guest list at a rehearsal party should include the *members of the wedding party* (except for the flower girl and the ring bearer), the *officiant, parents and grandparents of the bride and groom,* and *any siblings of the bride and groom* who are not in the wedding party. If the bride and/or groom have *stepparents,* they are invited with their spouses if they have remarried but should not be seated next to their former spouses. The *wedding party's husbands, wives, fiancées, fiancés, and live-in companions* should be invited, but dates are not included. Any *children of the bride and groom* from a previous marriage also attend, unless they are too young.

✢ *What type of invitation should be extended?* Invitations are generally written on informal or fill-in cards or may simply be handwrit-

Who's Invited to the Rehearsal Dinner?

Q: My fiancé says we are required to invite all out-of-town guests to the rehearsal dinner. I say we're not. Who is right?

A: The guest list for a rehearsal dinner traditionally consists of the bride and groom, all attendants and their spouses, the couple's immediate families, and the clergyperson and spouse. It's a nice gesture to include out-of-towners if your budget allows, but it's by no means a must. Sit down with your fiancé and discuss the situation. Perhaps the guests who are coming from a far distance can meet up informally at an easy-to-get-to restaurant.

ten or telephoned. If a good number of out-of-town guests are being invited, the written invitation is the best way to go; it serves as a tangible reminder of the time, date, and address of the party.

✤ *What happens during the dinner?* The rehearsal dinner is the perfect occasion for *the presentation of attendants' gifts,* whether from the couple to the bridesmaids and ushers or from the attendants to the bride and groom. Often the latter gifts are presented by the maid of honor and the best man and may be accompanied by a short speech or toast.

Toasts should be made during dinner, preferably not after; otherwise the night can drag on interminably. The host—often the groom's father—should make the first toast, welcoming the guests and expressing his feelings about the forthcoming marriage. He is generally followed with a return toast by the bride's father and then by toasts from ushers, bridesmaids, and anyone else who wishes to say something.

The attendants' toasts, while sentimental to some extent, are often filled with *anecdotes, jokes, and poems* regaling guests with tales from the bride's and groom's past. Sometimes the bride and groom stand and speak; even if they don't, they generally end the toasting by proposing a toast first to their respective parents and then to all their friends and relatives in attendance.

ETIQUETTE FINE POINTS

Who's Left?

After that, any number of people may attend, including out-of-town guests, close friends, aunts and uncles, and godparents. Junior bridesmaids may attend if the hour is not late, as may the flower girl and ring bearer (if supervised).

When *out-of-town* guests are staying overnight on the day of the wedding, the bride's family might spontaneously invite them home for *a late snack or even for dinner* after an afternoon reception. This is not at all necessary or expected. In fact, the last thing the parents of the bride may want to do is entertain, but often the afterglow of all the events leading up to that moment carries them on to an impromptu gathering with friends. The post-wedding entertainment, which can be provided by a close friend or relative, can be as simple as take-out pizza offered to guests who have changed into comfortable clothes or as elaborate as a next-day brunch.

The fun of the gathering is in hearing and sharing *postwedding stories and impressions.* Often the parents are so busy and swept up in the emotion of the occasion that they miss some of the details.

If the reception ends late and guests prefer to turn in for the evening, the after-wedding party can take the form of a *breakfast or brunch* the next day. In this case the gathering is probably planned, and it is generally the bride's parents or a friend who offers to host the occasion. Notes or informal invitations are sent to guests ahead of time so that they can plan their departure time around the party.

THE WEDDING PARTY: A BELATED RECEPTION

Couples *whose* wedding is small and private may decide to give a party in the weeks following the ceremony, to share their happiness with friends. No gifts are expected, only the good wishes of those present. Following are some guidelines for a postwedding party. While the couple are often the hosts of their own wedding party, the bride's or groom's family might want to host a wedding reception for the couple, particularly when the couple has married privately or away from home or did not have a reception at all.

When the Bride's Parents Host

The reception may include all the components of any wedding reception. It can be as formal or as informal as the couple wants. If the bride wore a wedding gown for the ceremony, she may wear it again at the reception party, *if* she wishes. They can even have a wedding cake ready to be cut and served to guests. Invitations would read:

Mr. and Mrs. William DeRosa

request the pleasure of your company

at a reception

in honor of

Mr. and Mrs. John Nelson

When the Groom's Parents Host

If the bride and groom were married in her hometown or elsewhere, and the friends of the groom and his family live too far away to attend, his mother and father might give a reception for them the first time they come to visit after the honeymoon. They may even host a reception if the couple visits them a short time before the wedding takes place.

Invitations to such a reception are generally fill-in cards or informals, with *"In honor of Priscilla and James"* or *"To meet Priscilla Holmes"* written at the top. They should be mailed two to four weeks before the party.

This party *does not* parallel the couple's wedding reception. There is no wedding cake, and the couple and any attendants who live near enough to be there do not wear their wedding clothes. However, when the party is held after the wedding and the groom's mother would like guests to see the wedding gown—and the bride would like to wear it—she may certainly receive in it and then change after everyone has arrived. Or some of the wedding pictures (or the proofs) might be on display for guests to peruse.

This party is usually in the form of a tea or cocktail buffet. The host and hostess stand at the door with the newlyweds and introduce them to everyone who has not met them. The bride's parents are invited as well, but they certainly don't have to attend.

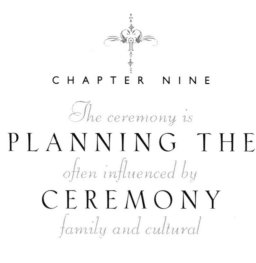

CHAPTER NINE

The ceremony is

PLANNING THE

often influenced by

CEREMONY

family and cultural

traditions.

❧ FIRST THINGS FIRST ❧

Planning the type of ceremony you want will likely be a collaborative affair. The ceremony, more so than the reception, is often influenced by family and cultural traditions—such as both your parents' religious preferences, your church affiliation, and the customs and traditions of your community. Many couples follow traditional ceremonial customs as a way to honor their family and their cultural heritage. It provides a spiritual connection to the generations that have gone before and infuses the ceremony with meaning.

Whether you choose to follow a traditional service, tinker with certain aspects of the ceremony to personalize it, or forgo a traditional ceremony altogether, you will need to make a few big decisions as soon as you become engaged. Following is a list of top things to do when developing the plans for your wedding ceremony.

1. *Choose the site of your ceremony.* Traditional venues may be a church, side chapel, synagogue, wedding facility, or home.

2. *Decide on the date and time of your ceremony.*

3. *Choose an officiant.* If the officiant is affiliated with the church or house of worship where the ceremony is being held, you will likely be discussing the date and time of the ceremony with him or her from the start. Note: *Never show up to see an officiant without making an appointment first!*

4. *Discuss the following issues with your officiant:*

   ✢ Reconfirm *the date and time* of your ceremony.

   ✢ Discuss any *issues or concerns* you may have, as well as any ways you might like to *personalize the ceremony,* including tinkering with the vows or including a reading or a musical interlude.

   ✢ Discuss the *length of the ceremony.* If yours is a Christian ceremony, for example, discuss whether communion will be part of the ceremony.

   ✢ Discuss the *number of guests* the site will comfortably hold.

   ✢ If your chosen officiant is a priest, rabbi, or minister, before doing anything you will need to let him or her know if yours is an *interfaith marriage* or if neither of you is a practicing member of that particular faith. Each religion has different standards, rules, and restrictions. You will need to discuss whether or not you plan to marry in a house of worship or at a secular site. Clergy often have restrictions on whom they can marry and where they can marry them. Catholic priests, for example, can marry couples only in a Catholic church.

A Chinese legend says that the gods tied an invisible red string around the ankles of a man and a woman destined to be husband and wife. With every year that passes, the string, which can never be untied, becomes shorter until the couple is finally united in marriage.

✢ If you haven't already done so, be sure to make a *reservation for the wedding rehearsal* at this meeting. You should do so as soon as possible—the site schedule that is heavily booked on your wedding day is likely to be equally tight on the day before, the traditional time to hold the rehearsal. Ask if there are restrictions or rules for the rehearsal, such as clothing regulations or guidelines on who may attend. Find out how long the rehearsal will run so that a rehearsal dinner can be planned. Note: *Make sure to include a few extra minutes in the schedule in case the rehearsal runs overtime.*

✢ If you and your partner plan to participate in *premarital counseling* from the officiant (and some religions require that you do so), this is also the time to set the dates for appointments.

✢ Finally, you'll want to provide the officiant with the *names* you want him or her to use in the ceremony. Also mention whether or not you will be taking the groom's last name.

ETIQUETTE FINE POINTS

Providing Church Documents

Many religions require that couples wishing to marry provide certain documents according to church or synagogue law. A baptismal certificate, first Communion certificate, and Confirmation certificate, for example, are often required in Catholic churches. If you plan to marry in a parish separate from the one you belong to, you may need to provide a letter of permission to marry from your priest.

NUTS AND BOLTS: QUESTIONS TO ASK AT THE CEREMONY SITE

Before you begin formalizing your plans, you must check with your officiant or the ceremony site manager to determine what is permitted and what isn't and to ensure access for your vendors. For example, it is imperative to get clearance to install your floral decorations at the ceremony site. It would be a colossal disappointment to finalize your floral plans only to find out that your selections weren't allowed at the site in the first place. Indeed, the answers your officiant or ceremony site manager provides about the wedding ceremony will likely inform many other decisions. For example, if photography or videotaping is allowed only during certain times in the ceremony, you will need to discuss this with the photographer. Following are important questions to ask your officiant or ceremony site manager:

Site Specifics

Be sure to get the site contact name and number and write it down in your planner, to give to any vendors or wedding consultants.

- Are any other weddings or ceremonies planned on the same day as your wedding? Does that give you a time restriction? (On the other hand, you may be able to share flowers with another bridal party—and floral costs.)

- Is there a room for dressing prior to the service?

- Is there a way to assure that space is left vacant for the cars that will carry the bride and her attendants to the front of the building? Is there enough space that a traffic congestion won't occur when the wedding takes place? If not, are the services of a traffic officer or off-duty police officer to direct traffic advisable?

- If the site is outdoors, is there some sort of podium for the officiant?

- Is the throwing of rose petals permitted outside the building?

✢ What fees are required for the use of the facility; the organist; the cantor; for additional musicians; for the sexton; for the minister or rabbi? If there will be other service participants such as altar boys or acolytes, is it the officiant's duty to arrange for them to be there? Should they be paid, and if so, how much? And should they attend the rehearsal?

✢ May a receiving line be formed at the ceremony site, if desired? In some instances there may be another ceremony following yours or there may not be enough room for a receiving line.

Flowers and Decor

✢ Are there any decorating restrictions or rules? What kinds of floral arrangements/decorations are permitted?

✢ At what time may decorations be delivered, and how will access be arranged? How do you arrange access for a florist to decorate?

✢ What is the site policy on the disposition of flowers after the ceremony? Is there a policy on removing the flowers after the ceremony? Couples often wish to use flowers as reception decorations, to deliver to shut-ins, area hospitals, or nursing homes, or to give to friends.

✢ Are candles permitted as decorations other than within the sanctuary?

✢ Does the ceremony site provide an aisle runner, should you want to use one, or do you need to order one from the florist?

✢ For a Jewish ceremony: Who will provide the *chuppah,* and may it be decorated with flowers?

Attire

✢ Are there restrictions concerning dress? Bare shoulders or arms? Head coverings? What about restrictions on attire for guests?

Photography

✢ Is photography and videography allowed? If so, when and how may photographs and/or a video be taken? Before, during, and/or after the ceremony?

✢ What are site rules on lighting, whether flash or videocassette lighting?

Music

If you're being married in a church or other house of worship, keep in mind that some sites stipulate that any musician performing in a wedding ceremony must be engaged through the in-house music department. In that case the house of worship may have its own music director or organist. Other religious sites forbid secular music.

✢ Does the site have any restrictions on the type of music, the types of instruments, or whether or not music is played with a microphone? Does it have any restrictions on recorded music?

✢ Does the house of worship allow secular, classical, or popular selections? Must the ceremony prelude, processional, ceremony, and recessional music, for example, be all sacred music?

✢ Are there certain hymns that can or can't be sung at the ceremony?

✢ Can additional music be inserted in the ceremony—such as a solo by a flutist, a trumpeter, a guitar player, or a vocalist—and if so, where?

✢ Does the site have modernized sound recording equipment, and can it provide audiocassettes as mementos?

Personalizing the Ceremony

Often couples like to include personal readings, musical interludes, or self-penned vows in the wedding ceremony. These are great ideas, but keep in

Clergy from Out of Town

Q: I would desperately love for my hometown minister to marry us in the church we now belong to, but I'm not sure of the protocol, and I certainly don't want to hurt the feelings of our current officiant. Any advice?

A: If you are having a clergyperson from out of town officiate at your wedding, and you want to marry in a church or synagogue he is not affiliated with, you should talk to the local clergy immediately. Explain that your hometown minister is an old friend and you've always wanted him to be involved in your wedding plans. In some cases it is required that the local officiant be present and participate in the service. In others there is no such requirement, and the church or synagogue is literally turned over to the visiting officiant. Sometimes a payment to the local clergyperson is customary for his or her help in making arrangements.

Your obligations?

✤ Check what the regulations are before asking the out-of-town officiant to perform the ceremony.

✤ Get permission to use the church or synagogue.

✤ Coordinate the communication between the out-of-town officiant and his or her contact person at the church or synagogue. Details may include borrowing a key to the building to have access to a robing room or to set up a Holy Communion.

✤ If the out-of-town clergy is to be the sole officiant, you should get a list from him or her of any ceremony needs ahead of time.

✤ Finally, it is your responsibility to pay the travel, lodging, and meal expenses of any clergyperson you invite from out of town.

mind that any additions will lengthen the total time of the ceremony and affect the timing of your reception.

✤ What latitude do you have in writing some or all of the ceremony by yourselves or including additional readings? If you are being married in a house of worship, ask your officiant to give you a copy of the liturgy for the wedding ceremony and to mark those places where you may add a reading. Find out whether the readings must be scriptural or can include secular pieces. Your officiant may even be able to provide a list of reading choices. Finally, find out whether the officiant needs to review your selections.

✢ Can you use a second officiant at the wedding? If you want a co-officiant at your wedding—a relative, perhaps, or a retired minister you are particularly close to—ask your officiant if this is permissible. If so, provide his or her name, telephone number, and address and send the reciprocal information to the visiting clergy. That way they can communicate directly if they wish and plan the order of officiating. If the visiting clergy is of another faith, your officiant may be unable or unwilling to include him or her. If your officiant agrees to include a co-officiant from another faith, discuss with him or her ways the service may be structured.

❧ ARRANGEMENTS FOR ❧ A CEREMONY AT ANOTHER SITE

Even if you plan to marry at a site separate from the officiant's church or synagogue, many of the same questions for the officiant still apply. In addition, you will need to ask:

✢ Are there any restrictions on the kind of ceremony you can have if it is not conducted in a house of worship? If so, what? If not, is there perhaps more room to deviate from the standard wedding service?

✢ What are the travel needs of the officiant? Would he or she prefer to come in a hired car? Can you reimburse the officiant for time, gas, and mileage if he or she chooses to drive?

✢ Will you need to provide an altar? A kneeling bench or cushions? An altar cloth? Candles? Any other liturgical items? If the answer is "yes" to any of these questions, ask for the names of resources who provide them. Ask whether makeshift arrangements will do, such as a table that can be used as an altar or a table runner that doubles as an altar cloth. If the ceremony site is a frequent wedding location, you may find that these items are already available.

❧ A CIVIL CEREMONY ❧

In general you will need to make few arrangements for a civil ceremony to be held at the office of a justice of the peace or at the town hall.

+ *What do you need for a civil ceremony?*   The ceremony itself is simple and brief. The only things you'll need to do are fulfill the legal requirements and, often, provide two witnesses.

+ *What arrangements are needed for a civil ceremony at another site?*   If a civil ceremony is to be conducted at another site, such as the bride's home, a garden, or a rented facility, the same arrangements need to be made as those for a religious ceremony outside of a house of worship (with the exception of the need for liturgical items that aren't required for a civil ceremony).

+ *Can the service be personalized?*   Yes. If the bride and groom wish to personalize the order of a civil ceremony, they should arrange to meet with the justice of the peace or whoever will officiate to discuss the length of the service, any requirements, and a list of elements they may add to the service.

❧ RELIGIOUS CEREMONIES ❧

Even with so many different religious rituals and cultural traditions being used in weddings today, there is generally one common thread. Most of the major religions share a mutual belief, and that is that marriage is a joyous occasion worthy of high celebration. Using happiness as the common denominator, today's brides and grooms from different religious and ethnic backgrounds are able to blend the cultural traditions of one with the rituals of the other, by weaving those aspects that matter most to them and their families into the events surrounding their marriage.

Deciding on a ceremony can be a challenge, especially when families and friends have a wide range of practices and beliefs, but there are ways you can foster understanding and help everyone be a part of your wedding. One

At-Home Ceremony Tips

- If you're having an evening wedding outdoors, line your walkway with white paper bags filled with sand and luminaria candles. Hang Japanese lanterns in the trees or on ropes from tree to tree.

- Borrow or rent chairs from a church, school, social club, or rental company for seating your guests.

- Hang a wedding banner on the front porch, or rent topiary or potted trees to place at the entrance.

- Recruit neighborhood children to usher, take guests' coats, and even give corsages and nosegays to special guests.

- Hire off-duty police or responsible teens as parking valets.

- Avoid having muddy footprints in the house—don't water the lawn the day of your ceremony!

solution is to provide a wedding program, with the help of your clergy, which explains the symbolic meaning of different parts of the ceremony so that guests can follow along. Programs can also provide translations if parts of the ceremony are in another language.

ETIQUETTE FINE POINTS

Interfaith Marriages

If your faiths have strictures against interfaith marriage and offer no way for you to incorporate the two faiths in one ceremony, you should either be married in a civil ceremony or hold two separate ceremonies, one right after the other. If you do the latter, you'll need to decide whether to invite guests to both ceremonies or invite all instead to a reception after the two private ceremonies.

Whether yours will be a marriage of mixed faiths, one that integrates age-old traditions and rituals into a modern ceremony, or one that follows religious tradition to the letter, your officiant can best help you choose the right ceremony rites for you.

Roman Catholic Ceremonies

One of the seven sacraments of the Catholic Church is marriage, and as such it is treated seriously.

PREPARING FOR THE CEREMONY

Interfaith marriages: Interfaith marriage is accepted as long as the partner of another faith complies with counseling requirements, and most priests will co-officiate with the clergy of the non-Catholic.

Marrying divorced individuals: Divorce is not recognized, however, so the bride or groom whose previous marriage ended not in annulment but in divorce is not permitted to be married in the Catholic Church if that partner is still living. It is likely that someone married not in a Catholic ceremony but in a civil service and later divorced may remarry in the Catholic Church, which does not recognize civil marriages in the first place.

Premarital counseling: The Catholic Church requires a prescribed series of religious and personal counseling sessions for both the bride and groom, even if one is not Catholic.

THE CEREMONY

✣ Inclusion of a nuptial mass is common, although not required. If it is conducted, it lengthens the approximately twenty-minute ceremony to about an hour. (It used to be that a nuptial mass could be conducted only if both the bride and groom were Catholic, but today this is not a requirement.)

✣ Only Roman Catholic guests are permitted to receive Holy Communion.

✣ Throughout the ceremony personalization and the participation of lay readers may take place, as well as the singing or playing of religious music.

THE SERVICE

I. At the beginning of the service, the groom stands by the priest at the altar and the bride processes, preceded by her attendants.

2. The bride is met by the groom, and the two remain in front of the altar, either kneeling, sitting, or standing throughout the ceremony. Their attendants either flank them or move to front pews in the church.

3. The priest then often welcomes those present and gives a homily about marriage.

4. After the homily, he asks if the couple has come freely to marry. They respond and join hands to exchange marriage vows.

5. The priest blesses the rings, the groom puts the bride's ring on her finger, and she puts his ring on his finger, and then the nuptial blessing is given, followed by the mass if one is included.

Episcopal Ceremonies

Like the Catholic Church, the Episcopal Church considers marriage a sacrament and requires that at least one partner be baptized in the name of the Holy Trinity.

PREPARING FOR THE CEREMONY

Interfaith marriages: Interfaith marriage is accepted, and Episcopal priests are usually willing to co-officiate with other clergy if the couple wishes.

Marrying divorced individuals: If either the bride or groom has been divorced, she or he must receive a dispensation to marry again from the area bishop. If this is not done, the marriage may not take place in the church.

Premarital counseling.   Premarital counseling with the priest who will marry you is customary.

THE CEREMONY

✣ Personalization is permitted in the form of any number of readings and the inclusion of religious music—usually solos, but sometimes hymns sung by the guests.

✣ The ceremony, with the celebration of Holy Eucharist, takes about forty-five minutes. Without Communion, the service is about twenty minutes long.

✢ The celebration of Holy Eucharist may follow the wedding ceremony if the bride and groom wish. All baptized Christians are welcome to receive Communion.

✢ The attendants stand on both sides of the bride and the groom throughout.

THE SERVICE

The Episcopal ceremony is taken from *The Book of Common Prayer* and has four parts, which follow the processional of the bride and her attendants:

1. The priest begins with the call to worship: "Dearly Beloved, we have come together in the presence of God to witness and bless the joining together of this man and this woman in Holy Matrimony."

2. It is followed by the declaration of consent.

3. The ministry of the Word follows, using one or more scriptural passages.

4. This is followed by the exchange of vows and blessing of the rings and then the blessing of the marriage

Mainstream Protestant Ceremonies

The wedding ceremonies of the Baptist, Lutheran, Methodist, Presbyterian, and other mainstream Protestant churches are familiar to many; they are the ceremonies most frequently portrayed in movies and television shows. Mainstream Protestant ceremonies, in general, are similar. Marriage is not a sacrament, but it is considered holy.

PREPARING FOR THE CEREMONY

Interfaith marriages: Interfaith marriages are permitted and co-officiants welcomed, although the more conservative synods or branches may not permit a co-officiated Christian/non-Christian marriage.

Premarital counseling: Premarital counseling is customary, usually conducted in a series of three or more private meetings with the minister who will conduct the ceremony.

THE CEREMONY

✢ Holy Communion may be part of the ceremony if the bride and groom wish. The bride and groom may add readings and music to the ceremony and may write their own vows to replace the ones included in the church's worship book.

THE SERVICE

The service, without additional readings and music or Communion, can take as little as fifteen minutes. When the minister enters, followed by the groom and his best man, who stand to the side, the bride and her attendants begin the processional.

The ceremony consists of three parts:

1. The welcome and introduction by the minister.

2. The exchange of vows and rings.

3. The final blessing.

In the charge to the couple, the minister may say, "Will you have this man to be your wedded husband to live together in holy matrimony? Will you love him, comfort him, honor and keep him in sickness and in health, in sorrow and in joy, and forsaking all others, be faithful to him as long as you both shall live?" He then repeats this charge to the groom.

Roman Catholic, Episcopal, and Mainstream Protestant Traditional Order of Service

While individual clergy members prescribe specific procedures and may require a certain processional, order of service, and recessional, most Christian wedding ceremonies follow this order:

1. Guests are ushered to pews.

2. Prelude music is played.

3. Grandparents and other honored guests are ushered to their seats.

4. The parents of the groom are ushered in.

5. The mother of the bride is ushered to her seat.

6. The aisle runner, if used, is rolled out by the ushers.

7. The music selected for the processional of the attendants begins.

8. The clergymember enters the sanctuary.

9. The groom and best man enter and move to the center side of the head of the aisle.

10. Attendants enter, ushers first, followed by bridesmaids, the maid of honor, and then the ring bearer and the flower girl.

11. If separate processional music accompanies the entrance of the bride, it begins.

12. The bride enters accompanied by her father, her father and mother, her mother, another escort, or by herself.

13. The ceremony is conducted.

14. The minister pronounces the couple husband and wife.

15. The bride and groom kiss.

16. The recessional music begins.

17. The bride and groom turn and walk up the aisle, followed by their attendants.

18. The ushers return and escort the family members from the front pews.

19. The remaining guests exit beginning from the front.

Eastern Orthodox Ceremonies

Marriage is a sacrament in Eastern Orthodox congregations, which can be Greek, Russian, Serbian, Syrian, Polish, or Yugoslavian, among other backgrounds.

THE CEREMONY

✠ The ceremony is filled with symbolism, beginning outside the church doors with the betrothal, when the rings are blessed and exchanged. The couple is then led by the priest into the church to stand on a white cloth in front of a wedding platform. A wedding icon is carried in the processional, and the couple is given lighted candles, which they hold during the service.

THE SERVICE

1. Much of the symbolism of the service, which can last up to one hour, is represented by threes. During the betrothal, the priest beseeches God's blessings upon the rings and proceeds to bless the groom and the bride with the rings. He does this three times, in the name of the Father and of the Son and of the Holy Spirit. He then places the rings on the ring fingers of the right hands of the couples, and the rings are exchanged three times.

2. The ring blessing is followed by the sacrament of Holy Matrimony, which is followed by three prayers.

3. This service, along with the Byzantine Catholic Church service, then uses crowns, whether metal crowns or floral wreaths, as a solemn part of the service, called "the crowning." The crowns, often attached to one another with a ribbon as a symbol that the two are now one, are placed on the heads of the bride and the groom and exchanged between them. The crowns have several meanings, the two most important being the conformation to biblical teachings that say God bestows His blessing upon His children in the form of crowns; and the identification of the bride and the groom as the beginning of a new kingdom.

4. The service continues with readings, with the presentation of the common cup to the bride and groom to symbolize that from that moment on they will share the same cup of life and that whatever life has in store for them they will share equally and with the expression of joy.

5. The priest takes the arm of the bridegroom and leads him and the bride around the table three times, as an expression of joy.

Jewish Ceremonies

Jewish weddings may be held anywhere that a canopy, or *chuppah*, can be erected and is most often held where the reception will follow. The *chuppah* symbolizes both the tents of ancient ancestors and the formation of the new home of the family being created beneath it. The *chuppah* can be decorated with flowers and may be constructed in a fixed position or held by special attendants.

PREPARING FOR THE CEREMONY

Intermarriage: Intermarriage is not encouraged but nonetheless occurs, usually with a Reform rabbi presiding. Some Reform rabbis will also permit a co-officiant of another faith, but Orthodox and Conservative rabbis, as a rule, will not.

Marrying a divorced individual: Usually, even in a Reform congregation, a divorced woman cannot be remarried without a get, an official rabbinical document of divorce.

THE CEREMONY

✢ The ceremony lasts about twenty minutes.

A QUESTION FOR PEGGY

Informal Receiving Line

Q: We are having a small wedding and don't feel the need for a receiving line. We would, however, like to acknowledge and speak with each of our guests personally outside of the mayhem that is the reception. Any ideas?

A: Instead of forming a receiving line at the ceremony site or reception, some couples stop at each pew on their way out of the church or synagogue. Guests rise and exit, greeting the bride and groom on their way. The couple should alternate sides rather than going all the way to the back on one side and then returning to the front to greet guests on the other side. This is indeed best done when the wedding is small. It would be much too time-consuming for a large wedding, leaving half the guests outside and half inside, waiting their turn. For a large guest list, the traditional receiving line is faster and more efficient.

Readings for Your Ceremony

Many couples include in their ceremony scriptural passages, poems, and prose pieces, often read by special friends and relatives. Within some religions readings may be selected from secular as well as scriptural sources. Within others readings must be confined to the scriptural. Talk to your clergyperson about the requirements of your faith.

Readings are generally taken from three categories: those that are scriptural and are about marriage, love, and the nature of joy; those that are classical poetry or prose and similar in theme to the scriptural readings; and original poetry or prose.

Following are a few selections that are popular with brides and grooms.

Scriptural

Love is patient and kind; love is not jealous or boastful; it is not arrogant or rude. Love does not insist on its own way; it is not irritable or resentful; it does not rejoice at wrong, but rejoices in the right. Love bears all things, believes all things, hopes all things, endures all things.

Love never ends; . . . So faith, hope, love abide, these three, but the greatest of these is love.

—*I Corinthians 13:4–8, 13*

Two are better than one, because they have a good return for their toil. For if they fall, one will lift up his fellow; but woe to him who is alone when he falls and has not another to lift him up. Again, if two lie together, they are warm; but how can one be warm alone? And though a man might prevail against one who is alone, two will withstand him.

—*Ecclesiastes 4:9–12*

Secular

Love is something you and I must have. We must have it because our spirit feeds upon it. We must have it because without it we become weak and faint. Without love our self-esteem weakens. Without it our courage fails. Without love we can no longer look out confidently at the world. We turn inward and begin to feed upon our own personalities, and little by little we destroy ourselves. With it we are creative. With it we march tirelessly. With it, and with it alone, we are able to sacrifice for others.

—*Chief Dan George*

You have become mine forever.

Yes, we have become partners.

I have become yours.

Hereafter, I cannot live without you.

Do not live without me.

Let us share the joys.

We are word and meaning, unite.

You are thought and I am sound.

May the nights be honey-sweet for us.

May the mornings be honey-sweet for us.

May the plants be honey-sweet for us.

May the earth be honey-sweet for us.

—Hindu marriage poem

Now you will feel no rain, for each of you will be shelter to each other.

Now you will feel no cold, for each of you will be warmth to the other.

Now there is no more loneliness, for each of you will be companion to the other.

Now you are two bodies, but there is only one life before you.

You will now go to your dwelling place to enter unto the days of your togetherness.

And may your days be good and long upon the earth.

—Apache wedding poem

How do I love thee? Let me count the ways.

I love thee to the depth and breadth and height

My soul can reach, when feeling out of sight

For the ends of Being and ideal Grace.

I love thee to the level of every day's

Most quiet need, by sun and candlelight.

I love thee freely, as men strive for Right;

I love thee purely, as they turn from Praise.

I love thee with a passion put to use

In my old griefs, and with my childhood's faith.

I love thee with a love I seemed to lose

With my lost saints,—I love thee with the breath,

Smiles, tears, of all my life!—and, if God choose,

I shall but love thee better after death.

—Elizabeth Barrett Browning

The Service

1. The bride and groom are escorted by their parents in the procession and gather, with their attendants, under the *chuppah*.

2. To begin the service, which is usually conducted in a combination of Hebrew and English, the bride and groom take a sip of ceremonial wine and are blessed by the rabbi.

3. The bride is given a plain gold wedding ring by the groom, and the marriage contract, or *ketubah*, is read aloud and presented to the couple.

4. A member of the family or a special guest then reads the Seven Blessings, after which the bride and groom again take a sip of wine, this time symbolizing the commitment of the marriage.

5. The ceremony ends with the groom stamping on a glass wrapped carefully in a cloth to prevent shards flying while guests cry *"Mazel tov!"*—meaning good luck and congratulations. The breaking of the glass represents the destruction of the Temple in Jerusalem and is a reminder that even on such a joyous occasion it is important to remember that others may not be so fortunate.

6. The service ends with the recessional, led by the bride and groom and followed by the bride's parents, the groom's parents, the attendants, the rabbi, and the cantor, if one is participating.

7. Following the recessional, the bride and groom retire to a private room for several minutes before they join the reception. This lovely tradition is known as *yichud*, or "seclusion." These few minutes give the couple a brief time to be alone before the excitement of the rest of the day. It symbolizes the couple's right to privacy. Tradition also says that the couple is to share their first meal together, so they are often brought a small plate of favorite foods.

8. The reception is often begun with a blessing of the challah, a loaf of braided bread that here symbolizes the sharing of families and friends. The meal often concludes with grace and seven special benedictions, sung in Hebrew.

Mormon Ceremonies

Members of the Church of Jesus Christ of Latter-day Saints (Mormons) may be married in one of two ways: in a *marriage ceremony* or a *civil ceremony*. The marriage ceremony, the "sealing ordinance," is for couples of great faith. This sacred ceremony is always held in one of the church's dedicated temples. Members of the Mormon faith believe that when they are married (sealed) in a temple by proper priesthood authority, their union may continue forever; they believe that marriage and family relationships can extend beyond the grave. Mormons proclaim that the family is ordained of God and that marriage between man and woman is essential to His eternal plan. Only faithful members may be participants in—and guests at—a temple wedding.

If Mormons choose to be married civilly, the ceremonies are simple, sacred ceremonies usually held in a church or a home. They may be attended by anyone. Bishops for the church are authorized to perform civil ceremonies but receive no pay for conducting such services.

It is typical after both types of ceremonies that a reception is held (often later in the evening) for any number of guests. Gifts for the couple are usually taken at this time.

Islamic (Muslim) Ceremonies

Marriage is a holy and desirable union under Islamic law. Although marriage is not a sacrament, it is a sacred covenant or contract.

PREPARING FOR THE CEREMONY

Interfaith marriages: There is no objection to interfaith union, but there may be objection to intercultural marriage, another issue entirely.

Civil preliminaries: Prior to the religious ceremony, the bride and groom are required to undertake civil preliminaries and may be required to go through a civil ceremony in addition to their religious ceremony.

THE CEREMONY

✣ A Muslim marriage ceremony usually takes place in a mosque, at the bride's home, or in an office. The main wedding reception should

Writing Your Own Vows

Your wedding vows are the expression of your personal commitment to one another. Most clergy are willing to allow certain adaptations of traditional vows, as long as the basic tenets of those vows are expressed in one form or another. These tenets, in most religions, are promises to be true to one another in good times and in bad and in sickness and in health; and to love and honor one another "until death do you part." They may also include pledges to cherish and respect one another. If you decide to write your own vows, keep in mind the following tips:

- Make sure your vows express who you are, reflecting your beliefs and sensibilities.

- If you decide to personalize your vows, avoid sweeping generalizations—make your words personally meaningful.

- Keep it brief. Simplicity and brevity can be far more eloquent than overblown metaphors.

- Even if you plan to memorize your vows, make sure you or the officiant has a written copy in case you go blank and forget what comes next.

- If you come from two different cultures or two different faiths, vows that commit to building bridges of understanding and honoring one another's traditions are particularly meaningful.

not take place until after the religious ceremony and also after the civil ceremony, if there is one.

THE SERVICE

1. When the groom, who is attended by a *serbala* (the youngest boy in his family, usually the son of a sister), arrives at the ceremony, he and his *serbala* are given floral garlands in welcome.

2. The ceremony is conducted by an imam, who reads from the Koran.

3. The bride, who is heavily veiled, and groom are seated apart during their wedding, often on opposite sides of the room.

4. The bride's father and two witnesses ask the bride if she has agreed to the marriage, and the imam asks the groom if he has agreed.

Assuming they have both agreed, the imam completes the marriage certificate.

5. A meal is served after this ceremony, but the bride and groom are still separated, sitting with their own families.

6. After the meal the bride leaves, puts on all the jewelry she has been given for her wedding, and returns to sit next to the groom. Her veil is lifted.

Hindu Ceremonies

Marriage is one of a series of holy sacraments in the Hindu faith, just as it is in the Roman Catholic Church. It is believed that marriage has a purifying quality.

PREPARING FOR THE CEREMONY

Interfaith marriages: Interfaith marriages are accepted.

Civil ceremony: It is important for the couple to be aware of the possibility that a civil ceremony may be required by law. Since the requirements for civil and religious ceremonies are separate, the civil ceremony may take place first, but the couple is not deemed married by the community until they have had a religious ceremony.

THE CEREMONY

✢ The wedding ceremony, which is conducted by a priest, can last all day in India. In the United States the ceremony has been shortened to about ninety minutes, although cultural traditions surrounding the wedding can last several days. It does not have to be performed in a temple and is often conducted in the bride's home.

✢ Throughout the ceremony, whether of a duration of ninety minutes or an entire day, the couple is instructed in lessons for married life. There is frequent chanting of mantras, or prayers in Sanskrit, which ask for blessings on the union. A traditional Hindu mantra is "I am the word and you are the melody. I am the melody and you are the word."

✣ The bride usually wears a sari made of a single piece of red fabric embroidered in gold. She is also adorned with 24-karat-gold jewelry, presented to her by the groom's family. The groom wears white trousers, a tunic, and a ceremonial hat.

THE SERVICE

1. At the beginning of the ceremony, the bride and groom, usually seated under a decorated canopy called a *mandaps,* may exchange garlands of flowers.

2. After emphasizing the importance of marriage, the priest ties the couple's right hands together with cord and sprinkles holy water over them.

3. The bride's father then gives his daughter to the groom.

4. A sacred flame is lit, and the bride and groom make an offering of rice to symbolize their hope of fertility.

5. The most important part of the ceremony is the Seven Steps, and until this rite is completed, the couple is not married. The Seven Steps symbolize food, strength, wealth, fortune, children, happy seasons, and friendships. The bride and groom together either take seven steps around the fire or walk around it seven times.

6. Now married, the bride and groom feed each other five times with little bits of sweet food, and the ceremony ends with prayers and readings.

Sikh Ceremonies

The Sikh wedding ceremony is called *Arnand Karaj,* which means "the Ceremony of Bliss." It solemnizes the union of the couple's souls and seals their religious, moral, and legal obligations.

PREPARING FOR THE CEREMONY

Civil ceremony: A civil ceremony may be required to legalize the union.

The Ceremony

✢ The ceremony may be performed in a *gurdwara,* the Sikh place of worship, or not. It most often takes place in the bride's home.

✢ It almost always takes place before noon, because according to Sikh belief morning is the happiest time of day.

✢ The bride wears either red trousers and a tunic or a red sari made from a single piece of cloth, and a red head scarf. She also wears all the jewelry the groom's family has given her. The groom wears a white brocade suit, a scarf, and a turban, or he may wear Western dress.

✢ Wherever the ceremony is performed, a central platform is used, upon which the Holy Book is displayed by the priest who conducts the ceremony. (It is not necessary for a priest to be present; actually any Sikh may be in charge of the ceremony as long as both families agree.)

✢ Guests sit on the floor around the platform, with men to the right of the Holy Book and women to the left.

The Service

1. Flower garlands play a role as they do in Muslim and Hindu weddings, beginning when the parents of the bride welcome the groom and his parents by placing garlands around their necks. The bride is brought to greet the groom, and they exchange garlands.

2. The couple stands before the priest and the Holy Book, and the bride's father hands one end of a sash to the groom and the other end to the bride. This symbolizes giving her away.

3. The wedding ceremony comprises four verses from the Holy Book that explain the obligations of married life. Each verse is read, and then it is sung. During the singing, the groom leads the bride around the Holy Book four times, sometimes with the help of guests to symbolize their support. After they have walked around four times, they are married.

4. A prayer and a short hymn follows, and the sharing of a sweet food by all the guests is symbolic of God's blessing on the marriage. Guests place garlands around the necks of the couple or throw flowers petals, a symbol of happiness.

Unitarian-Universalist Ceremonies

The roots of this society are Judeo-Christian, making it a pluralistic religion. It is not a church with ecclesiastical rules or rituals, so wedding ceremonies may be personalized and individualized, and couples are encouraged to design their own service from a combination of religious, spiritual, or other traditions that are meaningful to them.

Quaker (Society of Friends) Ceremonies

A Quaker wedding is the simplest of all Christian marriages, for it has no music or set order of service. Couples who wish to marry in a Quaker meetinghouse must apply for permission in advance, often two to three months; several levels of approval are required for the marriage to take place. The bride and groom pledge their lifelong love and loyalty to one another but do not exchange rings during the ceremony, for it is believed that the words of the pledge are sufficient. A ring may be given to the bride at the end of the ceremony, however.

❧ COMMITMENT CEREMONIES ❧

While many religions refuse to be associated with commitment ceremonies for gay and lesbian couples, others are willing to affirm same-gender unions in one way or another. Still, which services they will perform varies greatly. For example, within the Universal Fellowship of Metropolitan Community Churches, a couple may participate in a rite of blessing (a simple prayer that acknowledges the relationship and offers it to God) or a holy union (a covenant or contract between two people), but not a rite of holy matrimony. The Unitarian-Universalist religion performs a service of union; some Episcopalian priests will perform a commitment ceremony; and some

Presbyterians perform a holy union. Many other clergy, within the structure of their religion or outside it, will perform a ceremony that acknowledges the commitment of the couple.

Because many churches do not sanction a gay or lesbian union through wedding liturgy, gay couples actually have more latitude in planning the ceremony. Most write their own vows in some form or another, using both religious and secular sources, as they wish. In thinking about how to structure a ceremony of commitment, couples generally follow the standard guidelines of Jewish or Christian ceremonies. That structure includes the following:

THE INTRODUCTION

Any activity before the actual service begins, including the processional, a gathering together and welcome, and an invocation. Some gay or lesbian couples want a statement made about being gay, believing that their sexuality is so integral to their being and their relationship that they wouldn't think of not addressing it. Others choose not to address their sexuality, preferring a ceremony that focuses on love and commitment.

THE SERVICE

Consists of prayers, songs, readings, a homily, and an address by the officiant. If readings are included, some gay couples like to read from the Book of Samuel, chapter 18, verses 1–5, and chapter 20, verses 16–17. Lesbian couples often select readings from the Book of Ruth, chapter 1, verses 16–17. Unless the ceremony is taking place in a house of worship that prohibits the use of secular readings and music, the couple also has a wide range of sources from which to choose.

THE VOWS

The expressions of the couple's intent. The couple may borrow vows from any service book ("I, Jane, take you, Beth . . ."), write their own vows to be read by an officiant, or declare to each other with no prompting.

THE EXCHANGE OF RINGS

May be preceded by the rings being blessed.

THE PRONOUNCEMENT

The public proclamation by the officiant that the couple is recognized as married. This part of the ceremony can be worded several ways, such as "Since you have consented to join together in the bond of matrimony, and have pledged yourselves to each other in the presence of this company, I now pronounce you married" or "In the presence of this company, by the power of your love, because you have pledged to one another your vows of commitment, we recognize you as married."

THE CLOSING

The kiss, the blessing of the union, the recessional.

✦ MILITARY WEDDINGS ✦

Any enlisted man or woman on active duty or any officer or cadet at a military academy may have a military ceremony. The military wedding is different from other weddings in the following ways:

- ✣ Military weddings are formal in attire. Those who are entitled to do so wear full dress uniform, including the bride, if she, as a member of the military, so chooses.

- ✣ Other attendants wear civilian formal attire.

- ✣ Men in uniform do not wear boutonnieres.

- ✣ The American flag and the standard of the groom's and/or bride's unit is displayed.

- ✣ During the recessional, the bride and groom—if the groom is a commissioned officer—pass under an arch of drawn swords or sabers that is formed outside the church or chapel.

- ✣ At the reception, the cake is cut with the groom's sword or saber.

Otherwise the rest of the ceremony is conducted according to the religion and traditions of the bride and the groom.

Double weddings may honor two sisters, two cousins, or two best friends. Each couple should have the same number of attendants. All ushers are dressed alike. The bridesmaids' dresses, while not necessarily all the same, should be complementary. One difficulty of a double wedding is the seating of the parents of the two bridegrooms. They must either share the first pew or draw lots to determine who sits in the first row and who sits in the next.

THE CEREMONY AND SERVICE

✣ If the wedding involves two sisters, the ceremony begins with the two bridegrooms following the clergyperson to the altar. Each stands with his best man beside him. The groom of the older sister stands nearer the aisle.

✣ The ushers—half of them friends of the first and the other half friends of the second bridegroom—go up the aisle together.

✣ Then come the bridesmaids of the older sister, followed by her maid of honor, who walks alone.

✣ The older sister follows, holding her father's arm.

✣ Then come the bridesmaids of the younger sister, her maid of honor, and, last, the younger bride on the arm of a brother, uncle, or other male relative.

✣ The first couple ascends the chancel steps and takes their place at the left side of the altar rail, leaving room at the right side for the younger bride and her bridegroom. The father stands just below his older daughter.

✣ The younger daughter's escort takes his place in a pew with his wife or family.

✣ The service is read to both couples, with responses made twice.

✣ Generally, if the service includes a father "giving" two daughters away, he does so—first his older daughter and then the younger.

Then he takes the place saved for him beside his wife in the first pew.

✢ At the end of the ceremony the older sister and her husband turn and go down the aisle first. The younger couple follow. The bridesmaids and ushers of the first sister pair off and follow. The attendants of the second walk out last.

❧ SPECIAL CEREMONIAL TRIBUTES ❧

Children from a Previous Marriage

Children of either divorced or widowed parents should be included in the wedding party as long as they want to be. Including them in the ceremony, whether as attendants or in some other role, will help them adjust to the new family situation much more readily. They will feel they are part of the formation of that family.

One meaningful way to include children from a previous marriage in the wedding ceremony is by placing a family medallion around their necks after vows have been exchanged. The medallion, sometimes a circle with three intersecting circles inside, represents a promise of family love and inclusion. It is first blessed by the minister, priest, or rabbi, who then shares with those gathered the meaning of the medallion. He then gives it to the parent to give to the children. The children may then stand alongside the attendants or return to their seats for the conclusion of the service.

Honoring the Deceased

Increasingly, some couples are finding ways to honor deceased family members, either privately or publicly, in their ceremony. This is a way to remember loved ones, especially parents and grandparents, and give tribute to the importance of family and tradition. If you decide to include a tribute in your ceremony, be sure that it is neither morbid nor lengthy. A simple declaration of love, a moment of silence, or the lighting of a candle may be the most eloquent way to honor them. Often couples find it too difficult to publicly honor the deceased, so they make their memorials private. They may do so by offering a silent prayer, wearing something of the person who has died, or laying a bouquet of flowers on the front pew or by the altar.

Unity Candles

With the concurrence of their officiants, some couples include unity candles in the ceremony, as a symbol of the joining of their families. At the start of the wedding service, the bride's parents light a candle on one side of the altar and the groom's parents light one on the other side. At the conclusion of the wedding the bride and groom each carry their parents' candles to the center of the altar, where they light a single candle from their parents' candles. Once the unity candle is lit, the bride and groom blow out the smaller candles. If the marriage is a blending of two religions, lighting unity candles is a particularly meaningful way to symbolize the merging and acceptance of both traditions.

❧ BLESSING A CIVIL MARRIAGE ❧

Couples who missed out on a religious wedding originally can usually get approval from their church at a later date for a church or chapel ceremony for the blessing of the marriage. There is such a service in *The Book of Common Worship.* The widely used Protestant service book follows the traditional marriage service, except that the minister says, "Do you *acknowledge* [rather than take] this woman..." and makes other similar changes. No one gives the bride away, nor does the groom give the bride her ring again.

- ✥ *Who attends?* The service is generally attended only by family and close friends, and there are no attendants. This is, after all, a blessing and not a new celebration of the marriage.

- ✥ *What is the attire?* The bride wears a street-length dress or suit and the groom a dark suit. She may carry a bouquet or wear a corsage.

✢ *What can be included in the ceremony?*   There may be music, and the altar may be decorated with flowers.

❦   REAFFIRMATION OF VOWS   ❦

Traditionally couples who reaffirm their vows do so on a big anniversary, such as the twenty-fifth or even higher one. This practice is popular today as a way for some couples to celebrate earlier anniversaries. In addition to wanting to recommit to one another publicly, they may want to have the big celebration they missed out on the first time around. A big party will usually do the trick, as it sometimes will have to, since some clergy will not perform a duplicate of the first wedding ceremony. Most clergy, however, will conduct a simple reaffirmation of vows.

✢ *When is the ceremony held?*   The ceremony can occur during a regular Sabbath service or at a separate time.

✢ *What type of service is performed?*   The form of the service varies, depending on the wishes of the officiant and the tenets of the place of worship.

✢ *Who attends?*   The couple is joined by any members of their original wedding party, plus their children.

✢ *Can a celebration be held after the ceremony?*   Of course! Most reaffirmations of vows are followed by a party or reception, whether at the church, at home, at the home of friends, or at a reception site. Some couples make a reaffirmation of vows a destination affair, inviting family (and perhaps close friends) to a vacation location for both the ceremony and the party.

CHAPTER TEN

Each culture has its own

MULTICULTURAL

special ways of celebrating

WEDDINGS

and honoring the wedding

of two people.

✤ THE UNIVERSALITY OF LOVE ✤

*L*ove *is* a universal phenomenon, and the ceremonial commitment a couple makes to each other knows no physical boundaries. But each culture has its own special ways of celebrating and honoring the wedding of two people, many of them traditions that have been lovingly passed on for many generations.

The revival of these multicultural traditions among contemporary

Seeing the Bride Before the Wedding

Q: My mother insists that I not see my bride-to-be on the day of the wedding until the ceremony. Is this customary in today's weddings?

A: Most couples today have disregarded the musty old superstition of the bridegroom not seeing his bride before the ceremony on the day of the wedding. The superstition stems from the days when marriages were arranged and the groom might never have seen the bride. There was the chance that he might take one look at her and bolt—so it was often safer for them to meet for the first time at the altar! This, of course, is a custom that these days certainly does not need to be followed, unless of course it's something you both feel strongly about.

brides and grooms is proof of their lasting power and significance—and attests to the desire of modern couples to invest their ceremony with meaning and a personal and historical context. It's a way to honor their heritage and personalize their ceremony. If the bride and groom come from different cultural backgrounds, incorporating separate traditions into the wedding events can be a connective thread linking both families. Fusing traditions of old with twenty-first-century nuptials, couples are discovering, will only serve to enhance and enrich an already remarkable milestone event.

WEDDINGS AROUND THE WORLD

The year 2000 is an auspicious one for marriages; wedding experts estimate that the number of weddings held in 2000 are almost 10 percent higher than in previous years. Why have so many couples planned their wedding for that year? For many people, having a wedding in the year 2000 represents a clean beginning and good fortune. For the Chinese in particular, marrying in the year 2000, combined with selecting the right date, makes the union doubly blessed. The Chinese place great importance on numbers and dates and refer to the Chinese lunar calendar to determine good times to hold special events, like weddings. Eight, for example, is a number of particularly good fortune to the Chinese (in the Chinese language, the word *eight* sounds like "good luck"). In Ireland the last day of the old year is thought to be a particularly lucky day for weddings.

Today the Western wedding is truly a melting pot of old and new customs, drawn from cultures and traditions all over the globe. Following are some of the most popular of the multicultural customs that have been incorporated into traditional Western wedding celebrations.

Symbolic Acts

CROSSING STICKS AND JUMPING THE BROOM

African Americans in increasing numbers are weaving the traditions of their forebears into their ceremony and reception plans. At some African American wedding ceremonies newlyweds "jump the broom," a custom that originated during the era of slavery in early-nineteenth-century America. Slaves were not permitted to marry, so they developed their own ritual of crossing stafflike sticks that symbolized the strength and vitality of trees. The custom, intended to honor and bless their new life together, drew no objection from the slave masters, who permitted a couple to stand before witnesses, pledge their devotion to each other, then jump over a broom—a symbol of the start of the couple's homemaking. Forging a cultural link, many modern African American brides and grooms include the rituals of the crossing of sticks and "jumping the broom" in their ceremonies. The act of jumping the broom is generally held either after the officiant has pronounced the couple husband and wife or as the couple enters the reception room.

BREAKING THE GLASS

In a traditional Jewish ceremony the bride and groom stand beneath the *chuppah,* or wedding arch or canopy (often adorned with flowers). They sip wine during readings by various guests. Wine is poured into a new glass, and the bride and groom drink from it. The groom then places the glass, wrapped in cloth, on the ground and breaks the glass with his foot—an act symbolizing the destruction of the temple in Jerusalem that is meant to underscore the fragility of love.

Exchanging the Tartan Sash

In Scotland, at the end of the wedding ceremony, the groom takes off his colorful tartan sash—often the tartan of his clan or family—and places it on his bride, whether gently on her shoulder or over her head, with the sash running diagonally across her gown. It symbolizes the welcoming of the bride into the family and the joining of two into one.

In the Mexican Tradition

Brides and grooms of Mexican descent who are removed from their heritage by time and distance can reconnect by adding long-standing cultural traditions to their nuptials. In addition to the common customs of decorating the church with white roses and holding the mass at nine o'clock in the evening, they can ask those closest to them to be "godparents," giving a responsibility to each. One responsibility is to make three bouquets—one to place on the altar; one to keep as a memento; and one for the bride to toss at the reception. Another godparent holds a dish with thirteen gold coins (*arras*) and rings: the groom takes the coins from the dish and hands them to the bride as a sign of giving her all his possessions; he also promises he will use all he possesses for her support. Two more godparents carry a very long rosary rope (*lazo*), which they drape around the bride and groom as the couple kneels at the altar. Besides the appointing of godparents, musical tradition may also be included: at the reception the band can play music for *la vibora*, a line dance that the single women perform.

Food and Drink

Double Happiness

The Chinese to varying degrees follow the traditions of their forebears. Dowries for marriages are still honored in many families, whether in the form of a whole roasted pig, a live chicken, or some other representative swap. For the wedding banquet the bride often changes from her wedding dress into a long red cheongsam (red is considered a powerful, lucky color to the Chinese), which may be adorned with dragon and phoenix images, representing the union of man and woman.

The banquet revolves around a feast of elaborate courses, serving foods imbued with special symbolism for the Chinese, having such attributes as prosperity, happiness, and long life. Eight courses are generally served—eight, of course, being considered a lucky number. Popular foods for wedding banquets include shark's-fin soup, which represents prosperity; "red" foods, such as lobster (another good-luck symbol); and noodles, which symbolize longevity. Lotus seed, in soup or steamed bread, represents fertility. The Chinese icon representing "double happiness" is often hung on the wall behind the bridal party table.

A CUPFUL OF COMMITMENT

In *France* the bride and groom often drink a reception toast from a silver two-handled cup that is shaped like a small bowl on a pedestal called a *coupe de marriage.* The bride drinks first, then the groom, and in so doing make their commitment to each other. In *Germany* a couple's silver cup is made in the shape of a young girl wearing a full skirt, holding the cup over her head. The bride and groom drink from it at the same time to symbolize their joining together. You can start your own "marriage cup" tradition with your marriage—and save the cup for the next in the family to be married.

THE CAKE'S THE THING

In *Denmark* the traditional wedding cake is tall and round and is called a *"cornucopia."* It's customary for each guest to partake of the cake to ensure good luck for the newlyweds. In the *Caribbean* a rich rum fruitcake is the wedding cake, baked from a vintage recipe passed down through the generations. In *Ireland* the traditional cake is a fruitcake full of currants, cherries, almonds, spices, and a dollop or two of brandy or whiskey; it's often accompanied by a special toast, along the lines of "As you slide down the banister of life, may the splinters never face the wrong way." In the *American South* a groom's cake is often included in the wedding reception. Having a special groom's cake is a charming personal touch, and it's often baked in a shape that reflects the groom's interests. Some couples ask to have the groom's cake packaged in small boxes to send home with departing guests, "to dream on."

Music and Dancing

THE MONEY DANCE

Many European cultures perform a traditional dance called "the money dance" at the reception. The idea is that the men at the wedding pay for the privilege of dancing with the bride—sometimes women will do the same with the groom—after the bride and groom have had their special dance and the bride's and groom's parents have danced with the couple. That's when guests begin to cut in; but before they do, they pin a monetary bill onto the clothing of the bride or groom. Pins are provided, and the amount of money is not set but sometimes will go up to $100. A dollar bill is more the norm, and in some locales in the United States this custom is referred to as "the dollar dance." At the end of the dance both bride and groom are covered with cash.

Saying It with Bagpipes

Scottish wedding receptions often feature music for dancing jigs and reels, keeping up the high-energy custom of Scottish wedding days of old, when pipers played all day in the fields and fiddlers played all day in the house. Bagpipes continue to be a popular instrument at both Scottish wedding ceremonies and receptions, announcing the entrance of the bride and other important events.

THE CIRCLE DANCE

In many Jewish receptions the newlyweds are surrounded by reception guests, who dance in a circle around them. The bride and groom are often lifted above the circle in chairs.

CELTIC MUSIC

The musical traditions of the Celtic world are naturally celebratory, perfectly suited to the joyous events surrounding a wedding. Irish *céilí* bands play toe-tapping music for social dancing. The Scots' equivalent are *céilidh* bands and dancing. Irish set dancing is an elaborate form of social dancing, traditionally practiced by four couples in a square. Many modern Irish weddings feature performances by set dancers; others opt for less frenzied accompaniment, such as soothing music from an Irish harp.

Good-Luck Charms

HORSESHOES

Irish brides often wear little porcelain horseshoes on their wrists for good luck.

COINS IN SHOES

Swedish brides wear a gold coin from their mother in the right shoe and a silver coin from their father in the left shoe, while Irish brides traditionally put an Irish penny in their bridal shoes for luck.

The Mother Asks: Is a Money Tree Proper?

Q: *My daughter's fiancé wants to have a money tree at their wedding reception. I personally find this distasteful; can I say so?*

A: It is not appropriate to stand a "money tree" in the middle of a wedding reception for guests to clip dollar bills on. Money trees sometimes work for other venues, such as a fiftieth wedding anniversary party, where the couple is saving up for a cruise, for example. In the case of the wedding reception, remember that guests are guests—not sponsors. An alternative idea: If guests inquire about gift ideas for the bride and groom, one option is to tell them that sending checks as wedding presents would be greatly appreciated.

JORDAN ALMONDS

These are traditionally given to guests at weddings in the Mediterranean countries. They represent the bitter and the sweet sides of marriage.

THE EVIL EYE

A good-luck charm or pin in the shape of an eye is worn by attendants in Greece to protect against evil spirits.

PLATES

Plates are broken in Germany on the doorstep of the bride to drive away evil, and the remaining shards are considered good luck.

THE ART OF MEHNDI

Mehndi—the ancient art of painting beautiful designs on the hands and feet with henna—was practiced for centuries by friends of Pakistani, Moroccan, and Indian brides; it's still done in some villages. In these countries friends gather before the wedding to color and paint with henna the hands, feet, and sometimes arms and face of the bride in intricate floral patterns as good luck and protection against unfriendly spirits.

GIFTS FOR GUESTS

Japanese brides and grooms sometimes give their wedding guests *kohaku man-jyu,* round steamed buns with sweet bean paste in the middle. A pair of buns, one red, one white, is made and given to guests in a special box. Other gifts for guests include a pair of chopsticks imprinted with the date and names of the bride and groom, tied with a ribbon; a collection of origami cranes; or a bag of candied almonds. The reasoning behind this gift giving? The Japanese believe that guests bring so much luck with them that the bride and groom should thank them in return!

ORANGE BLOSSOMS

In a tradition that began in twelfth-century Spain, brides fashioned fresh orange blossoms into wreaths to crown their heads or carried them in their bouquets. According to legend, the orange blossoms represented purity and chastity and symbolized everlasting love.

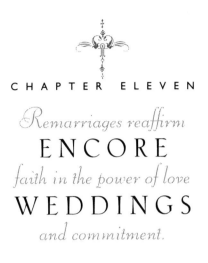

CHAPTER ELEVEN

Remarriages reaffirm

ENCORE

faith in the power of love

WEDDINGS

and commitment.

Few trends underscore the durability of marriage in modern culture more convincingly than the popularity of encore weddings. In spite of increasingly complex family divisions and the prevalence of divorce, the faith in forging a spiritual lifelong union with another person remains strong and steadfast.

Indeed, it is estimated that more than 40 percent of all weddings are encore weddings. An encore wedding is defined as the marriage of two people who have been married before. The "encore" wedding is a second, third, or fourth marriage for one or both members of the couple. More and more, questions are being asked about the proper etiquette surrounding encore weddings. Can a bride wear white again? Can the bride's father walk his daughter down the aisle again? Is it okay for the couple to register for gifts?

To these questions the answer is *yes*. There is nothing wrong with an encore bride wearing white. If the bride's father is able and willing, by all means he can walk his daughter down the aisle once more. Certainly a couple marrying for a second or third or fourth time may register for gifts. An encore wedding may be celebrated with an engagement party, the bride may have the same maid of honor she had for the first wedding, and the ceremony may be as formal as she wants. In other words, an encore wedding can be as festive as a first wedding often is and can follow the same traditional customs.

The nature of an encore wedding, however, often dictates a different sort of celebration. People who are marrying for the second time (or more) are often in a very different phase of life from that at the time of their first wedding. A couple planning an encore wedding is generally older, more established, and less dependent on parents for support. Other people may be in the mix—children being the most important, of course. If children are involved, and if first-marriage relatives and in-laws remain important to the couple, then you may want to invite them to your celebration, as long as your fiancé is comfortable with that.

Because plans for encore weddings are often undertaken by the couples themselves, who choose and blend the types of traditions and themes that best represent them, the result is a more personalized celebration. Another difference between first weddings and encore weddings is the party responsible for paying. The general rule for an encore wedding is that parents are not expected to foot the bill; that is up to the bride and groom. This does not mean, however, that any help that is offered must be turned down.

For these and other reasons, an encore wedding is often very different from a first wedding. In general the celebration for an encore wedding is not as large or elaborate or formal as that for a first wedding. The planning may be more streamlined, with the couple playing a hands-on role and making decisions based on personal choices. Gifts of camping equipment, say, or specialty foods might be presented to the couple instead of traditional gifts such as china and silverware, which the couple may already own. Yet although

The Consultant Asks: Can the Father Give the Encore Bride Away?

Q: I am the wedding consultant for an encore bride. In her first marriage her father escorted her up the aisle and "gave her away." She has been living independently, first when she was married and then ever since her divorce. She would love for her dad to do the honors again. Is this appropriate?

A: Yes, it is perfectly fine for the bride's father to escort her up the aisle, although for the encore bride who has already led an independent life and is not anyone's to "give away," it certainly isn't necessary. Still, if her heart is set on it, she should talk it over first with her dad to make sure he's comfortable with the idea of escorting her (not "giving her away"). If he isn't comfortable, she should not insist on his doing so.

the celebration of an encore marriage may be low-key compared with that of a first wedding, it is often a powerfully unique and personal experience. Weddings should be occasions of joy, and many remarriages are doubly so. They reaffirm faith in the power of love and commitment.

Ten Guidelines to a Joyous Encore Wedding

1. Keep it simple; don't let the details take over.

2. Find meaningful ways to include your children (if they concur) in the celebrations and in your future lives.

3. Reassure family and longtime friends that they will continue to play an important part in your lives.

4. Build your celebrations around those traditions and themes that are most meaningful to you, and have confidence in your choices. Make sure, however, that in making these choices, you have given consideration to those involved and that your choices will not alienate them or make them feel uncomfortable.

Do-It-Yourself Invitations

Q: So many encore couples host their own wedding celebrations. How are the wedding invitations worded?

A: They would read:

> The honour of your presence
>
> is requested
>
> at the marriage of
>
> Susan Walker Smith
>
> and
>
> David Michael Warren
>
> Saturday, the twelfth of June
>
> two thousand
>
> at half after four o'clock
>
> Village Lutheran Church
>
> Briarcliff Manor

5. Be realistic about the budget—in all likelihood it's just the two of you footing the bill!

6. Make sure you have put closure on your first marriage, legally, financially, and emotionally.

7. Plan together. Today both brides and grooms are actively involved in planning their weddings.

8. Remember that thank-you notes never go out of style. A written note should be sent for every wedding gift you've received, within three months of the date of receipt of the gift. And remember, grooms can write thank-you notes, too!

9. Be sure to thank anyone who has done anything for you—vendors, service providers, clergy, or friends—whether verbally or with a small token of thanks.

10. When the big day arrives, relax and enjoy your wedding!

ESSENTIAL ETIQUETTE FOR ENCORE WEDDINGS

When Children Are Involved

‡ *Who tells the kids?* A good percentage of couples marrying again have children from a previous marriage. If you have children from another marriage, it is your responsibility and yours alone to tell your own children about the new wedding; the same applies if your fiancé has children from a previous marriage. You should talk to your children without your fiancé present, so they will feel comfortable

The Ex-Spouse Asks: Why Wasn't I Told?

Q: *I am very hurt and perplexed. I heard about my ex-wife's remarriage the same way the general population did—in a newspaper announcement. While we didn't have children together, we divorced on good terms. Why couldn't my ex-wife have made a simple phone call to me in advance as a courtesy?*

A: It certainly would have been thoughtful if she had advised you. Even if there are no children, it is a discourtesy to let an ex-spouse hear this news from anyone other than the former husband or wife. When there are children from the first marriage, it is particularly important to let an ex-spouse know about the impending nuptials. The ex should be told early on, at (or close to) the time the children are informed. This courtesy allows an ex to better deal with the news and help the children deal with it.

about expressing any anxieties they may have. The two of you should then talk to them together, addressing their concerns and asking for their input in making plans. Remember, too, that your children should be the first people you tell about your engagement, even before you tell parents, other relatives, and close friends.

✥ *Should children be included in the wedding ceremonies?* Even if your children or your fiancé's children don't live with you or you don't see them as much as you'd like, it's always a good idea to try to include them in the wedding in some way. Second weddings, whether for the bride, the groom, or both, are often about building a family. No matter how you feel about it, your fiancé's children will become part of the new life you create, even if he sees them only on alternating weekends. Talk to your future husband about his feelings on this. It's likely that he feels strongly that any children should be included in the wedding. Most important: Ask the children if they want to be included. This sometimes becomes complicated if an ex-spouse is angry over the remarriage and objects to the children's participation in the wedding. If the ex can be convinced that the children's inclusion in your wedding plans does not detract from their relationship, he or she may be willing to allow it. Still, it's in the best interests of

The Bridegroom Asks: Must She Wear Her Old Ring?

Q: *Both my wife and I were married before. We are very happy together, except for one thing: She insists on wearing the wedding ring given to her by her deceased first husband. Frankly, it bothers me to see her wearing the ring. Is it appropriate for her to do so?*

A: When a widow or divorcée becomes engaged to marry again, she should stop wearing her rings from her previous marriage, whether or not she receives a new engagement ring. In deciding what to do with her first engagement ring, she may want to consider keeping it for a son to use as an engagement ring for his future bride, or she might have the stone or stones reset into another piece of jewelry for herself or for her daughters.

A divorcée does not continue to wear the engagement ring from her previous marriage. She may, if she wishes, have the stone or stones from that ring reset in another piece of jewelry. She does not need to return the ring to her ex-husband when she becomes engaged again.

everyone to make every effort to get to know your future stepchildren. Use the period before the wedding to spend time with them. That way, when the wedding day arrives, you both will be much more comfortable sharing this important moment together.

✢ *Can children serve as attendants in an encore wedding?* This is a great idea, especially if your children are happy about the marriage. You may ask them, siblings, or close friends—whomever you would like to have share these moments with you and serve as official witnesses to your marriage. Some encore brides have even asked their children—whether a son or daughter or both—to walk them down the aisle. Instead of "giving the bride away," the child is participating in forming a new family. (No more than one or two kids should escort you, however, as you don't want to crowd the aisles.) It's a wonderful, personal touch to hear the officiant ask, "Who will support this new family?" and hear the music of children's voices happily answering, "We do."

✛ *Can grown-up children be involved?* Of course! For older couples with adult children from a previous marriage, including these children (and even grandchildren) in the celebrations only adds to the joy and community of the occasion. If you both have children who have never met one another, it's a nice idea to bring them all together to announce your engagement, particularly if you are planning a wedding where all will be present. Still, arranging a gathering for your children to meet is not absolutely necessary. You needn't assume that you have to set the stage for all your children to become friends. In other words, don't push them together; give them some time to get used to the idea that you are remarrying.

Some adult children even ask to host or help out with the reception. This is a lovely gesture and requires only some minor wording changes in the wedding invitation. The invitation would list your children, as hosts, before your fiancé's children, and generally the names are then listed in age order, from oldest to youngest, in each family. For example:

Mr. and Mrs. Patrick O'Connor
Mr. and Mrs. Keven O'Connor
Mr. and Mrs. John Restin
Miss Kristin Restin
request the honour of your presence
at the marriage of their parents
Margaret Diane O'Connor
and
Stanley Restin
Saturday, the twelfth of June
two thousand
at half after four o'clock
Village Lutheran Church
Briarcliff Manor

Inviting Ex-Spouses

Q: My ex and I have a congenial relationship and are in frequent contact regarding parenting issues for our two children. Should he be invited to my new wedding?

A: It is better not to invite ex-spouses. It can be confusing to your children, who need to see you and your new groom as a family unit, separate from the ex. They also need to understand that while you are all still their parents, you are otherwise not connected to each other. And no matter how amicable your divorce, it may present an awkward situation for your guests. They may feel uncomfortable expressing happiness for you in front of a former partner with whom things did not work out.

Gifts, the Second Time Around

✣ *How do you let guests know that you don't want gifts?* Many encore wedding couples already own the wedding china, silverware, and other gifts traditionally given to first-time brides. They may even feel they want for nothing, desiring only to enjoy the company of family and friends in celebrating their happy event. Often, too, the issue of "no gifts" comes up when the guest list includes people who were at your first wedding, whom you don't feel are obliged to give you a gift the second time around.

First of all, you should make no mention of gifts on your invitations. Instead rely on word of mouth, mentioning to close friends and relatives that you hope guests know your wish about "no gifts." You can ask them to pass along this message to anyone who asks them what you would like. Although it may seem odd that there is a prohibition against asking people not to bring you gifts when all you are doing is trying to be thoughtful, there is a reason. The moment you mention gifts, you put an *emphasis* on gifts, which is the opposite of your intent. Indeed, friends and family who have attended a first wedding and given a gift are under no obligation to give another wedding gift to the same person, even if, as is usually the case, the marriage is to a different person. Still, there will be many who know this but will want to give you a gift anyway, as a way to share in the celebration of your happiness.

New friends who have never given you a wedding gift before also may want to give you something. For them it is helpful if you either register at a few stores for the fun things that you don't have or make a list for your parents and attendants to share, if asked. Your ideas could be anything from a two-by-four for a new deck to a bunch of movie tickets for a nearby theater to a welcome mat for your front door. You can keep your ideas restricted to reasonably priced items that would be fun for your friends to find or create to commemorate your marriage.

✚ *What happens to the monogrammed linens and sterling silver flatware from a first marriage?* It's really up to you and your fiancé to decide what's best and practical for the both of you. With regard to the linens, unfortunately their monogram may be a daily visible reminder of your previous marriage. Your fiancé could face a lifetime of having to see your former husband's initials everywhere he looks. Here's a suggestion: Why not pass them down to any children you have or give them away to close friends or relatives?

The flatware is a different story, however. Sterling silver flatware is exorbitant to replace. Again, ask your fiancé how he feels about using the flatware. It is very likely that you are both bringing belongings to the marriage, and the flatware can be thought of as no different from furniture or other household items from your pasts that work well together in your new home with one another.

Attire, the Second Time Around

✚ *Is an encore bride restricted in her choice of attire?* It used to be that second-time brides were advised to wear a pastel suit or, for a more formal wedding, a pastel or off white gown. This custom dated back to earlier days when white symbolized purity or virginity—thus making it an inappropriate color for a person who already had been married. Today this is no longer the case—white is thought of as a color of joy and celebration. You may wear as beautiful a white bridal gown as you can find—but make sure that it is appropriate to your age and figure.

Although it is preferable for an encore bride go the more low-key route, it is okay to wear a veil if you really want. These days wearing a veil can be regarded as a fashion choice—and for some religions it's required. Do, however, apply some common sense if you plan to wear a veil. You'd preferably choose a veil style that matches your gown, and one that isn't overly frilly or long.

Children on the Honeymoon?

Q: I am marrying for the second time, and my children are very important to me. I'm a little conflicted about what to do for a honeymoon. My children are feeling threatened by my marriage plans, and I'm concerned about leaving them right after the wedding. I'm anxious that this will confirm their worst fears, that I consider them to be less important to me than my new husband. Still, I would like to have some private time together with my fiancé. What can I do?

A: Talk to your fiancé about the possibility of dividing your honeymoon, with the first part a time for the two of you alone, and the second part a trip as a family. The family "honeymoon" needn't be an elaborate trip—it could be time spent at local sites or taking day trips to places nearby. It should reassure them that you are not abandoning them; it should also give you and your husband much needed time to relax and enjoy each other without the pressure of having to keep everyone entertained. Or you could go ahead and have a traditional honeymoon, just the two of you, and plan a special kids' party when you get home.

Encore Brides and the Blusher Veil

With a nod toward the tradition that said only a first-time bride could wear a veil, you should forgo a blusher veil that covers your face. This style is still an option reserved for the very young or first-time bride.

The Wedding Party, the Second Time Around

✢ *Can the wedding party of an encore wedding include attendants from previous weddings?* While your upcoming wedding should not be a flashback or replica of your first wedding, it is absolutely fine to include people who remain near and dear to you in your encore wedding, whether they were attendants in a previous wedding or not. If, for example, your sister was your maid of honor for your first wedding and you remain the best of friends, it's perfectly acceptable for her to serve as your maid of honor again. All you need to do is make sure your sister is comfortable with the idea. Tell her you feel so fortunate to have her by your side, supporting you and welcoming her new brother-in-law. It's a fresh start for you, and who better to have with you than your best friend?

Showers, the Second Time Around

✤ *What is the etiquette of an encore wedding shower?* A second shower is okay only if it's carefully planned—other than a few close friends and relatives, the guest list should not include people who came to a first shower. Of course, if you've changed jobs or moved to a new town since the first get-together, another party could be in order. But if your friends plan to invite people who have already "showered" you, a small luncheon or afternoon tea—sans gifts—would be a better way to go.

As for the shower gifts for an encore wedding, often theme showers work well, because they allow the couple to be specific about the things they really need. So, for example, if the couple wants to replace monogrammed linens from a previous marriage, a linen shower would be a great way to accomplish this.

A QUESTION FOR PEGGY

When Is a Prenuptial Agreement Advisable in an Encore Marriage?

Q: My fiancé has asked me to sign a prenuptial agreement before our wedding, which is the second marriage for both of us. He suggests that doing so will benefit me as well. What exactly is a prenup, and when is signing one advisable?

A: A prenuptial agreement is basically a contract between two people that defines the rights and benefits that will exist during the marriage and after, in the event of a divorce. Although anyone can have a prenuptial agreement, it is most often used when the bride or groom or both bring assets to the marriage that they want to protect in the event of divorce or death. This is particularly true for people marrying for the second or third time who have children from a previous marriage and who want to ensure that certain assets will be legally passed on to their children. Prenuptial agreements can be sensitive matters for brides and grooms, but they actually protect a couple and allow them to make their own rules about the distribution of their finances, should they someday seek a divorce or when either or both die.

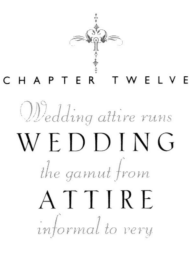

CHAPTER TWELVE

Wedding attire runs

WEDDING

the gamut from

ATTIRE

informal to very

formal.

Before Queen Victoria appeared in her white wedding gown and orange blossoms in 1840 and changed the Western world's thinking about what brides wore to be married, most brides donned their best dress of any color, perhaps pinned a flower to it, and that was that. Even before then, through the eighteenth century, the poorer bride went to her wedding in a plain white robe, a symbol that she brought nothing to her marriage and therefore her husband was not responsible for her debts. Other brides wore colors, often for their symbolism: blue for constancy, green for youth, and

Snappy Undergarments

Q: I am investing in a traditional wedding gown, white with beaded trim and lots of lace. It's occurred to me that I could ruin the whole effect simply by wearing inappropriate undergarments that are out of proportion with the dress. What do I need to be looking for?

A: Number one, you don't want to be uncomfortable on your wedding day. But that doesn't mean that you should just plop on your favorite sports bra and panties and go. Many wedding dresses need to be complemented with underwear of like proportions. You can find bras and bustiers made specifically for wedding gowns at bridal shops. Make sure any new brassiere is comfortable by wearing it for a day or two before the big day. Also, try out beforehand any other undergarment you don't normally wear, such as a garter belt or corset.

red for no particular reason. Never yellow, though, for that meant jealousy. Gradually white came to symbolize purity rather than poverty. Today white is regarded as the symbolic color of weddings and can be worn by anyone, whether a first- or second- or even third-time bride.

Today wedding attire runs the gamut from informal to very formal. There are many ways to blend old traditions with new, glamour with simplicity, and fantasy with fun. Many brides opt for a spanking new, custom-fit gown with all the trimmings; others feel that wearing an heirloom dress passed down through the family makes a more personal statement. Still others, who may find the formal route stuffy and constricting, feel the most important way to wed is barefoot on the beach, with loved ones, friends, and even pets in spectacularly informal attendance. For the bride especially, there are a multitude of choices, whether she selects a wedding dress indigenous to her heritage or searches for the most dazzling white confection she can find.

HOW FORMAL IS FORMAL?

When planning the wedding party attire, use the following chart as a general guide for fabrics, lengths, styles, and accessories. Remember that these are traditional guidelines only and that there are many nontraditional choices.

Dress for Bridal Party and Guests

	Most Formal Daytime	Most Formal Evening	Semiformal Daytime
Bride	Long white dress, train, and veil, gloves optional	Same as most formal daytime	Long white dress; short veil and gloves optional
Bride's Attendants	Long dresses, matching shoes; gloves are bride's option	Same as most formal daytime	Long or short dresses, matching shoes.
Groom, His Attendants, Bride's Father or Stepfather	Cutaway coat, striped trousers, pearl gray waistcoat, white stiff shirt, turndown collar with gray-and-black striped four-in-hand or wing collar with ascot, gray gloves, black silk socks, black kid shoes	Black tailcoat and trousers, white piqué waistcoat, starched-bosom shirt, wing collar, white bow tie, white gloves, black silk socks, black patent-leather shoes or pumps or black kid smooth-toe shoes	Black or charcoal sack coat, dove gray waistcoat, white pleated shirt, starched turn down collar or soft white shirt with four-in-hand tie, gray gloves, black smooth-toe shoes
Mothers and Stepmothers of Couple	Long or short dresses; hat—veil, or hair ornament optional; gloves optional	Usually long evening or dinner dress, dressy short cocktail permissible; head coverings optional: veil or hair ornament if long dress; small hat, if short dress, gloves optional	Long or street-length dresses; gloves, head covering optional
Female Guests	Street-length cocktail or after-noon dresses (colors are preferable to black or white); gloves; head covering optional	Depending on local custom, long or short dresses; if long, veil or ornament—otherwise, hat optional; gloves	Short afternoon or cocktail dress; head covering for church optional
Male Guests	Dark suits; conservative shirts and ties	If women wear long dresses, tuxedos; if short dresses, dark suits	Dark suits

	Semiformal Evening	Informal Daytime	Informal Evening
Bride	Same as semiformal daytime	Short afternoon dress, cocktail dress, or suit	Long dinner dress or short cocktail dress or suit
Bride's Attendants	Same length and degree of formality as bride's dress	Same style as bride	Same style as bride
Groom, His Attendants, Bride's Father or Stepfather	Winter, black tuxedo; summer, white jacket; pleated or piqué soft shirt, black cummerbund, black bow tie, no gloves, black patent-leather or kid shoes	Winter, dark suit; summer, dark trousers with white linen jacket or white trousers with navy or charcoal jacket; soft shirt, conservative four-in-hand tie; hot climate, white suit	Tuxedo if bride wears dinner dress; dark suit in winter, lighter suit in summer
Mothers and Stepmothers of Couple	Same as semiformal daytime	Short afternoon or cocktail dresses	Same length dress as bride
Female Guests	Cocktail dresses, gloves, head covering for church optional	Afternoon dresses, gloves, head covering for church optional	Afternoon or cocktail dresses, gloves, head covering for church optional
Male Guests	Dark suits	Dark suits; light trousers and dark blazers in summer	Dark suits
Groom's Father or Stepfather	He may wear the same costume as the groom and his attendants, especially if he is to stand in the receiving line. If he is not to take part, however, and does not wish to dress formally, he may wear the same clothes as the male guests.		

BALL GOWN

EMPIRE

A-LINE

BASQUE ("U" WAISTLINE)

BASQUE ("V" WAISTLINE)

You should start looking for a wedding gown as soon as the date is set. If yours is a formal wedding, in particular, where elaborate, custom-made gowns are often the rule, you may need to order your gown as far in advance as a year. Delivery times can be as short as eight weeks and as long as a year. Note: Be sure to make the delivery date a few days before your formal portraits are taken, not the actual wedding day. You can then plan a fitting between the delivery date and the photography date.

Fabrics by Season

SPRING Lace and tissue taffeta
SUMMER Chiffon, organdy, marquisette, cotton, piqué, linen
FALL/WINTER Satin, brocade, taffeta, velvet, moiré

Bridal Gown Styles

Following are some of the more popular and traditional bridal gown styles:

‡ Ballgown. "Cinderella"-style gown with big, poufy skirt.

‡ A-line. In the shape of an "A," slimmer at the bodice and widening from the bodice down.

‡ Empire. Dress with high waist that is cropped just below the bust, from which the skirt flares.

‡ Basque. The waist is several inches below the natural waistline and forms a "U" or a "V" shape.

Bridal Veils

Veils come in a variety of lengths and materials. They are often fashioned from lace or tulle. They may have delicately embroidered edgings and trims.

- Blusher veil. Short veil worn over the face that often falls below the neckline.
- Fingertip veil. Veil that falls to the tips of the fingers.
- Mantilla. Scarflike veil that drapes over the head and shoulders.
- Sweep veil. Veil that sweeps the ground.
- Chapel veil. Long veil that trails one or two feet from the gown.
- Cathedral veil. Long veil that trails from one to three yards from the gown.

FINGERTIP

BLUSHER

MANTILLA

SWEEP

CHAPEL

CATHEDRAL

Lifting the Veil

Some brides like to wear face veils for their wedding, and some religions even require that face veils be worn. If the bride chooses to wear a veil over her face coming up the aisle and during the ceremony, it should be short and about a yard square. It is either taken off by the maid of honor when she gives the bride's bouquet back to the bride at the end of the ceremony (if it is a separate piece attached to the headdress), or she or the groom may gently lift it back.

Bridal Trains

Trains are either sewn onto the dress or come detachable for ease of movement at the reception. Also, many sewn-on trains can be "bustled" at the back for an attractive look and more mobility, postceremony. Some of the most popular trains for floor-length dresses:

- ✣ Sweep train. Train draping from the waistline to six inches on the floor.

- ✣ Court train. Train that extends three feet from the waistline.

- ✣ Chapel train. Train that extends five feet from the waistline.

- ✣ Cathedral train. Train that extends three yards from the waistline; more often associated with formal weddings.

- ✣ Watteau train. Train that drapes from the shoulders.

Bridal Headdresses

Bridal headdresses may come attached to a veil, may be separate but placed over a veil, or may be worn without a veil. They may be as simple as a hat, a bow, or a hair comb. The bride should experiment with hairstyles to find the one that is most flattering and natural and that best complements a headdress. Plan a trial appointment with your hairdresser to establish the look you want on your wedding day.

Some popular headdress styles:

✢ Headband or bow. Worn around the head.

✢ Wreath of flowers. Worn snugly on the crown of the head or woven into the hair.

✢ Tiara. Crown rests on top of the head.

✢ Juliet cap. A small cap that hugs the crown.

BOW

WREATH OF FLOWERS

TIARA

JULIET CAP

The Wedding Consultant's Dressing Tips

The big day has arrived, everything is in order, your makeup has been expertly done, and your hair is beautifully coiffed. Your dress is a smooth, wrinkle-free miracle—but wait: you haven't put it on yet! Here are some tips from a seasoned wedding consultant on getting into your wedding attire without mussing the rest of you.

- **If the bride's gown is put on over her head, she should always hold a towel in front of her face if her makeup has already been applied. If you don't have a towel, be sure to hold your face forward while dressing so that nothing touches your face. This is not the time for spot removal, and it is all too easy for foundation or lipstick to rub off on the gown.**

- **Hairnet covers or bouffant-style shower caps will do in a pinch in protecting a hairdo while dressing.**

- **If the dress is close fitting, the bride's hair should always be styled *after* the gown is in place.**

- **A low stool is a great addition to the dressing room; the bride can sit without wrinkling her dress, her skirts around her over the stool, while she has her hair done and her veil, flowers, or other headpiece put in place.**

Shoes and Gloves

The bride's shoes are traditionally made of satin (if the gown is satin) or peau de soie, dyed to match the gown. Shoes should be comfortable—not only does the bride walk up the aisle in them, but she also has to stand in them (and perhaps dance in them) at the reception. Pumps are considered to be more appropriate for a formal wedding than open sandals—but that, too, is changing, especially if the bride is marrying on a hot summer day.

Some bridal stores offer beautiful beaded ballet shoes or fancy rhinestone-studded tennis-style shoes you can slip into at the reception for comfort.

Gloves, whether wrist length or below elbow length, are optional for formal and semiformal weddings. Fabric choices include satin, cotton crochet, and satin embroidered with lace, pearls, or beads.

Gloves and the Wedding Ring

If the bride chooses to wear short, loose gloves, she merely pulls one glove off at the altar so that her ring can be placed on her hand. But if she wears elbow-length or longer gloves, the underseam of the glove's wedding finger may be ripped open, and she need only pull off the tip to have the ring slipped on. (This can be cumbersome, however, so you may prefer wearing no gloves at all.) If the bride's gown is enhanced by long gloves, an alternative to cutting the seam of the ring finger is fingerless gloves.

Jewelry

The traditional jewelry is classic and neutral colored, such as a pearl necklace or a pearl-and-diamond lavaliere. Of course, wearing a piece of heirloom jewelry or jewelry with special meaning (a gift from the bridegroom, perhaps) is a loving gesture, even if it is composed of colored stones.

THE BRIDAL ATTENDANTS

Since in most cases attendants pay for their dresses and accessories, the bride has an obligation to consider the price of the gowns carefully. The second thing she should consider is figure flattery. When your attendants come in all shapes and sizes, you should look for gowns that will flatter one and all. Get their input and be flexible. You can have each bridesmaid choose a slightly different style to accentuate the positive for everyone. Some brides, respecting attendants' privacy, won't even ask for sizes or body measurements but will let the bridesmaids do their own shopping. If the bride has a "best man" as her honor attendant, he would dress identically to the groom's attendants.

Dresses

The number one rule: Bridesmaids' dresses should match the bride's dress in degree of formality. The material for the bridesmaids' dresses should complement the material of the dress of the bride. In other words, if the bride chooses

A Living, Breathing Wedding Bouquet

Countless tales have been told of unhappy bridesmaids who have walked down the aisle in dresses they either disliked or that were clearly unflattering. Some brides have hit on the clever idea of letting their bridesmaids choose their own dresses. It's practical, too: why not let each attendant pick out a dress she actually likes and can use again? It is perfectly proper for your bridesmaids to wear different dresses. There is absolutely nothing wrong with variations on a theme. Bridesmaids' dresses may be identical in texture and style, but not necessarily in color—or vice versa. The trend these days is away from costumey sameness. It is, however, a nice idea to give your attendants some general guidelines so that the wedding party doesn't clash visually. Have the attendants select dresses of similar lengths, styles, and colors, for example. You can have each bridesmaid wear a slightly different variation on one color—red, for example, with one attendant in rose, another in soft pink, and another in sunset red. One bride asked her attendants to pick floor-length dresses with short sleeves in various shades of purple. The result was a glorious blend of lavender, violet, and magenta—a living, breathing wedding bouquet!

to wear satin, the attendants' dresses should not be organdy or ruffled lace.

Be sure to factor in any religious requirements, such as covered arms and high necks. Check with your officiant to see if your ceremony site has any restrictions.

The dress of the maid or matron of honor may be different from that of the bridesmaids or her flowers of a different color. For example, for an autumn wedding the bridesmaids might wear deep yellow and carry rust and orange chrysanthemums, and the maid of honor might wear rust and carry yellow chrysanthemums.

If dresses are long, the hemline should be short enough to keep the attendants from tripping on the church or chancel steps.

Accessories

Attendants' shoes are generally the same type and color but don't necessarily have to be exactly the same shoe. They may be different shoes that are dyed

The Bridesmaid Asks:
What If I'm on a Tight Budget?

Q: *I have been asked by a dear friend to be a bridesmaid in her upcoming wedding. The problem is, I am on a strict budget and I am sure she will select extravagant dresses for us to wear. Can I hint that I have a limited income to spend on a dress and shoes? Or should I simply turn her down and tell her why?*

A: Tell her truthfully that you cannot realistically afford an expensive dress and that even though you would love to be a bridesmaid, it is simply out of the question economically. That way you give her the choice of finding someone else or selecting a less expensive dress. If you are really close, the bride may decide that her wedding would not be complete without you and offer discreetly to buy the dress for you herself.

to match. (If she is having them dyed the same color, the bride should ask her attendants to buy their shoes well ahead of time.) Some brides simply ask attendants to wear dressy black or white sandals with straps. Also, when bridesmaids' dresses are short or tea length, she needs to make sure all are wearing the same color panty hose.

The bride decides on a headdress for her attendants to wear, if she chooses, but she never tells her attendants how to wear their hair.

ETIQUETTE FINE POINTS

Covering the Head

If guests are required to cover their heads to enter your house of worship, make sure that appropriate coverings are provided for all. Most synagogues provide yarmulkes for men guests but may not transport them for a Jewish wedding at a hotel or other site; this you should do. For female guests at a Sikh wedding, place a box of head scarves at the door in case they did not bring their own.

YOUNG ATTENDANTS

Flower girls are generally dressed in white ballet-length dresses or in gowns similar to those of the bridesmaids but in a style becoming to a child. Flower girls usually wear small wreaths of artificial flowers on their heads or no headdress at all. They may have ribbons or flowers braided into long hair instead. Flower girls traditionally carry small bouquets or baskets of flowers, although they no longer—as a rule—strew them before the bride.

Very small boys—ring bearers, pages, or train bearers—wear white Eton-style jackets with short pants. When they are a little older they may wear navy blue suits instead. If a boy's suit is white, his shoes and socks should also be white; if it is navy, he wears navy socks and black shoes.

Junior bridesmaids wear dresses exactly like those of the older bridesmaids, although sometimes of a different color. Their flowers may or may not be different from the others.

Junior ushers dress in the same style of clothing as the other ushers.

THE GROOM AND HIS ATTENDANTS

Attire for the male members of the wedding party is rarely deviated from. In temperate climates formal evening clothes mean a black tailcoat and matching trousers, stiff white shirt, wing collar, white tie, and white waistcoat. Semiformal evening clothes are a black or midnight blue dinner jacket (tuxedo) and matching trousers, piqué or pleated-front white shirt with

TAILCOAT

WAISTCOAT

CUTAWAY

TUXEDO

SUIT

attached collar, black bow tie, and black waistcoat or cummerbund. In hot weather a white dinner jacket and black cummerbund are used. Evening clothes should never be worn during the daytime.

Formal day clothes are appropriate for daytime weddings and should be worn whenever a wedding is scheduled before six o'clock. The daytime equivalent of the evening tailcoat is a black or Oxford gray cutaway coat worn with black or gray striped trousers, pearl gray waistcoat, stiff white shirt, stiff fold-down collar, and four-in-hand black-and-gray tie or a dress ascot tie.

Less formal daytime clothes are the same except that a suit-style dark gray or black sack coat is substituted for the cutaway, the shirt is soft instead of stiff, and only a four-in-hand tie is worn.

In an informal wedding, although the bride may still wear a simple bridal gown or satiny slip dress, the men switch to lightweight suits or dark gray or navy blue jackets accompanied by white trousers and either white dress socks and white dress shoes or black dress socks and black dress shoes. Shirts are soft white with attached collar, and ties should be four-in-hand with a dark, small, neat pattern.

The groom may send ushers his own outfit's specifications and ask each to rent like clothing. Often, however, for the sake of uniformity, he may find it easier to order all the outfits himself from a rental agency. The groom may delegate this task to his best man. Shoes can also be rented, especially when everyone does not own the same dress shoes. The ushers, in any case, pay the rental fee. Formal-wear rental stores generally carry all accessories—such as gloves and cummerbunds—in stock. The groom provides his attendants' boutonnieres.

The Comfort Factor

Whether the groom buys or rents his wedding attire, he should consider comfort an important element in making selections. The coat should allow free movement of his arms and lie smoothly across the back. Sleeves should reach to the curl of his fingers when his arms are straight at his sides and should reveal one-half inch of shirt cuff. Pants should be hemmed even with the top of the heel of his shoe in back and have a slight break in front, so the hem rests on the shoes.

❧ THE MOTHERS OF THE BRIDE AND GROUP ❧

The elegance of the mothers' dresses should be keyed to the elaborateness of the wedding. Long skirts and dresses are considered appropriate for any wedding from noon on. They may vary greatly in formality—from shirtwaist tops and skirts to brocade evening gowns.

The mothers should try not to wear the same color as the bridesmaids or the bride are wearing. Nor should both mothers wear the same color.

At very formal weddings the mothers should wear gloves, which are kept on while they are in the receiving line. They should also wear something on their heads—a small artificial flower arrangement, a hat, a veil, or a bow.

❧ THE FATHERS OF THE BRIDE AND GROUP ❧

There is no hard-and-fast rule governing the clothes of the bride's father, but since he will be escorting his daughter down the aisle behind the ushers, the party will have a more unified appearance if he wears the same outfit they do. Thus the father of the bride almost invariably dresses like the other men in the wedding party.

At a formal wedding the bridegroom's father may wear the same type of clothes as those worn by the bride's father. He has, however, no official part in the ceremony and therefore may wear a dark suit if he is more comfortable.

CHAPTER THIRTEEN

The reception

PLANNING THE

should be a reflection

RECEPTION

of your personality.

The wedding reception is not just a celebration party; it's your chance

to share your good fortune with the family and friends who form the most

important relationships in your life. Whether you plan a grand affair with

elegant food and service or prefer a barefoot clambake under the stars, the

reception should be a reflection of your personality. Combining personal and

traditional touches gives homage to the people and influences that formed

you—and presents an introduction to the person you have become.

THE WEDDING TEAM: FORMING A SUCCESSFUL PARTNERSHIP

Planning a wedding reception is a creative process of exploration. The goal, really, is a simple one: It's about ensuring the physical and emotional comfort of your guests. You and your vendors are in partnership to meet that goal. It's all about applying the *concept* of your wedding to the *details*— and managing those details toward a common goal.

The success of your reception is dependent not just on the choices you make, but on your success in conveying your vision and desires to the people you have hired to help you. Ultimately the onus is on you to make sure that your vision is executed. But it is also to your benefit to place your trust and good faith in your vendor. Taking an antagonistic approach or assuming that the vendor is out to fleece you at every turn is a recipe for uninspired execution at best and ill will at worst. I can't tell you how many professionals have told me how much it means to be treated as a respected collaborator, not simply as hired help. Good manners and a personable approach go a long way toward making your wedding a positive experience for both you and your vendors. Establishing a partnership up front gives your vendors confidence to work to the best of their abilities.

FINDING THE PERFECT PLACE

Finding a reception locale is a top-priority decision, a process that begins once you have determined the size of your guest list—and the size of your budget. Your choice for the reception will affect the style of wedding you have, the food you serve, the entertainment you choose. Remember that typically the later in the day your wedding is, the more formal it is, and the more expensive the reception is likely to be. Remember, be thorough in selecting just the right space. Most sites require a hefty deposit the day you reserve it and have equally steep cancellation fees.

In addition to cost, there are a few other important considerations in selecting a reception site:

Helping the Caterer Help You

The caterer is an important member of your wedding team. It is his job to tailor his skills to meet your needs and wishes. You can make his job easier by viewing the relationship as a collaboration working toward a common goal: the success of the occasion. Here are suggestions and advice on ways to make working with a caterer a positive, joyful experience for all involved:

1. Decide at first what your vision is and see if the caterer can accommodate it. Think it through thoroughly, so that you can articulate your goals to your vendors.

2. Stick to your vision. Don't give in to the instinct to just to let the caterers do what they do. Speak up; gently insist on attention to detail. If you want a variation made or have a special request, say so. Don't let yourself get lost in an assembly-line wedding machine. A wedding consultant or events planner can be invaluable in helping fight for your vision.

3. Recognize the strengths of your caterer. Ask what his signature dishes are, as well as his most popular dishes.

4. Be up front with the caterer from the start on the amount of money you want to spend on catering—and stick to that figure. If you are firm about your budget, then it's the caterer's job to work within that figure. Have faith: reliable caterers are not in the business of inflating budgets, certainly not at the expense of customer relations.

5. Just as it's helpful to say up front if there is something you really want on the menu, it's also invaluable to specify any food you don't want. This is especially important if key members of the wedding party have allergies, for example, or if there are certain religious restrictions regarding foods. It's best not to find out about these things on the day of the wedding, and no one wants to risk offending anyone.

6. Even perfectionists need to know when to pull back a bit. You may have articulated a vision, but you don't necessarily need to know exactly how your caterers achieve it. It's all a creative process of exploration.

7. Remember that the kitchen and the front of the house—the wait staff, manager, bartenders—are two parts of the same team. You'll want to make sure the communication between the two is there so that plans are carried out.

8. Don't forget to check on any site restrictions before the caterer gets to work.

1. *Size and comfort.*　You may fall in love with a space the first time you see it, but until you determine its comfort capacity—not its standing-room-only capacity—refrain from booking it. No matter how lovely it may be, your guests will be uncomfortable if they have no room to move. Be on the lookout for potential bottlenecks—the entrance and coat check, for example, should be spaced so that arrivals to the reception will not have to wait in line. Consider the flow of the space, making sure aisles or hallways are not cluttered and won't precipitate traffic jams.

   On the other hand, if the guest list for your reception is small, don't pick too spacious a space. Otherwise tables could be miles apart, and the room will feel cavernous and empty. If you are planning hours of dancing, you will want a dance floor large enough to accommodate guests. If you plan to have food stations instead of a single buffet line, you don't want guest tables so close to the food stations that no one can move.

   Other comfort factors: sufficient rest rooms, a place for coats, and plenty of chairs, even if yours is an afternoon tea or cocktail reception where guests will stand more than they sit. You will also want to check the acoustics so that your music is neither too low nor too deafening. Finally, make sure the space offers good air circulation. A church hall may be a perfect space to decorate, but if it has few windows, it may need extra fans to provide better air circulation.

2. *Time availability.*　The lag time between the ceremony and the reception is often dependent on several factors—including whether formal photographs of the wedding party will be taken after the ceremony, and if so, the time it will take to do so; the distance from the ceremony site to the reception site; whether a receiving line will be held at the ceremony site or not; and the time availability of both spaces. The ideal lag time is just thirty minutes. While that may not be possible, you should avoid keeping reception guests waiting and aim for as short a lag time as possible.

3. *Level of formality.*　The degree of your celebration's desired formality is set by both the time of day of your wedding and the envi-

ronment you choose for the reception. While a morning or afternoon reception can be as informal or formal as you like, an evening reception usually requires a formal reception space, unless you let guests know to the contrary. Certain spaces, simply by virtue of their casual ambience, will be unlikely choices for formal weddings. No matter how you decorate, these casual spaces—such as a backyard garden or a hunting lodge—will never look like a country club or hotel and would be more appropriate for a morning or afternoon wedding that is informal or semiformal.

4. *Accessibility.* When scouting sites, also think about how your guests will get there. If access is difficult, consider hiring minivans or even a bus to transport guests to and from the reception site. If the parking lot of the club is the equivalent of blocks away from the entrance, arrange valet parking (the tab and tips are on you) so that guests don't have to walk far in high heels, or in rain, or in heat. Also, check for access for the disabled. No matter how enchanting, the tower room at the golf club isn't for you if many of your wedding guests are older or have disabilities and the room is up three flights of stairs.

5. *The layout.* You should also see how easily tables can be set up; if you want a bridal table, determine how many guests the other tables will seat comfortably, where speakers will be located if music will be amplified, whether you require a table where guests may pick up their table assignments or a table for gifts in case guests bring them to the reception, and where a receiving line is best placed.

❧ CHECKING OUT THE SITE ❧

Before you begin formalizing your plans, check with the reception site manager to determine if there are any restrictions and to ensure that all your vendors will have access to the space to do their work. Most sites do have some guidelines. Have all details spelled out before signing a contract. Also, be sure to communicate specific details to the site or restaurant manager, such as the final guest count. Make arrangements for outside vendors to inspect the place and later set up delivery times; make sure parking spaces are available for vendors who may need it (such as the band, the florist, or the photographer); and ask about the lighting. Here is a list of important questions to ask the site manager:

+ What policies and restrictions does the site have for food, beverages, music, flowers, decor? Are there restrictions on the use of candles? Are there restrictions on photography or videography lighting?

+ What are the laws in the state regarding the serving of alcohol? Does the site have a liquor license?

+ How large a band or orchestra is recommended?

+ Is there adequate wiring, and are there sufficient outlets for a sound system, or would the band or DJ have to bring extra cords and plugs?

+ What restrictions, if any, are there on floral decorations at the ceremony site? Some reception halls, for example, aren't keen on having flower garlands twined around statuary and staircases or have restrictions on moving furniture to make room for, say, potted plants or carpet runners. It would be a colossal disappointment and waste of time to finalize your floral plans only to find out at the last minute that your selections weren't allowed at the site in the first place.

+ At what time may decorations be delivered, and what access will the florist be given for putting them in place?

+ Who assumes liability if a guest becomes inebriated and has an accident?

+ Is there a place for the wedding party to change clothes, if necessary?

+ Is there a place where children can go to watch videos or play games, if necessary?

+ Does the site provide baby-sitting services?

The Father of the Bride Asks: Do I Need to Hire Parking Security for a Home Wedding?

Q: Our daughter is getting married and is having her reception in our backyard. Unlike that at hotels or wedding facilities, we don't have valet parking or official security. We have made plenty of room in our driveway and on the streets for parking, but we want to make sure our guests' cars are secure. What can we do?

A: You may want to arrange parking security for your guests' cars. For a reception that is held at a private residence, you should first call the police to find out about local ordinances so that guests' cars won't get ticketed or towed. If the area already has considerable traffic congestion, you may need an off-duty police officer or a security guard or even valet parking attendants. When hiring parking security, check that the company is fully insured and licensed, and ask that any parking attendants be neatly dressed and courteous. It is better to have experienced drivers and attendants than to hire neighborhood teens to move cars. Ensure that there are enough attendants to patrol the lots or areas where guests will be parking.

A WORLD OF RECEPTIONS

There are basically two ways to organize your reception. At a club, wedding facility, restaurant, or party boat, the services are often provided by the site. If you are thinking about a rental facility, your own home, or any other space that is just that—a space—you will need to make arrangements with outside vendors and suppliers for everything else. Here are specifics on the types of receptions you can choose from.

A Club, Hotel, or Wedding Facility Reception

Hotels, private clubs, and catering halls offer wedding packages that vary according to the time and style of your reception. When investigating possibilities, make appointments with facility managers to discuss your needs and hear their suggestions. Wedding facilities and many hotels and clubs have the capabilities to manage your entire wedding from soup to nuts, from the exchange of vows to your honeymoon departure.

Out-of-the-Ordinary Reception Sites

Q: I really want a different sort of reception site, not the standard reception hall or hotel meeting facility. Any ideas for a place that is different, but one that everyone will feel comfortable with?

A: Choices for reception sites are wide and varied. You don't need to limit your thinking to hotels, clubs, church fellowship halls, or wedding halls. There is a whole world of reception sites that are well outside the traditional. How about a country inn, a vineyard, a party cruise boat, or a city loft with soaring ceilings? You might look into town halls, libraries, aquariums, barges, riverboats, and art galleries. If you're looking for offbeat choices that are also affordable, check out historic homes and sites, museums, parks, botanical gardens, greenhouses, and conference retreats. Renting these sites can cost as little as one-tenth—in some regions even one-twentieth—the cost of a traditional wedding facility or hotel party room.

If you are planning a destination wedding on an island or at a resort area, and your guest list is limited to those family members and close friends who can afford the time and expense to attend, you may either choose to let a resort facility handle the preparations or opt for a casual celebration at the ceremony site or at a local restaurant. If you are planning a theme wedding that is not just decorative, but one where tradition is thrown to the wind, your plans will be different, too. For example, if your passion is country and western music and you want your party to feature square dancing, you will need a space that can comfortably accommodate that. If you choose a beach reception, your theme will be the great outdoors—and the rest of the plans will spring from that.

Most facilities have a minimum numbers of guests they will accept for the larger spaces or main ballrooms. If your guest list is small, consider a smaller secondary room.

If the reception site has an in-house catering service, refer to "Nuts and Bolts: Questions for the Caterer," page 272.

A Restaurant Reception

Having your reception in a restaurant is a smart idea for the busy couple who has little time to plan. It's all there in one place: food, service, ambience, and a built-in cleanup crew. Some wedding parties rent out the entire restaurant for a block of time; others celebrate in the restaurant's private party room.

Although some large receptions can be accommodated in a private room of a restaurant, most restaurant receptions are small ones. A restaurant is often chosen for lunch or dinner after a civil ceremony or after a marriage attended only by family and close friends. Unless you are inviting guests to order off the restaurant menu, the food and choice of beverages are ordered ahead of time. Having a set menu, whether served by waiters at a sit-down meal or offered buffet style, is most often the economical choice. It also eliminates any complications in paying the check. Many larger restaurants have party menu choices and even reception consultants to help out. You'll surely want to have a wedding cake, no matter how simple, and toasts to the newlyweds.

The Tented Reception

The bride and groom considering the use of an outdoor tent for their reception have a long list of options. Tents today run the gamut from simple to palatial. There are arches for entryways, bridges and pathways, parquet floors, stained-glass panels, and chandeliers. You can get a colored tent that matches your wedding colors or a climatized tent with generators for heating or cooling or ceiling fans to keep air circulating.

Because the choices for tents can be mind-boggling, if you are thinking about using a tent, it is a good idea to talk to your caterer or club manager, who may be able to recommend reputable suppliers and offer advice on tent size and the best locations. You will want recommendations; whom you rent the tent and supplies from is crucial to your budget. There is often a big discrepancy in costs from one tent supplier to another. Another tip to remember: Never order a tent over the phone; go in person to see what you are paying for.

In general you need at least one 60-foot-by-60-foot or 40-foot-by-100-foot tent per two hundred people, for dinner and dancing. You can include rest rooms, but they're extra footage, and if you are having a cocktail hour, that's extra, too. In fact, it's all extra. You'll need to consider sound system hookups, a generator and a backup generator, ground cover, a dance floor, which permits are required by local ordinance, and what supervisory and other personnel are required for tent installation and maintenance.

Home Reception

Saving money may not be the primary reason people choose to have a home reception. Pride in home and family is often the overriding reason. Keep in mind that you must give hired staff, such as a caterer, space to work, with little interruption. The space could be as simple as a small pantry with the door closed or as elaborate as the entire kitchen.

❧ RECEPTION FOOD AND DRINK ❧

Once you have located a reception space that meets all your needs, it is time to brainstorm with vendors on the specific type of menu and services you want. In choosing the menu for your reception, don't forget to keep your guests in mind. You will want a menu to please most everyone, but you don't have to settle for bland or boring. Your main objective is to have a festive occasion, while making your guests feel comfortable. You don't want to alienate your reception guests, presumably the people who mean the most to you, by forcing a quirky, trendy, or bizarrely alien menu on them. But you can find foods that will excite your guests, that perfectly fit the season and the setting—and choices that are a meaningful expression of your personality. Be creative in choosing your menu—but never at the expense of your guests.

❧ SERVE IT UP: ❧
TYPES OF RECEPTION SERVICE

Many of your menu decisions will revolve around the size of your guest list, the season, the time of day, the formality of the occasion, and, finally, your budget. Before you think about the types of food and beverages you want to serve, consider how you'd like to serve them.

Sit-Down or Seated Meal

A sit-down meal is a meal at which reception guests are seated and served by a wait staff. Guests locate their tables, usually preassigned by you. At a large

The Lavish African American Reception

According to Harriette Cole, author of *Jumping the Broom*, the tradition of celebrating an African American wedding with a lavish reception feast represents the couple's entry into the community. In the past, the entire village was often invited to break bread in celebration of the new couple, so the food served was very important—as it is today. These rituals help keep the spirit of family and community alive, and food takes on a sacred symbolism.

reception, table numbers are noted on place cards that guests pick when they arrive at the reception. Don't assume that this is the most expensive kind of reception, because staff costs are often moderated by the fact that guests at a sit-down meal eat what they are served and can't go back for seconds, as they can at a buffet. Therefore food costs are often easier to manage.

The types of sit-down services include the following:

1. *Plated service.* Guests are served their meal with the full menu already arranged on their plates.

2. *Russian service.* Plates are already at the guests' places when they sit down. Courses are served from platters by a wait staff. Often one waiter serves the vegetables, another the meat, and another the salad.

3. *French service.* Two waiters do what one waiter does with Russian service, with one holding the platter and the other serving.

Buffet

At a buffet guests select what they will eat, either from one long table filled with choices or from several stations situated strategically throughout the room. Guests serve themselves or are served by a staff standing behind the buffet table. The advantages of a buffet are that you can serve a varied menu from which most people will find things they like. With a buffet you can have a more informal environment. You can provide small or large guest tables. The disadvantage is that buffets often cost more. People tend to eat more, simply because they can return to the serving table as often as they wish.

There are two types of buffets:

1. *Single buffet table.*   A long table is covered with a plain white tablecloth. The centerpiece may revolve around your decorating scheme, but it may also be a simple bowl of white flowers. Stacks of plates, napkins, and cutlery are arranged on the table if guests are to take their plates to chairs or small tables. If they are returning to assigned tables, cutlery, napkins, and beverage glasses are already set on the tables.

    Buffet servers stand behind the buffet tables to assist guests. If there are no servers, guests help themselves. Guests pass along the length of the table, going in one direction, and return to their seats or find a place to sit. If there are no assigned tables, very often a waiter will carry beverages on a tray and serve guests where they find a seat. Whether there are assigned tables or not, if there is staff, guests leave their used plates when they go back for more and take a clean plate from the line. An ever-alert staff whisks away used plates before guests return to their seats. At a small house reception where there is not that kind of staff, guests may take their own plates with them when they go back for more.

2. *Food stations.*   Food stations are a variation on buffet service, the difference being that each station is often dedicated to a particular kind of food. Stations set up in strategic locations around the reception room permit excellent mobility. They allow guests to move from one station to another and not have to stand in line at one table. A chef may even be placed at a food station, making crepes to order or slicing roast beef.

    Food stations can be theme oriented—you can have a quesadilla station, a dim sum station, a pasta station—or feature a certain type of food. You may, for example, have a seafood station on one side of the room and a salad bar station on the other. The variety and breadth of foods offered will please the majority of palates, and the food stations provide a fun, interactive way to serve food. Food stations may also be set up for dessert after a sit-down dinner. You might want to offer a Viennese coffee station, an Italian pastry station, a make-your-own sundae station, or a cappuccino and cake station.

Passed-Tray Receptions

Ideal for cocktail receptions, passed-tray service is just that—waiters circulating through the room with trays of hors d'oeuvres and stopping to offer them to guests. This is an easy way to serve, but it can be expensive, since most caterers, hotels, and clubs charge a per-person fee for the hors d'oeuvres. They might figure on each person eating approximately six or seven servings, for example. If that is all you will be serving, guests may leave hungry, and the longer your reception is, the hungrier they will be. One way to augment passed-tray service is to include a buffet table containing crudités, cheese and fruit, and more substantial fare for guests to munch on between the elegant hors d'oeuvres being passed around.

❧   DO YOU NEED A CATERER?   ❧

If you are planning a small reception and have the help of family and friends, you probably don't need professional help in preparing and serving reception food and beverages. By preparing food in advance and freezing it and by keeping the menu and the decorations as simple as possible, a small wedding reception can be both inexpensive and, within reason, easy to manage.

Planning a larger reception in your home or anywhere else that provides no services, however, can be a lot of work. Entertaining a large group of guests with any degree of pleasure and relaxation requires the aid of professional catering services. Caterers, in other words, let you be a guest at your own party.

The rule of thumb: *Hiring a caterer is recommended for a reception of more than thirty guests.* Depending on the size of the catering company, they can provide just the food or the works: food, beverages, wedding cake, serving staff, crystal and china, tables, chairs, and linens; some even provide tents, dance floors, and party decorations—or can recommend reliable suppliers and vendors.

Little Buffet for Little Kids

If you plan to have children attend your wedding, one lovely way to serve them at the reception is to set up a separate children's buffet table of kid-friendly height. You can do the same thing at your wedding buffet reception. Locate a shorter table—decorate it with colorful linens or butcher-block paper with crayons—and include such kid-pleasing foods as stacks of peanut-butter-and-jelly tea sandwiches, fish sticks and chicken fingers, mini raviolis, and brownies and cookies.

The best way to find a reliable caterer is to ask friends for recommendations. Never, ever, use a caterer without checking his or her references, especially if you have picked a name out of the Yellow Pages.

You may choose to use the on-site caterer at your reception location. Banquet facilities often offer wedding packages that include on-site catering. It's a convenient and cost-efficient alternative to renting a space and hiring independent vendors.

If, on the other hand, you have your sights set on an off-site caterer, set up a preliminary meeting with the caterer. Be sure to set up a time to meet at your reception site before proceeding too far into your planning. A caterer's experience can be extremely valuable in assessing how well equipped the site is, deciding where to place tables, determining how many guests can be accommodated comfortably and how much staff will be required, and any number of other details essential to the perfect reception.

SELECTING THE
CATERER FOR YOU

Most people would agree that food and food service are among the most important elements of your wedding celebration. So if you've decided to use a caterer, finding the right person or company is one of the most important goals of your wedding planning. When you start to interview caterers, consider the following criteria:

Portfolio Some caterers keep albums containing photographs of previous receptions. Look for creative touches: fruits and vegetables skillfully cut into beautiful shapes or arranged in eye-catching ways; interesting and complementary color schemes; a variety of dishes; well-organized and attractive presentations, if you're considering a buffet. In other words, the food should be pretty enough to stand on its own.

Creativity and variety.   The catering menu reflects the chef's breadth of preparation know-how and awareness of food trends. If a menu seems fussy and complicated, the chef may be overreaching—especially problematic when you consider the challenges of efficiently serving large groups of people. On the other hand, if the menu appears uninspired, offering the same old standards prepared the same old ways, then that's exactly what you are likely to get.

Flexibility.   Most caterers have set menus with several selections to choose from in each category. The best caterers are happy to accommodate special requests or tailor the menu to your needs. Beware of inflexible caterers. Any caterer who is adamant about not veering from his or her patented script is a caterer you probably don't want to work with.

Taste, presentation, and service.   Most caterers are more than happy to set up a food-tasting session (see "The Wedding Team: Tips on Tastings," above). Ask for a variety of dishes, from hors d'oeuvres to a main course to a dessert. Note *how* the food is served as well as how it looks and tastes. It's important to keep in mind that three-quarters of the success of your reception will depend on service. Make sure you know how the caterer plans to time each presentation.

Details indicating quality and freshness. Tastings are invaluable in helping you evaluate the caterer's attention to fresh, quality ingredients.

❧ NUTS AND BOLTS: ❧
QUESTIONS FOR THE CATERER

When interviewing a caterer, be prepared. Take a list with you on the nuts-and-bolts issues of catering. Consider the following questions:

- ✛ How do you plan to serve guests arriving at the reception? Will champagne or drinks be ready for arriving guests? How soon will appetizers be introduced (ideally twelve to fifteen minutes after the drinks are served)? How do you coordinate switching from serving hors d'oeuvres to serving dinner?

- ✛ What is the ratio of serving staff to guests? (Ideally, for high-end service that ratio should be ten to one or one and a half tables per waiter. For medium-end affairs, the ratio is more like twenty to one.)

- ✛ What does a sample place setting consist of?

- ✛ Is insurance against china and crystal breakage included in the costs? If not, what are additional insurance costs?

- ✛ What are the selections of table linen colors? Are there choices for china, silver, and crystal? Can you provide tables and chairs if necessary? What about tents, marquees, heaters, portable toilets, and other miscellaneous items?

- ✛ How do you charge for meals for band, DJ, photographers, videographers?

- ✛ Can you provide the cake and serve it? Do you have a cake portfolio?

- ✛ What is the price difference between brand-name liquors and house brands?

- ✛ What is the price difference between an open bar just for the cock-

Tips on Tastings

Most reliable caterers offer potential clients tastings of their foods, from hors d'oeuvres to main courses—and it's a smart idea to take them up on it. Tastings are increasingly important; it's the only dress rehearsal for food you have. Here are some invaluable tips on things to watch for during your tasting:

❀ If you have hired a *wedding planner or consultant,* you should include him or her in the tasting; it's the wedding planner's job to be the clear-eyed troubleshooter and to make sure you get the service you want.

❀ Looks for signs of good-quality foods and ingredients. If the ends of cheese slices appear dry and discolored, that could mean that the cheese was cut hours before—or even yesterday. Are the vegetables brightly colored and not soggy? Is the salad fresh and not wilting? Are baked breads soft and chewy and not stale and hard? Even little things, like butter having a refrigerator taste, can be a clue to a caterer's attention—or inattention—to detail.

❀ Notice the *attentiveness of the staff.* If you're attending a buffet tasting, note whether food is allowed to sit out for long periods without being replenished. The caterer should have sufficient staff to keep the presentation as fresh looking at three P.M. as it was at noon.

❀ Ask if it's possible to *meet the chef* at your tasting. Be sure to thank the chef and offer positive feedback. Once you empower a chef with your attention and confidence, the results can be amazing.

tail hour and an open bar throughout the reception? A consumption bar (where drinks are charged on a per-drink basis) versus an open bar?

✢ At what time do servers go on overtime pay? What would the overtime charges be?

✢ Are gratuities and taxes included in the total bill? What are delivery charges? Are the fees for setup and cleanup included in the total bill?

For on-site caterers:

✢ Ask to see a book of on-site wedding cakes and whether you can sample a selection. Ask whether you can provide your own wedding

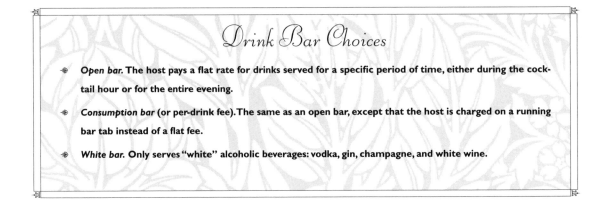

cake at no extra cost. If not, what is the extra cost? Can arrangements be made for your baker to finish decorating the cake on premise?

✣ Will a manager be on-site during the reception to oversee the event?

❧ THE WEDDING DRINKS ❧

Your beverage choices are varied. If alcohol is against your religion, don't serve it unless you don't mind if your guests drink. If you do serve alcohol, decide on how much and how it will be served. Some receptions offer champagne and wine only; others hold an open bar during the cocktail hour and serve wine, beer, and champagne during dinner; still others keep the bar open throughout the festivities.

You will be charged in one of two ways: a flat package rate, which is a per-person, per-hour charge; or a per-drink rate, where the bartenders keep a tally of every drink they pour. Find out what the per-person charge covers before deciding. If it is based on an average of five or six drinks per person for the duration of the reception, and you are also serving wine with dinner and champagne for toasting, you might opt for the per-drink rate instead—it is unlikely that each guest will consume that many glasses of liquor along with the wine.

THE FINE ART OF SEATING ARRANGEMENTS: WHO SITS WHERE?

At most sit-down dinners or formal buffet receptions, it is customary for the bride and groom to determine seating arrangements. This takes tact and diplomacy; you will want all your guests to feel they are each seated in a special spot. That's why it's a good idea to start considering seating early in your planning. It's also fun to mix and match guests, trying to find compatible dinner table partners. Avoid the possibility of hurt feelings by taking the time to think through your reception seating arrangements.

1. *Seating parents.* It is customary to have separate parents' tables, one for the bride's family and close friends and another for the groom's family. It is fine to put both sets together, but this can become unwieldy, as each set generally comes with its own entourage of extended family and close friends. When the bride's and/or groom's parents have been divorced, however, and all are in attendance, it is usually not a good idea to seat them together. Even if relations between the divorced parents are amicable, the extended family and friends of each make it difficult logistically to seat them all at one table.

2. *The bridal party table.* The bridal party table is often a rectangular table set against one side or end of the room. The bride and groom sit at the center of the long side, facing out so that guests can see them. No one is seated opposite them. The bride sits on the groom's right, with the best man on her right; the maid of honor sits on the groom's

A QUESTION FOR PEGGY

Assigned Seating: Pros and Cons

Q: My fiancé and I have agreed on everything but this: whether or not to assign seats. Since we're having butlered hors d'oeuvres and food stations instead of a sit-down dinner, I like the idea of not assigning seats (other than the bridal party table). I think it will keep the party fluid and guests mingling. My fiancé has a number of elderly relatives to whom he'd like to offer assigned seating. What do we do?

A: Here's a compromise. In addition to the bridal party table, have one other assigned-seating table reserved specifically for your elderly relatives. It's not only a way to make them comfortable, it's a way to honor them as well.

A Lighter Bar

If few members of your family or wedding celebration drink alcoholic drinks or if you have to cut costs some-where, here is a creative way to trim the alcoholic-drinks budget without going completely dry: Have a soft bar instead of a full bar. At a soft bar guests may order champagne, beer, nonalcoholic beer, red and white wine, reg-ular, diet, caffeine and noncaffeine iced tea, juices, coffee, tea, and mineral water. It is a good idea to know your guests' taste before going with this option, however. If your guests are used to cocktails, it might be wise to have a full bar and fewer guests instead.

left, and the bridesmaids and ushers alternate along the same side of the table. If the group is large, the table can be made into a U shape, with the bride and groom at the center of the center table. The wedding party's husbands, wives, fiancés, and significant others should be seated here, too, if there is room. When the wedding party is large or when the couple wants to seat the attendants with their spouses and significant others, two large round tables may be used to seat the entire bridal party and their partners. In this case the bride and groom would sit with the maid of honor and best man, their respective partners, and possibly some of the attendants and partners. Children or siblings of the bride or groom who were not in the wedding party may also sit with them.

3. *No bridal party table?* Many couples prefer to wander about and mingle with their guests rather than being seated at a formal table. There should always, however, be a table reserved for the bride and groom and their attendants to sit down and rest. The newlyweds may go to the buffet table just as the other guests do; in some cases a waiter fills a plate and brings it to them where they are seated. The bridesmaids and ushers need not all sit with the bride and groom at the same time, but all should gather together during the toasts and the cutting of the cake.

Place Cards

If you plan a seated dinner for more than twenty guests, you will probably want to use place cards. At some point in your meetings with the site manager or catering director, ask for a diagram of the number of tables and their placement. Make several photocopies of the diagram so that you can play around with the seating arrangements. Once you've made final decisions, number each table and place card accordingly. Delegate someone to have them arranged, in alphabetical order, on a side table at the reception entrance. After leaving the receiving line, each guest passes the table and finds the place card with his or her name on it, checks the number written on the card, and then locates the table with the same number. Some couples choose to make place cards for the parents' tables and the bridal party tables only. In this instance you should delegate a friend to take the place cards to the reception site before the ceremony, if possible, and place them in their proper location.

❧ PLANNING TRANSPORTATION ❧

If your ceremony site is not within walking distance of your reception site, you'll need to consider your mode of transport from one place to the next. If you plan to hire limousines, begin looking for a reputable company the minute your ceremony and reception sites are confirmed. The sooner the better: rented limos are in high demand at peak times. Then consider the following:

1. *Determine the number of cars you need.* Considerations include one for the bride and her father to the ceremony and for the bride and groom to the reception; a second car for the bride's mother, any children in the wedding party, and any attendants who will ride with the bride's mother and father to the reception; and a third car for the rest of the bride's attendants. If the sky's the limit and you want to hire additional cars for special guests, grandmothers, or whoever, count them in.

2. *Interview local transportation services over the phone or in person.* Ask their advice on the number and size of cars you will need for your wedding party. Ask if you have a choice in the types of cars. Find out their minimum number of hours and what services are included in the rates. An important issue is how the drivers will be attired—make sure they will be properly dressed for the occasion.

3. *Confirm driving times.* Drive the route to get the timing down if you have to. When it comes to weddings, it's far better to be early than to keep everyone waiting.

4. *Make sure the members of the wedding party have transportation home from the reception site*—especially if you will not be using the limousine service to do so. Be sure your attendants know their transportation arrangements. Enlist the best man to make sure all members of the wedding party (plus parents and close relatives) have transportation ready at the reception site.

5. *Don't try to cram in the entire wedding party with you on the way to the reception.* Even if the car is a huge stretch limo, enjoy the luxury and the romance of having your mate alone with you, if only for a few minutes. This will very likely be the first time you have been alone all day and most probably the last time you will be alone until you leave the reception. Savor the moment.

CHAPTER FOURTEEN

Flowers symbolize

FLOWERS FOR

the full blooming of

YOUR WEDDING

new love and a

new life.

Fragrant, lovely, and romantic, flowers are the key decorating elements of the wedding celebration. Flowers not only add visual pleasure and a note of festivity to the proceedings, but they also symbolize the full blooming of new love and a new life. Fresh blooms and greenery—whether cascading from an altar, twined around an arch, spilling over a flower girl's basket, or tucked lovingly into a groom's lapel—represent the flowering of a couple's love.

Many of the traditions of old retain a place in wedding events, long after their origins have been forgotten. For example, the tradition of flowers strewn along the path the bride walks has its roots in ancient times, when a path of flowers and fragrant herbs was thought to keep evil spirits away. Centuries ago wedding reception halls were decorated with sweet-smelling jasmine to entice angels to attend and bless the event. In a tradition that began in twelfth-century Spain, fresh orange blossoms were fashioned into wreaths to crown the heads of brides. Hundreds of years later England's Queen Victoria would wear fragrant orange blossoms in her hair in her marriage to Prince Albert. Brides who could neither afford nor find fresh blossoms used wax ones; many a wax bridal wreath has become a treasured family heirloom, passed down from generation to generation of brides.

Modern couples may not know the tradition behind the ritual, but they do appreciate the beauty and purity that flowers bring to a wedding celebration. These days flowers at weddings are used in nearly every aspect of the celebration, from the decoration of church pews to topping the wedding cake. Flowers can be seen everywhere: in the hands of attendants, given to parents, stepparents, and grandparents, in centerpieces, on mantels, wrapped around candles, topping buffet tables, even adorning serving platters. You might even decide to place plants at strategic locations, such as main entryways.

Whether you select flowers for their symbolic meaning, for seasonableness, for mix-and-match qualities, for color, size, or fragrance, or simply for aesthetic pleasure, you'll find the process of choosing a delight. Make it a personal quest. Make your wedding flowers an expression of your heart.

HOW TO CHOOSE YOUR FLOWERS

You should choose your wedding flowers based on the following factors:

1. *The formality of your wedding.* The more formal the wedding, the more formal the flowers, such as formal bouquets, which are traditionally all white and generally one type of flower.

2. *The time of day.* For an evening wedding, for example, white or brightly colored flowers stand out, especially if the ceremony is held in candlelight.

The Maid of Honor Asks:
What Do I Do If Flowers Make Me Achoo?

Q: *Flowers make me sneeze, and the bride has generously agreed to let me come up with alternative ideas for a floral bouquet. Are there any traditional alternatives to flowers?*

A: Absolutely. Many brides and bridesmaids who are allergic to real flowers do just that. They may use a beautiful arrangement of silk flowers, a Victorian-era fan with satin rosettes and ribbons, or a prayer book topped with a single flower (brides could use a single silk orchid, symbolizing rare beauty, or a rose, for love).

3. *The colors you and the bridal party will be wearing and the color of the table linens.* Some brides actually plan their bridal party colors around the flowers they love.

4. *The season.* Flowers in season will not only be fresher, they'll last longer and cost less, because they don't have to be shipped from far away.

5. *The interior design of the wedding site and reception site.* A church with a high ceiling, for example, demands taller plants.

6. *The constraints of your budget.* There are many ways to cut costs on flowers, including sharing ceremony flowers with another wedding couple, having friends help you do your own arrangements, using borrowed potted plants, using your ceremony flowers at the reception, or renting plants.

7. *Whether the site is indoors or out.* If you're marrying outdoors, you may need only supplement a blooming spring or summer garden site with a few flower arrangements here and there and bouquets, boutonnieres, and corsages.

8. *The unifying theme of your wedding.* Are you planning a country-style wedding with baskets overflowing with wildflowers and simple bouquets, or do you favor a traditional, formal celebration and see understated elegance carried throughout from attire to decorating?

Do you have a color scheme in mind, or are you considering all white for flowers and decorations? Will you have accessory themes? Are you making floral choices based as much on fragrance as on color and texture? If you are having a *real* theme wedding—romantic Victorian, for example, Hawaiian luau, fifties style—you'll want to come up with some concepts for flowers and decorations that match the theme.

WEDDING FLOWERS CHECKLIST

The *first* thing you should do is draw up a list of all your floral needs. A copy of this list should be presented to the florist at your first meeting. Determine what, if any, of the following items you would like to have: ribbons, greens, candles, vases, pots, or containers you may also need.

The range of floral decorations can go far beyond bridal party bouquets and altar decorations. You may want a plant for each entranceway, flowers to garnish serving platters, flower sprays for candles, bouquets for wedding helpers and grandparents—even a beribboned flower twined around the cake knife. The following is a general checklist of floral needs. By no means must you follow this list to the letter: it is simply a guide for you to work from, whether you are collaborating with a florist or floral designer or are planning to do the arrangements yourself. (For more information on flowers for the wedding party and family and friends, see chapter 12.)

The Bride and Her Attendants

- ✣ Bride's bouquet
- ✣ Honor attendant
- ✣ Bridesmaids
- ✣ Flower girl
- ✣ Tossing bouquet
- ✣ Floral hair decorations

The Groom and His Attendants

- ✣ Groom's boutonniere
- ✣ Best man
- ✣ Ushers
- ✣ Ring bearer

Family Flowers

+ Parents and stepparents of the bride

+ Parents and stepparents of the groom

+ Grandmothers and grand-fathers

+ Other special guests

For the Ceremony

+ Entranceway

+ Altar

+ *Chuppah*

+ Pews

+ Candles

+ Roses for parents, if necessary

+ Aisle runner

For the Reception

+ Centerpieces

+ Buffet tables

+ Cake topper, cake knife

+ Cake table

+ Mantel, stairway, entrance-ways

+ Place card table

+ Garnish for serving platters

+ Rest room arrangements

+ Flower petals for tossing

As Gifts

+ Party hosts

+ Out-of-town guests

+ Weekend hosts

+ Thank-yous to friends and helpers

❧ FLORAL THEMES ❧

There are many ways to use flowers to personalize your wedding. Here are some ideas to make your celebration special and unique.

Seasonal Flowers

Although the advances of modern technology have resulted in the year-round availability of formerly hard-to-get flowers, you can still cut costs by using seasonal flowers that are in bloom locally. They don't need to be shipped, they can be cut close to the time they will be used, and they tend to be hardier than those that are forced in a greenhouse, out of season. Following is a list of seasonal flowers:

Springtime Flowers	Summertime Flowers	Year-Round Flowers
apple blossoms	asters	Flowers that are readily available year-round—grown in greenhouses but not rare or difficult to grow:
cherry blossoms	calla lilies	
daffodils	dahlia	
dogwood	daisies	daisies
forsythia	geranium	baby's breath
iris	hydrangea	bachelor buttons
lilacs	larkspur	carnations
lilies	roses	delphiniums
lilies of the valley	stock	gardenias
jonquils	Queen Anne's lace	lilies
larkspur		orchids
peonies	**Fall Flowers**	roses
sweet peas	asters	stephanotis
tulips	chrysanthemum	ivy
violets	dahlias	
	marigolds	
	Shasta daisies	
	zinnias	

The Language of Flowers

As you begin making decisions about flowers, you might incorporate those that have special traditional meaning. In the early 1900s romance was often communicated with flowers. A young man would present a red rose, which symbolized love, to a young woman. She would return a purple pansy, which silently relayed the message "You are in my thoughts." Traditionally no words were spoken that would commit either party during this courtship, so knowing the language of flowers was of paramount importance if an accord was to be reached. Today it is a charming idea to select flowers, and even herbs, that convey special floral messages between the bride and the groom.

acacia—friendship

agrimony—gratitude

ambrosia—love returned

anemone—expectation

apple blossoms—hope

aster—elegance

azalea—temperance

baby's breath—innocence

bay laurel—glory

calla lily—beauty

camellia—loveliness

carnation—devotion

chrysanthemum—abundance

daffodil—regard

daisy—gentleness

forget-me-not—remembrance

freesia—innocence

gardenia—purity

heather—future fortune

heliotrope—devotion

ivy—fidelity

larkspur—laughter

laurel—peace

lilac—humility

lily—majesty

lily of the valley—happiness

myrtle—remembrance

orange blossom—purity

orchid—rare beauty

parsley—beginnings

peony—bashfulness

Queen Anne's lace—trust

rose—love

rosemary—remembrance

sage—immortality

stephanotis—marital happiness

thyme—courage

tulip—passion

violet—modesty

zinnia—affection

The Language of Color

Colors have meaning in many cultures. You may want to develop your floral color scheme around a particular color for its symbolic meaning.

✢ *Red or fuchsia.* The color of love in China and India.

✢ *Green.* The ancient color of fertility. A color symbolizing luck to modern-day Italians and Irish.

✢ *Red and yellow.* The marriage colors of Egypt, the Orient, and Russia.

✢ *Blue/turquoise.* Attached to wedding ceremonies in Western countries ("... something borrowed, something blue").

✢ *Purple.* Represented wealth in ancient Greece. The classical color of the soul.

✢ *Blue and gold.* Reinforces power, dignity, and rank.

Birth Month Flowers

Another special way to personalize and add meaning to floral choices is to combine the traditional birth month flowers of the bride and groom.

Month	Flower
January	carnation
February	violet
March	jonquil
April	sweet pea
May	lily of the valley
June	rose
July	larkspur
August	gladiola
September	aster
October	calendula
November	chrysanthemum
December	narcissus

Fragrant Flowers and Herbs

A popular trend is including fragrance in your overall wedding theme, using flowers, herbs, and greenery not just for their visual appeal but for their perfume.

Bay laurel	Magnolia blossoms
Carnation	Mint
Freesia	Narcissus
Gardenias	Roses, especially old-fashioned or tea roses
Jasmine	
Hyacinth	Stephanotis
Lavender	Violets
Lilacs	Wisteria
Lily of the valley	

❧ SELECTING THE FLORIST ❧ FOR YOU

In starting your search for the right florist, ask for recommendations from friends, local caterers, or local nurseries. A florist who is closely affiliated with nurseries or wholesalers can often get good prices on flowers and plants in bulk. If you are holding your celebration in a hotel or reception hall, get the names of florists who have worked wedding celebrations there. Some florists may be contracted to do arrangements for hotels and reception halls on a regular basis—in that case you can view their handiwork firsthand. When you have some names and are ready to interview people, always make an appointment. It is unrealistic and discourteous to think you can walk in unexpected and snare the florist's undivided attention.

At the first meeting, there is nothing wrong with saying up front that you aren't ready to sign a contract but that you are looking for someone with whom you can work. Use the following criteria in your search for a florist:

Florists vs. Floral Designers

Q: What is the difference between florists and floral designers?

A: In the last few years "floral designers" have become popular. Floral designers, unlike florists, generally do not work out of a shop and are particularly versed in creative, nontraditional themes. Floral designers can create a unifying look for your entire wedding, integrating not only flowers into the decor, but lighting and textiles as well. You'll have to decide whether you want to work with a full-service florist, who can provide soup-to-nuts floral needs in-house, or with a floral designer, who generally creates a design and then executes it by outsourcing jobs. Although many floral designers do not have a shop, they often have a full staff to handle every aspect of the floral plans.

1. *Creativity and compatibility.* Try to find a florist who is willing to embrace your ideas, offer advice and suggestions, show you examples, and agree to your budgetary parameters. Look for a florist who will work with you as a collaborator, but who also offers creative input and advice on ways to do things more efficiently. If, for example, your wedding is small but is located in a large site, ask for recommendations on ways to make it intimate. The florist may do this with greens, flowers, or even decorated screens. You'll want a florist you feel comfortable with.

2. *Wedding experience.* Look for a florist who is experienced in the business of wedding decorating. The florist should be capable of managing all the details, including the timing and the delivery arrangements you require.

3. *Portfolio.* Ask to see the florist's album or portfolio containing photographs or illustrations of previous weddings for which the florist has provided flowers.

4. *Flexibility and range of options.* Discuss your wedding flowers checklist and the range of options for each item. Determine how many of your ideas, large and small, can be accommodated within your budget. The best florists are happy to suggest alternatives that allow you to achieve your vision and stay within your budget, and you will experience less stress if you remain flexible on floral choices. If on the first pass your wish list results in a budget-busting estimated bill, simply rethink your options. Ask your florist to recommend inexpensive backup choices. Start over with the basics and make a list of your priorities. What is the most important floral expenditure? The bridal bouquet? The reception centerpiece? Can you splurge on these and rely on simple choices for the less important arrangements? If your

choices are made with loving care, it won't matter whether you used an expensive or exotic flower to express your joy. The magic of flowers is that there is beauty and elegance in the simplest of forms.

❧ NUTS AND BOLTS: ❧ QUESTIONS FOR THE FLORIST

Be sure to discuss the following once you've committed to a florist.

1. *Discuss your overall reception decor with the florist.* Check with your caterer and cake maker to coordinate the overall floral design and ensure that the color schemes match. Often wedding cakes are decorated with real flowers and greenery, so that will need to be coordinated as well. If the caterer is providing the table linens, you will need to select colors that complement the floral design or vice versa. If the florist cannot visit your ceremony and reception site, provide a sketch of the layout and describe its existing color schemes. You may also want to consult with the site manager on the types of decor that work well in the space.

2. *Can I get an item-by-item breakdown of the prices before I sign any contract or agreement?* Confirm your arrangements and ask if there is a deposit. Check whether the contract includes delivery costs and any gratuities. Add confirmation call reminders to your planner.

3. *When and where should deliveries take place?* If you have contracted with the florist to deliver and install the floral decorations, you should provide a list of all flower deliveries that need to be made. You'll need to discuss the best place and time to deliver each component of the decor. Where, for example, do you want the bride's and her attendant's flowers delivered: the bride's home if everyone will be dressing there or directly to the ceremony site? If yours is a morning wedding, will the flowers stay fresh if they are delivered the night before? Include dates, times, instructions for access, and accurate names, telephone numbers, and addresses. Copy the information

into your planner as well and mark on your calendar to make a reminder call a day or two before the big day.

4. *Can you take care of the little extras?*

   ⁜ If you will be lighting a unity candle, it can be decorated with flowers.

   ⁜ Flower petals to toss can be provided by the florist.

   ⁜ Special floral gifts for helpers need to be discussed up front. The florist might suggest simple nosegays, corsages, or flower arrangements to be delivered after the wedding day.

   ⁜ You may include thank-you flowers for bridal showers. If you know friends will be giving you a shower, flowers delivered before or after as a thank-you can be discussed and ordered at the same time you are ordering your wedding flowers.

   ⁜ Welcome flowers for some out-of-town guests staying in hotels or inns can be included in the florist contract. (Be sure to write the cards beforehand and give them to the florist.)

❧ FLOWERS FOR THE CEREMONY ❧

If you are having your ceremony in a church or synagogue, ask the minister or rabbi to advise you on the types of decorations that work best there, whether flowers or greenery for the altar or chancel, *chuppah,* pulpit, or candelabra. The ceremony flowers may be as simple or as elaborate as the setting, your budget, and the formality of the ceremony.

In a Church or Synagogue

Traditionally an arrangement or two of flowers that blends with the bridal party flowers is all you need to provide for your ceremony. Placed on the altar in a church or on the reader's platform in a synagogue, they are lovely to look at when guests arrive and serve as a background for the ceremony.

Helping the Florist Help You

Be prepared for your appointment with the florist so that you can both use the time efficiently. The more information you provide and the better your research and planning, the more successful and satisfying your collaboration. Here are tips and advice on how you can work with the florist to achieve your goals:

1. Trust the florist. Trust helps give your florist the opportunity to be creative and do his or her best work.

2. Have some flexibility in choosing your flowers. A florist is not unlike a chef: when at the market to purchase the flowers for your floral arrangements, your florist will be most inspired if he or she can use the best flowers available—and the best may be what is in season at that time, not the exotic you've included on your must-have list.

3. Listen to the florist's advice. It's the florist's job not only to fulfill your needs and desires, but also to advise you on the best ways to make it all happen—and that may entail offering solutions that run counter to your original vision. You may be determined to use columbines in your bouquets and table arrangements, for example, but because of their lack of sturdiness, they may not be the best choice. It is the florist's job to provide you with an informed opinion.

4. Bringing along photographs of floral arrangements you like—and those you don't like—is very helpful. Providing your wedding colors up front is also an excellent way to match fabrics with complementing flowers. Give the florist swatches of your gown and your bridesmaids' gowns, if you have them, or a color wheel with the family of colors you've chosen to work with. Photographs of bridal party attire are helpful, too.

5. If you are giving flowers—corsages or nosegays, for example—to special people at the wedding, consider each person's personal preferences and style when making a selection.

6. It's a good idea to work up a wedding flowers checklist before you visit the florist—or at least know what is essential to you and what is not.

7. Remember that the floral plan is a work in progress right up until the week of the wedding.

Candelabra and a standing unity candle can be wound with garlands of greens with a few flowers tucked in. When permitted in a synagogue, the *chuppah* or canopy can be decorated with garlands of flowers as well. If your budget permits, you can add more floral focal points.

If a stairway with railings forms the entrance to your ceremony site, you can drape the railings with garlands, leading the way to the door. Double doors at a church entrance could be adorned with floral wreaths, a beautiful welcome to guests.

The ends of pews may be decorated with satin ribbons or ribbons and flowers, marking the path the wedding party will walk. In a very large church or cathedral with soaring ceilings, height can be added to pew decorations with arrangements on standards placed at the ends of every three or four pews, leading to the altar.

At Home, a Club, or a Wedding Facility

Ceremonies that take place outside of a church or synagogue can be beautifully decorated. It is a good idea to take photographs of the areas that will be used, thus having a reference when you are planning your decorations. If a sweeping staircase is the site of your processional, you can drape it in floral garlands. If guests are to be seated in rows, facing the altar or *chuppah*, frame the aisle in well-secured standing arrangements or tie ribbons at the sides of the chairs closest to the aisle. A backdrop of greens and flowers can frame the bride and groom. If a fireplace is the center of the backdrop, it can be filled with greens and the mantel decorated with green roping or an arrangement of greens or flowers.

An altar may easily be made by covering an ordinary table with a white silk, lace, or damask cloth. Whether or not there is a cross or other religious objects on the altar depends on the service, your faith, and the officiating clergy. Often there is simply a kneeling bench for the couple. If there is a railing, it can be covered with greens, and a tall stand holding a flower arrangement at each end of the rail makes a lovely frame for the ceremony. Depending on the size of the room, an aisle runner may be used. If the ceremony site is a club or a historic facility, check to see what elements are available. It is very likely your florist can provide a kneeling bench, stanchions for flowers, and an aisle runner.

Assuming that your reception will be held at the same place, you will want to carry over the same floral theme from the chapel to the reception rooms.

Outdoors

You may think that because your ceremony is outdoors you will have little need to embellish nature. That is often not the case. You may want to add such festive ornamentation as potted plants placed at strategic spots, hanging baskets of flowers that match your color scheme, an arched trellis woven with flowers or colorful ribbons, streamers, and garlands. If the wedding is at night, candles or Japanese lanterns provide a romantic ambience. In the evening, scents are particularly pungent; you may want to marry in the proximity of a sweet bay bush or night-blooming datura.

Don't forget to formulate a backup plan with the florist in case of inclement weather. Unless your wedding is being held under a tent, you will need to consider a floral design for the backup indoors site. Formulate with the florist a set plan of where the floral arrangements will be situated, and if the site is located at a different address, make sure delivery instructions are changed.

FLOWERS FOR THE RECEPTION

The options for reception flowers are as unlimited as the number of sites. Arrangements can be added to each table, to the place card table, to serving stations or buffet tables, and even in rest rooms. Flowers can encircle the wedding cake, coil around entranceways and archways, and frame the musicians' bandstand. Pots of beribboned topiary and standards may form a backdrop for the bridal party table.

Flowers for Destination Weddings

Q: I am having a destination wedding and am doing my planning long-distance. One aspect of the wedding I'd really like to control is the choosing of flowers. How can I ensure a successful floral display from so far away?

A: One of the most popular wedding trends is marrying in a romantic, exotic locale far from home. Destination weddings are generally planned and coordinated long-distance. What you need to do first is find a reliable florist. To do so, you can take one of several tacks. You can:

- Inquire about coordinating the flowers and decorations through the wedding site or hotel manager. Many popular destination wedding resorts offer complete wedding packages that include floral selections.

- Ask your local florist if he or she is affiliated with any florists at the wedding location.

- Find a florist through a network of large floral organizations, such as FTD.

- Check the Internet for lists of florists. One, *weddingpages.com/home,* includes a city directory of florists and other vendors in many cities in the United States.

The long-distance florist may send or fax sketches of plans and photographs of previous weddings. Ask about local blooms; for a Hawaiian wedding, for example, take advantage of the exotic local flowers.

Centerpieces should be either low enough so that guests can easily see one another when seated or elevated in tall vases so that they are above the diners' heads. Bridesmaids' bouquets can form the floral focus at the bridal party's table or be placed around the cake on a separate table. At an evening wedding, candles or candelabra decorated with greens and simple flowers may serve as centerpieces.

If the reception is held outdoors, you can embellish the setting with the same flowers and plants you used for the outdoor ceremony. Decorations don't have to stop with flowers, however. An evening wedding outdoors may be lit by Japanese lanterns, glittering Christmas lights strung through the trees, or candle luminarias placed on the pathway to the site.

FLOWERS FOR THE BRIDE AND
HER ATTENDANTS

The formality and style of your celebration determine the wedding attire and the flowers that complement it. It is helpful to know what is traditional for bridal flowers as you plan. Bouquets, by definition, are simply clusters of flowers tied together or anchored in a bouquet holder. The shape of the bouquet generally determines the best flowers to use.

Do all the bride's attendants' flowers have to be identical? While they should complement their gowns and echo the style of the bride's bouquet, attendants' bouquets carried in semiformal and informal weddings can be of different flowers, with each bridesmaid carrying a nosegay of her favorite flower in the same hue as those of the other bridesmaids. One difference may be the size of the bouquet, which is generally determined by the height and size of the attendant. Bridesmaids come in all shapes and sizes, and as you adapt their gowns to flatter, so can you adapt their flowers. Give their heights and measurements to the florist, who can customize their bouquets. A six-foot bridesmaid holding a tiny nosegay looks as uncomfortable as a petite bridesmaid struggling with a large cascade.

You can also provide a personal touch by asking each bridesmaid what her favorite flowers are and surprising each with specially designed bouquets.

Bouquets

FORMAL BOUQUETS

Formal bouquets are traditionally all white, generally of one type of flower or a combination of two or three different flowers, such as roses, gardenias, stephanotis, and lilies of the valley. The flowers can be fashioned into a cascade or a formal bouquet or nosegay and are adorned with satin ribbons, chiffon, or organza. A formal bouquet can also be as simple as a single calla lily or white rose.

SEMIFORMAL BOUQUETS

Usually arm bouquets or nosegays, semiformal bouquets often are colorful bouquets, either a combination of mixed colors or different flowers of the same hue or color scheme, such as pinks or corals. Semiformal bouqets can also be all white but often are touched with color by the addition of softly tinted ribbons.

INFORMAL BOUQUETS

Informal bouquets can be just as elegant as formal bouquets but offer greater variety in shape and flower choices. An informal bouqet can be a gathering of flowers taped at the stem and tied with ribbons or something as simple as a cloud of baby's breath.

BOUQUETS TO TOSS

If the bride decides to keep her wedding bouquet as a keepsake, she may opt for a "breakaway" bouquet, which allows the bride to keep part and separate another part to toss, if bouquet tossing is part of the wedding festivities. Or she can order a completely separate "tossing" bouquet, often similar to but not as elaborate as the one she carries.

Bouquet Shapes

Hand in hand with the formality of a bouquet is the shape of the bouquet. There are four basic bouquet shapes:

NOSEGAYS

Nosegays are circular, densely arranged arrays of flowers, approximately eighteen inches in diameter. Within this circle there may be *posies,* which are petite nosegays made of tiny buds, or *tussy-mussies,* another type of small nosegay composed of tiny buds carried in Victorian-period silver cone-shaped holders. Tussy-mussies are often made of flowers that have traditional meanings, true to their Victorian origins. *Biedermeier nosegays* are arranged in rings of flowers, with each ring including only one flower variety. Nosegays can be carried with either long or short gowns.

ARM BOUQUETS

Arm bouquets are crescent-shaped arrangements, curved slightly to fit on the arm. Because they are larger than nosegays, they usually are best suited to long gowns.

CASCADES

A bouquet that cascades is one that gracefully trails blossoms and/or greens from its base. It can be any shape, from nosegay to tear-shaped, and looks best with a long gown.

SPRAYS

Sprays are flowers gathered together in a triangular-shaped cluster. Sprays can be carried with either long or short gowns, since they can be of varying sizes.

A QUESTION FOR PEGGY

Alternatives to Bouquets?

Q: I don't care for formal bouquets, and I don't want my attendants carrying them, either. Can I choose to carry something other than a bouquet, even if everything else about my wedding is traditional?

A: Neither the bride nor her attendants are restricted to carrying bouquets. They may walk down the aisle carrying a single long-stemmed flower (or two or three). They may wear flowers pinned to their dresses, wrist corsages, pomanders (blossom-covered globes held by a loop of ribbon), flower- and ribbon-decorated fans, or flowers attached to a prayer book. Additions to bouquets may be potpourri or tiny bells that ring sweetly as the bridal party walks down the aisle.

ETIQUETTE FINE POINTS

How to Carry a Bouquet

It simply doesn't look right to have one attendant clutching her bouquet tightly at chest level while another has it dropped below her waist. Usually a nosegay is held with two hands, centered just below the waist. An arm bouquet is rested along the lower half of one arm, with any falling sprays held in front. Attendants walking on the right side hold an arm bouquet on the right arm with the stems pointing downward to the left, and those on the left hold their flowers on the left arm with stems toward the right.

Experiment with loosely tied bouquets and single flowers—and make sure all the attendants are carrying the flowers the same way. Whatever you do, try not to press the bouquet against your gown, for it can get crushed and mark the gown with pollen.

FLOWERS FOR THE HAIR AND VEIL

Fresh or wax orange blossoms were once the flowers that crowned the bride's veil, but today an array of flowers is often used, woven into bandeaux or circlets and Juliet caps with veils or worn tucked into a chignon, French twist, or French braid. Flowers can wreathe the heads of the bride's attendants, too, or be as simple as a small spray attached to the back of upswept hair. If you want to gather your veil into fresh flowers, make sure it is delivered early enough so that the florist can determine the prettiest look and the most secure way of attaching the flowers to the veil.

FLOWERS FOR THE GROOM AND HIS ATTENDANTS

A boutonniere, worn by the groom and his attendants on their left lapels, makes for a festive and understated grace note to the men's attire. Subtle and small scale are the key words: the groom and his groomsmen should never appear to be wearing corsages. A boutonniere may be any flower, but it should be a hardy variety that won't wilt or crush easily. Usually the groom wears a flower that is one also used in his bride's bouquet, and groomsmen wear a boutonniere that complements that of the groom. A small-scale white or ivory rose, lily of the valley, stephanotis, or freesia are equally elegant and may or may not be wired with greens.

Wedding party boutonnieres are usually delivered to the ceremony site where the groomsmen gather, well before the wedding begins. But if all are dressing in the same location and traveling to the ceremony site together, their boutonnieres can be delivered there instead. Pins are provided by the florist, but reminders to the groomsmen that their boutonnieres are pinned on the left lapel should be made only by the bride or wedding consultant.

A QUESTION FOR PEGGY

Freeze-Dried Bouquets

Q: What's a good way to preserve my bridal bouquet?

A: Many florists now have the technical capacity to freeze-dry flowers—preserving them for all time in much the same state they were in when fresh. You can preserve your bridal bouquet and keep it on display with the freeze-dried method. After the wedding, bridal bouquets are taken apart and each component freeze-dried separately. Then the arrangement is put back together and the bouquet is placed in a glass box, frozen in time and on display for your children—and even your grandchildren—to see.

FLOWERS FOR CHILDREN

If your wedding party includes a flower girl, she may hold a tiny nosegay, a diminutive bouquet, or a small basket of flower petals. Traditionally fresh rose petals from the flower girl's basket are strewn behind the bride during

Floral Bouquets

Floral bouquets for brides originated tens of centuries ago as aromatic nosegays of fresh herbs, which were carried to ward off evil spirits and to ensure good fortune for the couple. Lavender, rosemary, and rue snippets were strewn at their feet for the same purpose. The mothers of early European brides tucked sprigs of myrtle into bouquets. These sprigs, removed later by the bride, were planted, tended carefully, and watched over, to be clipped and given to the bride's own daughter on her wedding day.

the recessional. But fresh petals are notoriously slippery, so many brides choose dried flowers instead.

Children are also enchanting carrying hoops decorated in satin and festooned with flowers in the spring and summer or swathed in evergreens in December. An old English tradition, and popular in France, this custom is also practiced today in the South.

Children from a previous marriage of either the bride or the groom who are not wedding ceremony participants might receive flowers to wear or hold.

When the Celebration Is Over

If you have no plans to use your ceremony and reception flowers again, recycle them! Arrange to have them delivered to area nursing homes and hospitals, local charities, or public buildings such as Town Hall. Another choice is to offer to leave them for the next worship service in celebration of your marriage. A wonderful idea is to have centerpieces from the reception delivered to a loved one who was unable to attend the wedding, accompanied by a note from you.

CHAPTER FIFTEEN

The right music

MUSIC

helps make a wonderful

day even better.

Music adds joy, solemnity, fun, and a sense of tradition to a wedding day. It serves as a ceremony cue, as pleasant background to conversation, as a call to dance the night away. The right music helps make a wonderful day even better. In fact, no other single element of your celebration has the power to engage the emotions the way music does.

Fortunately there are numerous ways for the bride and groom to orchestrate and personalize their wedding music—and few professionals are more enthusiastic than musicians when it comes to talking about what they love.

If you plan to marry in a house of worship, *check with your priest, minister, or rabbi about any site restrictions.* More and more churches and synagogues have established specific rules regarding music selections, and it is wise to know them before making plans. Some houses of worship are so strict that such well-known pieces as the "Bridal Chorus" ("Here Comes the Bride") from Wagner's *Lohengrin* and Mendelssohn's "Wedding March" are not allowed at all because each is a secular, not a sacred, piece of music.

Your officiant may refer you to a house music director, who can then review the parameters of the musical choices available to you and provide you with acceptable options. But don't take his or her word for it—you need to *hear* the music before you commit to it. He or she should play samples of traditional and popular choices to help you decide what to use for the prelude, the processional, and the recessional and during the ceremony. You can also find musical CDs that play nothing but wedding favorites. Look for such titles as *The Wedding Album* (RCA/Ariola International) and *Wedding Favourites* (London: Decca Record Co.). Following are some guidelines to use when planning your ceremony music.

✤ *Ask about acoustics.* Your music choices may not be the best for the acoustics of your ceremony site. Ask the officiant or music director what type of music and instruments sound best in the space.

✤ *Find out if you can use visiting musicians.* If you are indeed allowed to bring in your own musicians, you will need to know whether there are any sound limitations and the types of music that work best in the space. The officiant or music director may even be able to provide the names of musicians who have played in and are familiar with the site.

✤ *Consider your guests' preferences.* Make sure you don't include any music that might offend some guests' sensibilities. Some guests might consider a popular secular tune disrespectful in a church ceremony. If you are having your ceremony in a house of worship and plan on including hymns to be sung by the entire congregation, keep your guests in mind when making your selections. The more familiar or beloved a hymn, the more participation from your guests—and the more joyful your celebration will be.

✣ *Consider the services of the house organist.*   It makes sense to use the services of the house organist in the church or synagogue where your ceremony will take place. Who knows better than he or she the ins and outs of the organ, the acoustics, and the timing of religious ceremonies? Using the house organist might also save you on costs for ceremony music. If you hire an outside organist, you may have to pay a fee, which is standard practice endorsed by the American Guild of Organists. You must also coordinate it so that the outside organist has access to the organ to practice. Find out times that the church or synagogue will be open and when the organist can have practice time. If your ceremony is at another site, you will need to make the same arrangements.

✣ *Discuss how and when payment will be made.*   If a house of worship provides a bill, the fee for the organist is often included and you can write one check. If not, he or she must be paid directly, either in cash or by check, before or directly after the service. This is traditionally the best man's job, so one possibility is for him to take care of this after he has delivered the groom to the room where he will wait for the ceremony to begin.

✣ *List the songs and the players.*   If you are providing a program for your ceremony, you will want to list the music that is performed during the prelude as well as during the ceremony. Be sure to get the correct names of each piece and add the composer, information that may be of interest to your guests. It is also a good idea to list the names of the musicians. Check and double-check the spelling of everything you include.

❧   THE ORDER OF CEREMONY MUSIC   ☙

When working with the music director or organist, organize your choices into the four basic musical components of your ceremony.

THE PRELUDE

It is a happy beginning indeed when guests arrive at a wedding to the joyful sounds of music. The prelude music should begin at least a half hour before the ceremony starts. It can be played simply by a lone organist or performed by a string quartet; it can showcase the smooth strokes of a harpist or the ethereal trills of a woodwind ensemble.

Sampling of prelude music:

+ Air (Handel)

+ Rondo (Mozart)

+ "Jesu, Joy of Man's Desiring" (Bach)

+ Largo (Handel)

+ Concerto no. 1 (from Vivaldi's *The Four Seasons*, "Spring")

+ Pavane (Faure)

THE PROCESSIONAL

The processional music begins as the mother of the bride is seated, the groom and his best man enter, and the bride and her father (or other escort) and attendants are ready to begin their walk. The music can be simply that of an organ or, at a home wedding, a piano. A trumpeter can accompany the organ, adding a joyful and regal note. Music played during the entrance of the bride and her attendants should be joyous and formal at the same time.

The same piece can be played throughout the processional; sometimes the bride is accompanied by a different piece of music.

ETIQUETTE FINE POINTS

Walking the Walk

Many people are confused about the proper way to walk down the aisle. Thankfully, a slow, graceful walk has replaced the customary hesitation step, which often looked forced and stilted. Whatever processional music you choose, make sure that it has an audible cadence to help everyone keep time.

Sampling of processional music:

✢ "The Bridal Chorus" (*Lohengrin*)

✢ "Wedding March" (from Mendelssohn's *A Midsummer Night's Dream*)

✢ "The Prince of Denmark's March" (Clarke)

✢ "Wedding March" (Guilmant)

✢ Air (Bach)

✢ Canon in D Major (Pachelbel)

✢ "Arrival of the Queen of Sheba" (Handel)

✢ Trumpet Voluntary (Clarke)

✢ Trumpet Tune (Purcell)

THE CEREMONY

Many couples like having guests participate in the ceremony in the singing of hymns or a favorite song. This brings a communal spirit to the proceedings, especially when the ceremony is a brief one. In addition to one or two hymns, other musical interludes may be added at appropriate places during the ceremony. These can be vocal, performed by a soloist or a children's choir, or instrumental, performed on a harp, a trumpet, or a combination of both. Work with your officiant and, if there is one, the music director or organist to determine where in the service music should be placed. Make sure, if soloists are to perform, that practice time with the organist or other instrumentalist is scheduled.

Sampling of ceremony music:

+ "Ave Maria" (Schubert)

+ "One Hand, One Heart" (Bernstein and Sondheim)

+ "Jesu, Joy of Man's Desiring" (Bach)

+ "Joyful, Joyful, We Adore Thee" (Beethoven)

+ "The King of Love My Shepherd" (Hinsworth)

+ "The Lord's Prayer" (Malotte)

+ Biblical Songs (Dvorak)

+ "Libestraum" (Liszt)

+ "In Thee Is Joy" (Bach)

THE RECESSIONAL

The music you choose for your recessional should be the most joyous of all. It is a jubilant time, and the music should reflect that jubilation. Often the bell note on the organ or bells in the bell tower are rung to add to the festive ambience. Look for upbeat, joyous music, the kind that will have you and your attendants fairly floating down the aisle and out the door.

Sampling of recessional music:

+ "Ode to Joy" (Beethoven)

+ Trumpet Voluntary (Clarke)

+ "Wedding March" (from Mendelssohn's *A Midsummer Night's Dream*)

+ Trumpet Tune (Purcell)

THE POSTLUDE

Sampling of postlude music:

✦ Overture (Handel)

✦ Rondeau (Mouret)

✦ "Le Rejouissance" (Handel)

✦ MUSIC AT THE RECEPTION ✦

Music can make a party, and your reception should be just that: a full-tilt celebration of your nuptial vows. Whether you hire a disc jockey playing recorded music or have the house jumping with a full-fledged swing band, music sets the tone. While budget and personal taste are important considerations, the kind of music and musicians you select depends largely on the time of day your reception is held.

BRUNCH, LUNCH, OR TEA RECEPTION

If you are having a brunch, lunch, or afternoon tea reception and no dancing, a single pianist, harpist, or violinist, a string quartet, or taped background music are appropriate choices. The music you select for such an occasion is meant to be background music, and classical or light romantic selections set the mood for relaxed elegance.

AFTERNOON COCKTAIL RECEPTION

Guests are mobile at cocktail receptions, moving from table to table, standing, and talking. Let your

Helping the Musician Help with Your Reception

The musician is an important part of your wedding team. It is the musician's job to tailor his or her skills to meet your needs and wishes. You can make that job easier by viewing the relationship as a collaboration working toward a common goal: the success of the occasion. Here are suggestions and advice on ways to make working with musicians a positive experience for all involved:

1. *Find out first of all whether there are any site restrictions. Coordinate the equipment needs of your musicians with the offerings of the reception site; for example, make sure that amplified musicians will have sufficient outlets and electrical power to play. Ask whether the reception site already has a sound system or piano on the premises.*

2. *Always consider the space. Do not hire an orchestra unless you are going to be in a large space, or you'll risk deafening your guests and making it impossible for them to hear one another. Alternatively, the sound of an unamplified flutist may be lost in a large space, making it appear as if you have no music at all.*

3. *If you're on a budget, find musicians who can do double duty. When your ceremony and reception are small or held at the same location, it is entirely possible to have the same musicians play for both. Select a musician with the ability to play both classical and popular music. The benefit to you: being able to work with just one person to coordinate musical selections.*

music move with them. This type of reception is perfect for strolling musicians, instrumental combos and quartets, or a single pianist. The music itself should be livelier than that at a tea reception, but still never showy or obtrusive. This is not the place to have a vocalist—most guests would feel obliged to stop conversing and give the singer their attention.

DINNER DANCE RECEPTION

The music for a dinner dance reception may range from a dance band to a full orchestra to a disc jockey. Remember, the smaller the guest list, the smaller the group. If the guest list and reception space are large, use this handy rule of thumb to help you decide what kind of group to hire. For an orchestra or band, you will need five or six pieces per 150 guests; six or seven

4. If your reception is large and long lasting, you don't necessarily need music going the entire time. You can play CDs or have a lone guitarist, pianist, or flutist playing background music during cocktails and dinner and bring in the band just before dancing begins. Ask the band representative if any of the band members would be willing to perform solo during cocktails and dinner—for a fee, of course.

5. If you have hired more than one group, make arrangements for the two to coordinate their performance time. For example, if your reception is five hours long and your band is willing to play for one and one-half hours, during which they take two half-hour breaks, the strolling guitarist will need to be on call during those breaks.

6. Make arrangements for meals for the musicians. You are expected to feed any members of the band or the DJ at some point during the reception. Talk to your caterer about providing meals not only for the musicians, but also for the photographer, videographer, and any other professionals you have hired. A club or caterer will often give service providers a different meal from those for your guests or the same meal at half the price.

7. Be sure to give the musician a rough idea of the timing of everything—when dancing will start, when the cake will be cut, when toasts will be held.

8. Just as you should be specific about the music you want played, it is equally important that you are specific about songs you do not want played. If you absolutely cannot bear to hear "Endless Love" played at your reception, by all means let the musicians know ahead of time.

pieces per 200 guests; and a full orchestra for 300 guests or more. This is just a general guide—some groups can produce a sound that is bigger than they are.

❦ SELECTING THE ❦ MUSICIANS FOR YOU

If you've decided to use musicians, keep in mind that reception bands should be booked many months in advance, so you'll want to start looking for musicians as soon as you're engaged. Word of mouth is often your best resource, so ask everyone you know for recommendations. But don't take their word for it; be sure to listen for yourself. You can do this by seeing the musicians in concert or playing at another wedding; you could ask to attend a practice session. If the band has made a tape or video of their performances, by all means get it. When you start to interview musicians, look for the following qualities:

1. *A varied repertoire.*   Remember to look for a varied repertoire, especially if your guest list includes a wide range of ages and styles. Quality and proficiency count, but so does diversity. Have your musicians mix it up, combining upbeat tunes with tender ones. Don't subject your guests to three hours of waltzes or three hours of blasting rock selections. Remember, your guest list might very well comprise different generations. Make sure that the musicians you hire are capable of moving from one kind of music to another, especially if your reception includes dancing. For an ethnic wedding, you'll need to find musicians who can play traditional ethnic music.

2. *The same band you hired.*   Often a band comprises a variety of interchangeable instrumentalists and vocalists, so make sure you get in writing that the group you heard on the tape is the one that will be playing at your wedding.

3. *A well-rounded playlist and savvy pacing.*   Often musicians provide a list of their selections. Having a playlist makes things easy—you and your partner simply check off the music you want to hear. A seasoned reception band will generally offer a large, wide-ranging repertoire and have a good sense of the audience. It is their job to pace the selections and know when to move from waltz to rumba to rock.

4. *Flexibility.*   You'll want to find experienced wedding musicians who are happy to play special requests. You may want to select songs for special moments, such as music for the bride and groom's first dance, for the bride's dance with her father, and for parents of the couple. In that case you should communicate your choices to the musicians in writing.

5. *Tasteful presentation.*   Sometimes a DJ or bandleader will also offer

Top Ten "First Dance" Songs

1. "The Way You Look Tonight"
2. "Just the Way You Are"
3. "I Will Always Love You"
4. "Unforgettable"
5. "Wonderful Tonight"

6. "The First Time Ever I Saw Your Face"
7. "Love Will Keep Us Together"
8. "Endless Love"
9. "We've Only Just Begun"
10. "All I Ask of You"

to serve as a master of ceremonies. Quite frankly, there is no real reason to have a master of ceremonies at a wedding reception. A good bandleader or DJ knows how to keep things moving without constantly announcing the next song or offering a running banter over the microphone. The only time the bandleader or DJ needs to speak to guests at all is to ask for their silence to allow an officiant to say grace, for example, or a best man to propose his toast. You certainly don't need to be hailed over the microphone as you enter the reception, nor do you need anyone telling jokes that are amplified. And an announcement that a flambée dessert has just come out of the oven is over the top. *Be clear up front about the behavior you expect from the bandleader or DJ to avoid a misunderstanding.*

NUTS AND BOLTS: QUESTIONS FOR THE RECEPTION MUSICIANS

When interviewing musicians or DJs, make a list of questions to ask and provide any pertinent information. Make sure that the songs you definitely want played will be played. Questions you might ask include the following:

✛ How many breaks will be taken, how often, and for how long? (The standard is one per hour, for five to ten minutes.)

✛ Will you provide taped or synthesized music during your breaks?

✛ What will you wear?

✛ Are any other costs not included in the quoted fee? (Travel time, music between breaks . . .)

✛ Are you willing to go into overtime, and if so, what is the charge? What is your cancellation policy?

✛ Will the contracted musicians be the ones at my reception?

✛ Will the band (or DJ) take requests from guests at no extra charge?

✛ Do you sing in any other languages? (Important for ethnic weddings.)

✛ Do you have a playlist? (Most bands know from two-hundred to five-hundred songs, from swing to top forty to oldies to ethnic.)

✛ Ask for everything in writing. Understand precisely what you will be getting in return for the price you are paying. Find out how many hours of playing time is contracted, how many breaks the band will take, how overtime hours will be billed, what the required deposit is, when the balance is due, whether a refund is available if you cancel, and any taxes or other charges.

CHAPTER SIXTEEN

Consider the

PHOTOGRAPHY AND

style that best articulates

VIDEOGRAPHY

your vision.

Your wedding photographs and videotapes are a tangible record of a wonderful time in your lives and a gift for generations hence. That's why choosing the right person for the job is so important. The craft of wedding photography knows no bounds, with styles ranging from classical to artistic to journalistic. When you go looking for the right photographer for your wedding, consider the style that best articulates your vision.

Each photographer has a distinct style, which is reflected in the portfolio of his or her work. Before you choose a photographer, decide on the photographic style you prefer, then seek out those photographers whose work reflect that style.

1. *Traditional.* A traditional photographer generally treats every image as a posed portrait, even shots you may think of as candid. That doesn't mean the photographs will appear forced or posed, but there will likely be few spontaneous "action shots" included in the mix. Traditional wedding photographers look to capture perfect moments with artistry and dignity and generally produce excellent, albeit formulaic, shots of the wedding party, families, and planned events.

2. *Classical.* These photographers specialize in expertly composed, well-lit portraits. They try to keep an unobtrusive presence at the reception in order to set up perfect, classical images. You won't find them mingling or telling the crowd to "look at the camera" to come up with magic moments.

3. *Photojournalistic or reportage.* A wedding photographer who takes a photojournalist approach is one who considers it his job to record events, not stage them. This photographer will take the group shots you want but will also include candid and spontaneous images. There are few formal "grip and grin" roundups of guests smiling for the camera. The photographer prefers capturing close-ups, spontaneous reactions to events, and sensitive impressions of a wedding led by events, not orchestrated by the photographer.

4. *Commercial.* These photographers will perfectly capture shots of the centerpieces, cake, flowers, and decor and could be hired just for this purpose, supplemented by another photographer to handle people pictures. A commercial photographer's sense of style may be

more formulaic and less spontaneous than a journalistic photographer. Just the same, this type of photographer is a professional and capable of taking magazine-quality images.

5. *Photographic artist.*   Similar to a photojournalist, a photographic artist rarely takes traditional shots but prefers to find artistic ways to photograph elements, people, and events. The photographic artist is adept in the medium of black and white and at producing beautifully composed photos, likely to be less candid than full of drama and artistic beauty.

❧ SELECTING THE ❧ PHOTOGRAPHER FOR YOU

Once you have agreed on what type and style of photograph will make you the happiest, you can begin seeking a wedding photographer in earnest. When you have some names and are ready to interview people, consider the following criteria in your search for a photographer:

1. *Portfolio.*   Don't be dazzled by special effects or complicated setups. Look for a clean, straightforward style. When you visit a photographer or videographer, always ask to see samples of his or her work. This is the most telling element of a photographer's background. A so-so photographer can't hide behind impressive references. The picture tells all.

2. *Price and service comparisons.*   While your first consideration is your ability to relate to the work the photographer has done in the past, you will need to incorporate into your decision-making process price and service comparisons.

3. *Compatibility.*   If you like the photographer's work but don't like the photographer, look elsewhere; your annoyance will show up in your photos. If in a visit to a professional studio you are shown the work of several photographers but prefer the work of one, ask

Helping the Photographer Help You

How well your photographs and videography turn out is in large part dependent upon your success in conveying your vision and desires to your photographer and videographer. Ultimately the onus is on you to make sure that your vision is executed and that your vendors do their jobs to the best of their abilities. Here are a few tips on how to make your collaboration with your photographer a smashing success.

1. *The most important thing is to trust the photographer—and on the wedding day let them do what they do best. Most people have never worked closely with a photographer and are not that familiar with wedding photography.*

2. *To trust the photographer, you must first communicate your needs. Make it clear to the photographer exactly the vision you have and type of look you want.*

3. *It's very helpful to have ready a list of special people you want photographed before the wedding day. It's even more helpful to have ready a guest to direct the photographer to these people and organize group or single portraits. This frees the photographer to concentrate on taking the pictures.*

4. *It's imperative that all parties agree ahead of time on exactly the style you want. Both time and money can be wasted if you don't settle your differences before the photographer starts shooting.*

5. *Decide up front if you want traditional photography or what is sometimes called "reportage" photography—a looser, more journalistic approach. If you decide on a combination of both, be specific about which shots you want done more traditionally and which you want done more photojournalistically.*

6. *Bringing along samples of photographic styles you like and want to emulate when you meet with the photographer is a great idea and a big help to the photographer.*

7. *The more time and thought you put into discerning exactly what you want, the more the results will be personally tailored to you. Scour bridal magazines, look at Sunday wedding announcements, ask your married friends for suggestions or recommendations.*

8. *Don't feel pressured to do something you're not comfortable with. Some people, for example, find the videotaping of the ceremony intrusive but feel pressured to have it done because "everybody does it." Remember, this is your record of your wedding, and it's yours to shape as you desire.*

9. *Let the photographer know at what stage you want to view the photographs. Some photographers like to give their clients a finished photo album, while others prefer to give clients a contact sheet and let clients pick and choose their favorite shots to be printed.*

10. *Keep in mind that many photographers appreciate the opportunity to be a little creative—and sometimes the results can be the most endearing shots of the wedding.*

All About the Photography Contract

Q: What do I need to consider when working up a contract with a photographer?

A: When you find the photographer you want and agree to the date and terms, have him or her write up *an itemized cost breakdown,* including in the contract the date, agreed-upon arrival time, length of shooting period, how many photos/hours of video will be taken, breakdown of package cost and inclusions, extra charges, schedule for reviewing proofs, and delivery of finished album and/or edited video.

Make sure that *price guarantees for additional prints, enlargements, and extra album pages/prints and upgrades* are included in your agreement. Ask whether the photographer offers a *package discount* when you buy extra albums for parents and other relatives. All packages are negotiable to a point. If you'd prefer not to have a finished album from the photographer, choosing to purchase loose photographs instead, discuss your options.

Finally, provide your photographer with a *copy of the site's photography regulations and restrictions* regarding the use of cameras, flash photography, lights, and tripods. You will also need to provide the names and phone numbers of the site managers so that the photographer can scout out the wedding locations. Otherwise you can show him or her the sites yourself.

Once your decisions are made, make sure you get an *itemized contract,* providing a complete record of what is available and of what you want. Be sure to ask the photographer to cover all options in full detail. If you haven't discussed these points during the interview process, this is your last chance. You should have a record of the number of hours, the number of staff (assistants may be needed for a very large wedding), delivery and payment schedules, and final product such as albums or the number of prints.

---

for that one person and only that person to be assigned to your wedding.

4. *Details indicating quality.* When reviewing a photographer's portfolio, look for clean, sharp images that convey emotion and feeling. Keep in mind that you are being shown the photographer's showcase work. It won't get any better than what you see, so be sure you like what you see.

5. *Wedding philosophy.* The one factor that makes the difference between two equally competent professionals is their wedding philosophy. Ask the people you interview how they feel about weddings to try to ascertain if they are truly enthusiastic and dedicated—or if this is just another job.

❧ NUTS AND BOLTS: ❧
QUESTIONS FOR THE PHOTOGRAPHER

Be prepared: take a list of questions with you when interviewing photographers. Following are some sample questions.

- ✢ If you are planning formal portraits ahead of time, does the photographer have a dressing room in the studio? Is there a "prop" bouquet for you to hold, or do you need to provide one?

- ✢ Is a wedding package offered? If so, what does it consist of? For example, does the photographer provide an album for the bride and groom and smaller albums for their parents and perhaps grandparents? Is the package mandatory, or are there options, such as a greater number of prints or additional 8" × 10" prints?

- ✢ What is the number of photographs in the standard album?

- ✢ What is the size and cost of extra albums?

- ✢ What does it cost for additions to a package?

- ✢ What is the number of pictures to be taken before and during the ceremony and at the reception?

- ✢ May the proofs be purchased? Can the negatives be kept? How long does the photographer hold on to negatives after the wedding (in the event that something happens to bride and groom's wedding album)?

- ✢ How long will the photographer stay at the reception? What is the per-hour fee for overtime?

+ Is the photographer familiar with the ceremony and reception sites?

+ Are there extra charges for site visitation and/or travel time?

GETTING THE PHOTOGRAPHS YOU WANT

Once you have studied the different styles of wedding photography, you can decide which photographs you want taken in a formal portrait style and which you'd prefer to be captured in candid, natural shots. You'd be wise to select a photographer who does both types of photos well, because you'll probably want some of both. Or, particularly in the case of a very large wedding, you may even use two different photographers: one whose specialty is formal portraits and ceremony shots, the other whose candid style you prefer for the reception. Sometimes one studio will handle both kinds of photography.

Before signing a contract with a photographer, make a list of the photographs you want and how many copies you think you'll want to give to parents and attendants.

Engagement Photographs

In the past, engagement photographs were typically black-and-white head-and-shoulder shots of the bride alone, taken for publication alongside the engagement announcement. Today, however, the bride and groom frequently appear in engagement portraits together. The portraits are then often framed and given to family members. Whatever you decide on—a photo of you alone or both of you—is fine. It's entirely a personal choice.

The Parents Ask: Black and White or Color?

Q: *Our daughter is getting married this year, and we have a major disagreement over photography. We would much prefer that the wedding photographs be in color, while my daughter loves the look of black and white. Is one more appropriate than the other?*

A: There is a decided trend toward black-and-white wedding photography, particularly among the burgeoning school of brides and grooms who prefer a more candid, photojournalistic approach. Although black-and-white film is less expensive, it is more expensive to process and print than color. If you want some black-and-white shots, make sure your photographer is skilled in this area. Many brides and grooms hire photographers who are willing to switch back and forth, capturing, for example, the processional in color and the recessional in black and white; this can be the best of both worlds, particularly when it is negotiated as part of the package. To accommodate your preference for color, discuss in detail with your photographer any events you want to be captured in color and those your daughter wants in black and white. Be mindful that black and white won't preserve the day's colors, but it can confer a timelessness that can add power and beauty to some images.

Although engagement pictures are now usually taken in color, the photographer will also provide 5" × 7" black-and-white prints for you to submit to the newspaper along with your engagement announcement. Find out whether the newspaper prefers glossy or matte prints.

You will likely have the engagement portrait taken before you have begun the search for a wedding photographer. Try to use someone you might consider booking as your wedding photographer. It's a good introduction to the way the photographer works—and an introduction as well to the quality of the work. If you find he or she fits the bill, you'll have a head start on your working relationship.

Portrait Photographs

The portrait photograph is traditionally the photograph you send in with your newspaper wedding announcement—and it is usually the shot that ends up on the living room wall or perched lovingly atop your parents' piano. Photographers usually shoot a formal portrait in the studio, against seamless paper, in a controlled lighting situation. You may, however, prefer having your picture taken at home or even at the bridal salon on the day of your final fitting.

ETIQUETTE FINE POINTS

Timing for Portrait Photographs

Any formal portrait of the bride that will be submitted to the newspapers is generally taken one to two months before the wedding. In general, newspapers need to have it in their possession anywhere from ten days to three weeks before it runs. This means that your gown and accessories also need to be ready that far in advance.

Because you will want the formal portrait to look as though it were taken on the day of the wedding, you may want to have your hair and makeup done in the style you will wear on your wedding day. To ensure a picture-perfect portrait, make sure that your gown is wrinkle-free, that your headpiece is placed correctly and complements your hairstyle, and that you are wearing the jewelry you plan to wear on your wedding day. You'll want to wear makeup, neatly applied. Most important: Sleep well the night before. You want to look and feel well rested—even the most flattering lighting will not hide fatigue or stress.

Today the formal bridal portrait that appears in the newspaper often includes the groom. Make a decision on whether you want a portrait of the two of you together before the wedding. If so, book the portrait appointment at a time that is convenient for both of you, and make sure the groom's attire has been fitted, if necessary.

The formal bridal portrait can also be a lovely gift for parents and grandparents. Ask the photographer for prices on extra 8" × 10" prints.

Ceremony Photographs

Flash attachments have historically been the bane of every wedding officiant's existence. With the advent of high-speed film and high-tech cameras, the flash is no longer necessary to take quality ceremony photographs. But that doesn't mean that cameras are welcome in every church, chapel, or synagogue. Many officiants will not permit the clicking and whirring of cameras during the ceremony, an occasion they consider sacred. So before you contract with a photographer for ceremony shots, be sure to ask the officiant precisely when photographs are permitted and when they aren't.

If photography is not permitted during the ceremony at all, you can have the photographer take simulated ceremony shots before the wedding or re-create them afterward. If the ceremony photos are to be staged before the wedding begins, they should be taken well before, never as guests are being seated. The photographs should be completed at least an hour before the start time of the ceremony.

If you are having photographs taken between the wedding and the reception, don't think you have to rerun the entire wedding ceremony to get the right shots. Keep it brief! Simply select specific images you want to re-create. Otherwise the process will drag on, and guests will be left with an overload of downtime between the wedding and the reception.

Possible re-created photos might include the following:

+ The bride and her father walking up the aisle

+ The bridesmaids, maid of honor, flower girl, and ring bearer walking up the aisle

+ The groom and best man turned as they would to watch the bride walk up the aisle

+ The bride and groom standing or kneeling at the altar and/or exchanging vows

+ The bride and groom with their children

+ The entire wedding party as they stand for the ceremony

+ The bride and groom kissing

+ The bride and groom walking down the aisle after the ceremony

If there are other special moments or people you want photographed at this time, be sure to delegate a friend to ask these people to stay over after the ceremony. Included could be shots of grandmothers being ushered to their seats or the organist or soloist at work.

Reception Photographs

There are three kinds of reception photographs.

PORTRAITS

Posing for pictures with your respective families can get a little complicated these days. If your parents are divorced, it is simply not appropriate to ask them to flank you in a photograph in a semblance of a united family. Instead a portrait of you with each of them individually is fine—and if they have remarried, have a portrait taken of you with each of them with their spouse. The placing of this photo on your list of portraits can make your parent and stepparent very happy. If enmity toward the new spouse is great, you don't have to do it—just don't try to re-create the family you once were.

Provide, in advance, your list of "must have" shots to the photographer so that he or she can be thinking about suitable backdrops. Possible formal shots might include the following:

- ✢ The bride alone
- ✢ The groom alone
- ✢ The bride and groom together
- ✢ The bride and her maid or matron of honor
- ✢ The bride with her parents (or each parent, plus stepparent, as applicable)
- ✢ The groom with his parents (or each parent, plus stepparent, as applicable)
- ✢ The groom with his best man
- ✢ The bride with her mother
- ✢ The bride with her father

- ✣ The groom with his mother
- ✣ The groom with his father
- ✣ The bride and groom with all their attendants
- ✣ The bride with her attendants
- ✣ The groom with his attendants
- ✣ The bride and groom with the bride's family (parents, siblings, aunts, uncles, cousins)
- ✣ The bride and groom with the groom's family (parents, siblings, aunts, uncles, cousins)
- ✣ The bride and groom with their siblings, if they are not all in the wedding party
- ✣ The bride with "generations"; her parents and grandparents
- ✣ The groom with his parents and grandparents

PLANNED EVENTS

For planned events—both the traditional ones, such as the cake cutting, and those that personalize your wedding—ask an attendant, close friend, or even the catering manager to direct the photographer to the site of each so that he or she can be thinking in advance about the best way to take the picture. Provide the photographer with a list of events and the approximate times they will occur. These can include the following:

- ✣ The bride and groom arriving at the reception
- ✣ Guests going through the receiving line
- ✣ Close-ups of the cake table, centerpieces, and other special decorations
- ✣ The best man toasting the bride and groom
- ✣ The bride and groom cutting the cake

- The bride and groom feeding each other cake

- The groom toasting the bride

- The bride and groom's first dance

- The bride dancing with her father

- The groom dancing with his mother

- The bride tossing her bouquet

- The groom tossing the bride's garter

- The bride and groom leaving the reception

CANDID PHOTOGRAPHS

Let your photographer know up front the kinds of candid photographs that mean the most to you. If you want shots of every table, let the photographer know so no one is left out. If you don't want table shots but prefer shots of people in action, say so. If you love capturing totally spontaneous moments, again, just let your photographer know in advance. Good candid shots can be breathtaking.

If you want work-in-progress shots, you might book the photographer to start before the wedding begins, taking "getting ready" pictures as you and your wedding party prepare for the ceremony. These shots could include the following:

- The bride putting on the finishing touches—a necklace or a garter

- The bride's mother helping her with her veil

- The bride kissing her mother good-bye as she prepares to leave for the ceremony

- The bride and her father arriving at the ceremony site

A QUESTION FOR PEGGY

What If the Photos Don't Turn Out?

Q: Do we have any legal recourse in the event that our photographs or videotapes don't turn out? Are the professionals expected to pay a damage fee or will they offer to re-create portions of the day?

A: While nothing will replace lost photos or footage, you shouldn't have to pay for someone else's errors or accidents. Make sure your contract clearly delineates not only your right not to pay if work is not delivered, but also the return of your deposit and the professionals' financial responsibility to pay *you* if they don't deliver. If they will not agree to the latter, check on industry wedding insurance with your insurance agent to see what coverage is available and at what cost.

In addition, your ceremony and reception sites may require liability insurance of any vendor or service you bring in from the outside. Check early on to see if it is required, and if so, make sure the professionals you hire have liability insurance and proof of insurance to be sent to those who require it.

❧ VIDEOGRAPHY: ❧
WHAT'S YOUR STYLE?

A wedding video can be a wonderful addition to your collection of memories. It will be there on your first anniversary, and it will be there on your twentieth. It provides a wonderful record for your children, capturing like no other medium the mood and the moments of your wedding day.

When reviewing a videographer's work (ask to see tapes of previous weddings), you'll be looking not just for artistic quality, but for a personal sensibility that matches your own. Do you want a wedding video that is a lush visual record of a beautiful day in a beautiful setting? Or do you want a video that focuses on telling a story, one that has a point of view? Do you want a videographer who presents a cinematic sensibility? One who is proficient at editing and cutting the film? Is a sense of humor important to you? Are you interested in capturing special little moments and not just the standard orchestrated ones (like cutting the cake)? Consider these criteria when deciding on the style of your video.

❧ VIDEO OPTIONS ❧

While the costs of videotaping a wedding have gone up in the past few years, so have the credentials and professionalism of dedicated, full-time professionals, as well as the quality of the equipment they use. Standard video packages include your entire wedding story, from the time you arrive at the ceremony (or even before, if you wish) until you depart from the reception. Finished tapes are usually one and a half to two hours long, edited from three to five hours of raw footage.

A wedding video usually includes the entire service and all or part of the reception. The final product you receive is generally *an edited, color videocassette tape with sound.* The editing is done in a studio, and the edited tape can contain not only scenes from your ceremony and reception, but old family photographs, an image of your invitation, interviews with guests, reflections by your parents, and messages for each other. Naturally the more special effects, music, extra photography, and other elements that are added, the more your tape will cost. To produce this tape, the videographer leaves the camera running throughout the ceremony and reception to gather plenty of raw footage from which to edit and select highlights.

A less expensive option: *a tape edited in-camera.* This makes for a choppier video that lacks continuity and transition from scene to scene, one that doesn't include special effects, interviews, or still photography.

A third option, and the least expensive, is *a wedding highlights tape.* Usually lasting only about fifteen minutes, a highlights tape is a fast-paced clip-to-clip view of special moments of the day. It makes an ideal gift to send to those who were not present. Sometimes a videographer will provide a highlights tape as an extra to couples who contract for a full tape.

SELECTING THE VIDEOGRAPHER FOR YOU

Consider the following criteria in your search for a videographer:

1. *Equipment.*   Because videocameras and their locomotivelike high beams can be even more obtrusive than 35-millimeter cameras, you will want to look for a videographer who has the kind of commercial-grade equipment that requires less lighting.

2. *Style and content.*   You'll want a videographer who shares your style and content sensibility.

3. *Credentials.*   Talk to more than one professional, and view any previously made wedding tapes. It's a big investment of your time to preview tapes, but it is worth it to make sure your financial investment will be a good one, for seeing the videographer's work will give you the opportunity to see his or her training, experience, talent, and style.

4. *Details indicating quality,* such as the following:

- ⸸ Steady, not shaky images

- ⸸ Clean, crisp focus

- ⸸ Continuity of sound

- ⸸ A mix of distant and close-up images

- ⸸ Seamless editing from one scene to the next

⸙ NUTS AND BOLTS: ⸙
QUESTIONS TO ASK A VIDEOGRAPHER

Be prepared: take a list of questions with you when interviewing videographers. Following are some sample questions.

- ⸸ Will background music be dubbed on the tape? If so, who selects the music?

- ⸸ Can credits be added so that the names of the wedding party and others can be listed on the tape?

- ⸸ How much editing do you do? Are you the only person involved in editing the final tape?

- ⸸ What special effects are usually used, and when can we decide whether we want them?

- ⸸ What do additional copies cost?

- Are there additional costs for a video portrait of the wedding portrait and other groupings?

- Who keeps original video footage?

- What happens to the footage if it is the property of the videographer?

- How long is the original kept on file, in case we want to order extra copies?

- Can we buy the original footage, and if so, for how much?

- How soon will we be able to view original footage?

GETTING THE FOOTAGE YOU WANT

Both your preferences and your budget can determine what you arrange to have taped. Do you want the videographer recording the wedding party getting ready for the ceremony? You and your father arriving at the ceremony? The mothers being seated? Guests arriving? Do you want the ceremony taped, if your officiant permits it, or just the reception? Do you want your guests "interviewed" by the videographer, or do you think this will only be an unwelcome intrusion? Looking at the tapes of friends or those provided by the videographer may help you decide exactly what elements of your day you want recorded.

The Ceremony

The videotaping of your ceremony must be cleared with your minister, priest, or rabbi before you sign any contracts with videographers. Any specific guidelines should be discussed with the videographer, such as the placement of equipment, lighting restrictions, and whether events can be restaged later.

A Little Discretion, Please!

Let your videographer know that as far as you are concerned, discretion is the better part of valor. You are not looking to have intimate conversations recorded by hidden mikes or someone's inebriated behavior captured on film. At the same time, you do want to be able to hear your exchange of vows and the like. Viewing a videographer's previously made tapes can clue you in to whether the microphones will be powerful enough to do the job.

Most churches and synagogues allow videographers to tape from a specific location, either from the side of the altar or the rear of the balcony, to prevent disruption. Lights are generally not allowed, so newer equipment that requires little or no extra lighting is essential. Often a wireless microphone is attached to the groom's lapel so vows can be recorded clearly.

If your ceremony will be taped, meet with your videographer in advance to describe the ceremony plans. You will need to answer such questions as Will you face each other? Is there a soloist? How many members of your bridal party will there be? Will you have a receiving line at the ceremony site? Will guests shower you with rose petals, bubbles, or birdseed as you leave the ceremony?

The Reception

First decide what video memories and planned events you want recorded at your reception. Then give the videographer you hire a specific list of events planned for the reception. He or she will need to know if there is a receiving line, whether guests will be seated at assigned tables or mingling through the room, whether there will be dancing, and the timing of the cake cutting and other festivities.

CHAPTER SEVENTEEN

The wedding cake

THE WEDDING

has always been a

CAKE

focal point of the

nuptial festivity.

Wedding feasts through the centuries have evolved in much the same ways as have many traditions and rituals, with simple dinners developing into more elaborate displays of celebration as customs changed. Throughout, the wedding cake has always been a focal point of the nuptial festivity, from the symbol of fertility baked by the ancient Romans, to the cake of meal that Native American brides offered their grooms, to the storybook confections of modern times.

As wedding customs have become more elaborate, so have the expenses.

Today the wedding cake is not an insignificant part of the wedding budget. For example, wedding cakes that serve two-hundred guests and more can cost anywhere from a few hundred to several thousand dollars. Costs can be determined as a flat fee or on a per-slice basis, ranging anywhere from $1 to $10 a serving. Thus wedding cake planning deserves the same thoughtful attention you give to the other aspects of your wedding celebration.

The factors to take into consideration when choosing a wedding cake are your budget, the formality of your wedding, and whether or not the reception site requires that you use an in-house cake or pay an additional fee to bring one from the outside. You will also need to decide whether the cake will be the only dessert; if not, perhaps a simpler cake will suffice.

❦ WHO'LL MAKE ❦
THE WEDDING CAKE?

✢ *Where to find a wedding cake.*   Your wedding cake may be ordered from the caterer, a restaurant, the reception site, a professional bakery, a grocery bakery, or a master baker. If the wedding is small, a close friend or relative who is a skillful baker may offer to make your wedding cake. On the other end of the spectrum are individual tiered cakes made and decorated for each guest. Your cake can even be a convincing fake for display only; guests are served from a separate iced sheet cake cut and served from the kitchen.

❦ CAKE VOCABULARY ❦

Don't know the difference between a marzipan paste and a fondant finish? The world of wedding cakes is extraordinarily varied. You can choose a cake with a traditional look and an adventurous taste. Inside a classic tiered facade, for example, may be a carrot cake filling. You may even want to mix textures—combining a tender cake with a smooth filling, for example, or using a hard-finish royal icing over a smooth-finish fondant. You may even want to mix and match flavors: for example, devil's food with hazelnut; German chocolate with French cream; Amaretto with chocolate mousse; fudge truffle with strawberry cream. But don't worry: a good baker will be more than willing to help you choose a texture, filling, and icing that marry nicely.

Here's a primer on some of the terms you will be discussing with your baker.

Buttercream

Cakes iced in buttercream are the best value in terms of price per slice. Buttercream is smooth and creamy, but not too sweet. It takes flavors well, remains soft so it is easy to cut, and is perfect for finishes like basket weave, swags and swirls, fleur-de-lis, and rosettes. Genuine buttercream is made with real butter, so cakes iced with buttercream need to be kept in a cool place; heat and humidity make it bead, run, and drip. Some bakers counter this effect by adding shortening to the icing to give it a measure of stability. If your cake will be kept cool in an air-conditioned reception room, the added shortening is unnecessary. If you demand true, all-butter icing, ask the baker to forgo shortening altogether.

Whipped Cream

Whipped cream is a light, soft icing that, like buttercream, becomes temperamental in heat and humidity. A whipped cream cake must be kept refrigerated until just before it is served. Bakers may also use stabilizers when working with whipped cream. If you don't want stabilizers used, discuss with your baker whether this will affect the appearance of the cake.

Fondant

Rolled fondant icing is a combination of sugar, corn syrup, gelatin, and usually glycerin. It can be rolled out in sheets and wrapped around each tier of

Helping the Baker Help You

When choosing a wedding cake, give the baker the specifics regarding the size and type of wedding you are planning. Here are some tips on working successfully with a baker.

1. You should include the particulars of the reception site, such as the following:

    ◈ Number of guests, so that the baker can determine what size cake is right for the number of guests you expect. (A tip from the experts: Because cake is generally bought on a per-serving basis, many caterers suggest that you not order a piece of wedding cake for each of the guests at the reception, unless yours is a sit-down dinner. Underbuy: figure, for example, for 300 reception guests, ordering a cake that will feed 225. It will save you quite a bit of money, and you will probably *still* have leftover cake.)

    ◈ Room decor.

    ◈ Ceiling height.

    ◈ General temperature.

    ◈ Linen colors.

    ◈ Wedding party colors.

    ◈ Floral scheme (flower types and colors).

2. You'll want to provide the baker with the names and numbers of your other vendors, including the caterer, florist, and wedding planner. Provide the name and number of the site location manager to coordinate details and delivery. It's also important to provide clear directions to the reception site. If necessary, drive the route between the bakery and the reception site yourself to ensure that your directions make sense.

the cake, presenting a smooth frosting with a porcelainlike sheen. It serves as the perfect base for flowers and decorations piped in royal icing (see following) because of its smoothness. A cake iced in fondant cannot be refrigerated, however. While this is not a problem for the cake, it may be for a filling that requires refrigeration.

Royal Icing

Although soft when it is piped onto a cake, royal icing dries to a hard finish. It is what bakers use for creating latticework, flowers, and beading around the edges of the cake—in other words, for decorative touches only, not to ice an entire cake.

A QUESTION FOR PEGGY

Flowers on the Cake

Q: Is it okay to decorate the wedding cake with real flowers?

A: Generally it is better not to. Some flowers are poisonous or have been sprayed with a chemical insecticide.

Spun Sugar, Pastillage, and Marzipan

Finishing touches can be created with any of these decorative icings, all of which are edible. Spun sugar is caramelized sugar that is pulled into strands and quickly formed into bows and other shapes. It melts into a gooey mess in heat and humidity, so it isn't a good choice for a non-air-conditioned room. Pastillage is a paste of sugar, cornstarch, and gelatin that hardens as it dries to a porcelainlike finish. It is used to create realistic-looking flowers and decorations. Marzipan is also a paste, made of ground almonds, sugar, and egg whites. It is sometimes rolled in sheets, like fondant, but it is usually molded into flowers and other decorative shapes and painted with food coloring.

✣ *Selecting a baker.* Make an appointment to meet and review any baker's portfolio, whether he or she is the baker at the club, the one used by the caterer, or one you find and interview yourself. Ask to see photographs of the baker's work. You'll want your cake to look good, but looks aren't all—you'll want it to taste as good as it looks. Most reputable bakers offer tastings of cakes, fillings, and icing. Sample a baker's work before signing a contract.

Be sure that any contract you sign—whether with an outside baker or with a caterer—spells out all the details of your arrangements, including flavors, ingredients, decorations, and of course date and time of delivery. Some reception sites charge an extra cake-cutting fee if your cake is not ordered through them; be sure to ask. Inquire about extra charges for cake stands and pillars and delivery. Ask if a deposit is required and whether it is refundable.

✣ *Bringing in an off-site cake.*   If your cake is to be baked at another site and transported, it is a good idea to follow up yourself and tell the site caterer or club manager when the cake will be delivered. A cake consisting of more than three tiers is generally transported unassembled and put together and decorated on-site. Find out from the location manager if there is space for the baker to work and the best time to do so.

✣ *When to order the cake.*   You'll want to order your wedding cake at least six to eight weeks in advance. If yours is a limited engagement period or a last minute nuptial, you can get good-quality cakes at short notice from professional bakeries and grocery store deli bakeries.

THE WEDDING CAKE DISPLAY

The wedding cake is generally in place and on display when guests enter the reception location. It is sometimes placed on the bridal party table or in the center of a buffet table, but most often it is put on a small table or cart of its

Cake Toppers

The little plastic bride and groom figurines of old may be the quintessential wedding cake topper, but times—and trends—change. Cake toppers are an art form all their own these days, with pieces created from ceramic, porcelain, handblown glass, clay—even crocheted yarn. The fashion nowadays in nuptial cake toppers is a delicate confectionary cascade from the highest tier down of fresh, silk, buttercream, or pastillage flowers and ivy or ribbons—or some combination thereof. Before you go crazy investing in a personalized cake topper, however, consider the entire design when planning the cake topper. A tiny plastic model of the car you drove on your first date, for example, may detract from an elegant-looking cake. Inform your baker of your preferences in advance.

own. If this is the case, you can personalize the display by using a favorite family tablecloth or your mother's wedding veil over an undercloth. You can use a cloth from the caterer with swags caught up by fresh flowers, a design that may be repeated on the cake with similar-looking flowers made of edible icing. You might want to wrap the handle of the cake knife with a ribbon or flowers and place it on the table next to the cake. Or perhaps you have a special cake knife to use, such as a family heirloom. Sometimes the presentation of the cake is an event in itself. The cake is kept hidden in the kitchen until it is time for you to cut it. The lights are lowered, the music stops, and the room becomes hushed. The cake is wheeled into the middle of the room and spotlighted. Then everyone gathers around to witness the cutting of the cake.

❧ THE ART OF CUTTING THE CAKE ❧

No matter what the presentation, the cutting of the wedding cake continues to be a traditional part of the reception. At a sit-down reception the cake is cut just before dessert is served. At a luncheon, tea, or cocktail reception,

it is cut closer to the end of the reception. If the cake has been on display throughout, the bridesmaids simply gather around the bride and groom at the appointed time. Notify the caterer or club manager of the approximate time you plan to cut your cake so that the kitchen staff can be alerted to remove the cake for serving after the cutting. The photographer also should be alerted in advance in order to set up the shot. Here is the traditional sequence of events in cutting the cake:

+ *Cutting the cake.* To start, the bride puts her right hand on the handle of the cake knife and the groom puts his hand over hers. It is easiest if they pierce the bottom tier of the cake with the point of the knife and then carefully make two cuts, removing a small slice onto a plate provided by the caterer in advance, along with two forks.

+ *The first bites.* The groom gently feeds the bride the first bite, and she feeds him the second. This tradition is meant to symbolize their commitment to share with and support one another, and as such it is inappropriate for either to stuff the cake into one another's faces or comically offer up too large a bite.

+ *The wedding cake kiss.* At this point the couple generally share a kiss, and the caterer then has the cake whisked away and cut so that guests may be served.

The Groom's Cake

The tradition of sending wedding guests home with a piece of a second cake, called a "groom's cake," has its origins in early southern tradition. It is a tradition that almost disappeared but today is experiencing a revival of sorts. The modern-day groom's cake is often a chocolate cake, iced in chocolate, or baked in a shape, such as a football or a book, that reflects an interest of the groom. If it is to be used as a second dessert, it is placed on a separate table from the wedding cake and cut and served by the wait staff. At a small, at-home wedding it may be cut and served when the wedding cake is served. Having a special groom's cake is a charming personal touch. Some couples ask to have the groom's cake packaged, festively wrapped and tied with a ribbon, in small boxes to send home with departing guests.

✢ *Slices for parents.*   A lovely gesture before the cake is taken away is for the bride and groom to cut cake slices for their parents. Tradition has it that the bride serves her groom's parents, and he serves hers.

✢ *Saving the top layer.*   If the top layer is to be saved, be sure to tell the caterer in advance so that it isn't cut and served to guests.

ETIQUETTE FINE POINTS

Cutting the Whole Cake

If the wedding is small or at home, you'll want someone in charge of cake cutting once you and your mate have made the traditional first cuts. In this case it is a good idea to review the art of cake cutting in advance.

Each layer needs to be removed to be cut.

About two inches in from the outside, cut all the way around the layer (the cut runs parallel to the outside of the layer, circlelike). Individual slices are cut from this section, and each is lifted onto a cake plate to be served to guests.

The process continues until the center of the layer is reached.

CHAPTER EIGHTEEN

The day is yours

AT THE

to savor

CEREMONY

This is the moment when all your careful planning and organizing crystallize, when time-honored customs embroidered with fine detail combine to create magic. As the hour approaches, take a deep breath and relax. The day is yours to savor.

❧ GETTING READY ❧
The Bride and Attendants Get Ready
DRESSING

The bride generally dresses at home, although many wedding sites offer "getting ready" rooms where the bridal party can dress for the ceremony. If room permits, the bridal attendants will dress there as well. In any case, they should all get together at least an hour before all are scheduled to leave for the ceremony. The bride's mother and her honor attendant help the bride with the finishing touches. Sometimes a professional hairdresser and makeup artist are on hand to help prepare the bridal party for the wedding.

It is the duty of the maid of honor and bridesmaids to check that the bride is wearing something old, something new, something borrowed, something blue. The maid of honor makes sure that an emergency kit of pins, makeup, tape, and other essentials is nearby and ready to go.

BOUQUETS

If the bride's attendants are all present, their bouquets should be delivered to the house or to the gathering place at the ceremony site for the bride and her attendants. Also deliveries should be made for the flower girl's nosegay or basket, the bride's mother's corsage, and the bride's father's boutonniere.

PHOTOGRAPHS

Pictures of the bride and her attendants getting ready are taken, if desired. The photographer then leaves for the ceremony site to take other pictures as the guests arrive and to set up for ceremony shots.

TRANSPORTATION

The bridesmaids travel together, the bride's mother accompanies them or any children who are in the wedding party and/or the bride's children from a previous marriage. The bride usually rides with her father. If the groom has children from a previous marriage, they would be taken care of by the groom's parents or other family members. The flower girl and ring bearer will ride to the ceremony with the bride's mother, if they are not delivered directly to the ceremony by their parents before the ceremony takes place.

The Groom and Best Man Get Ready

DRESSING

The groom should be dressed and ready to go at least an hour before the ceremony. The groom usually spends the hour or so before he is to leave for the ceremony with his best man.

The groom and his best man should arrive at the ceremony site at least fifteen minutes before the hour of the ceremony. Once there, the best man drops the groom off in a private room, such as the vestry or officiant's study, and returns to the sanctuary to retrieve his and the groom's boutonnieres from the head usher. After returning to the groom, he helps him pin on his boutonniere on the left side with the stem down. The best man waits with the groom until the signal comes that the ceremony is about to begin.

ETIQUETTE FINE POINTS
The Best Man's Last-Minute Duties

It is the best man who makes sure that all the necessary papers are together and that the bride's wedding ring is safe in his pocket. If the couple will be leaving directly from the reception for his honeymoon, the best man should have checked that all bags are packed and clothes to change into after the reception have been readied. The best man also traditionally has arranged for the newlyweds' transportation from the reception.

The Ushers Arrive

ARRIVAL

The ushers should arrive at the ceremony site about an hour before the ceremony is to begin. If a head usher is appointed, it is his duty to make sure that the other ushers have transportation to and from the ceremony.

FLOWERS

Boutonnieres delivered to the ushers and the bride's father are pinned on the left side with stem down. Any other boutonnieres—for the groom's father, perhaps, or the couple's grandfathers—are distributed. Ushers are also responsible for presenting corsages to those designated to receive them, such as mothers, grandmothers, and any special friend helping out. The bride has provided a list to the head usher, who then parcels out the tasks among his ushers.

PROGRAMS

If a ceremony program has been printed, the ushers are usually responsible for handing them to guests as they seat them; however, this job can also be given to children who are relatives of the bride and groom and do not have another part in the ceremony.

PEW CARDS

Some couples choose to enclose pew cards in the invitations of certain spiritual guests. The recipients are usually close relatives, such as grandparents, or others close to the couple or their families (godparents or longtime friends). The pew cards alert the ushers that the recipients are seated in forward pews.

If pew cards have been issued, the ushers should not ask for them but should wait for guests to present them. It should be determined ahead of time if certain ushers will escort particular guests who hold pew cards. If the groom's brother is an usher, for example, he would escort his grandmother and mother, just as the bride's brother would escort his own grandmother and mother.

THE AISLE CARPET

Some couples like to have a white carpet rolled up the aisle before the bridal attendants and bride come down the aisle. Some houses of worship have them available as a service or for a small fee. If not, most florists or limousine services can provide them. The "white carpet" is actually just a pressed fiber strip, although sometimes canvas runners are still used. (Ask your officiant's advice. Some feel that aisle carpets are a terrible trip hazard.) Confirm when and how it is rolled out and how many ushers are required to place it successfully. It is a good idea, if possible, for the ushers to rehearse this maneuver. The head usher designates which ushers will be responsible for rolling out the aisle carpet and which ones will place and later remove any ribbons along the ends of the pews.

LAST-MINUTE DETAILS

A last-minute check is made by the ushers. If the room is stuffy or hot, they can open windows. They can make sure that pews are clear of papers or other debris. They should familiarize themselves with the location of a telephone, in case of emergency, and the rest rooms, should a guest ask.

The Guests Arrive

ESCORTING GUESTS

The ushers show all guests to their places. They should ask any guests they do not immediately recognize whether they wish to sit on the bride's side—the left—or the groom's—the right. Just as the reserved pews are divided more or less evenly, so should the rest of the church be divided.

In taking guests to their seats, each usher should offer his crooked right arm for the women guests to hold on to, with their escorts walking behind them. Or the usher may lead the way as the couple follows him to their seat. If a male guest is escorted by himself to a seat, the usher should walk on his left.

GREETING GUESTS

If the day is warm and the weather good—and if the parents of the couple are so inclined and have arrived early—the parents of the couple may want to greet guests for a while outside the ceremony site as guests arrive. Their presence is a welcoming one for guests. They should keep conversations brief and warm, however, so as not to detain everyone outside.

Ushers needn't walk in stony silence when escorting guests down the aisle. They may indeed smile warmly and exchange a few quiet remarks. It's a time of joy and fellowship, and the seating of guests should never be done in absolute silence or with somberness.

SEATING FAMILY

SEATING PARENTS

The parents of the bride always sit in the first pew on the left, facing the chancel; the groom's parents sit in the first pew on the right. If the church has two aisles, her parents sit on the right of the left aisle (as they enter the church from the back), and his parents sit on the left of the right aisle. This way both are seated in the center section of the house of worship.

SEATING WIDOWED PARENTS

Widowed parents of either the bride or groom should not necessarily be expected to sit in lonely splendor at their child's wedding. If they prefer having someone by their side during the ceremony, it is perfectly correct to do so. The guest of the widowed parent does not have to participate in any way, however, such as standing in the receiving line—unless he or she is engaged to the widowed parent or is helping to host the reception. Every effort should be made to treat the companion as an honored guest.

SEATING PARENTS WHO ARE DIVORCED

When either the bride's or the groom's parents are divorced, it is best to have specific advanced instructions for seating, in the interest of amicability. They most likely would not sit together.

Unless the bride is estranged from her mother, her mother (and stepfather, if her mother has remarried) is seated in the front pew. Members of her immediate family—the bride's grandparents, aunts, and uncles—sit immediately behind her (preferably in no more than one or two rows of pews). The bride's father, after escorting his daughter up the aisle and presenting her to her groom, sits in the next pew back, behind the bride's mother's family, with his wife and their family members.

If there is rancor between divorced parents but the bride has remained close to both, the situation is much more difficult. Perhaps she has lived with her father since the divorce. Maybe her mother is hosting the wedding, either entirely or with the bride's father. Sometimes a bride's father (or mother) has remarried and her other parent resents the ex-partner's spouse. If, for example, the bride's mother strongly resents the new wife, it would be more tactful for the new wife to sit farther back in the church, preferably with a friend. In these circumstances the father might not even attend the reception. Grandparents and other relatives on his side might be excluded entirely, unless the bride has remained close to them.

Even if the wedding is given by the bride's father, the seating arrangements remain the same. The bride's mother (and her present husband, if the bride is comfortable about his being there) sits in the first pew. The bride's father and stepmother sit in the front pew only when the bride is estranged from or not close to her mother or is closer to her stepmother. Ordinarily the father's family sits in the third or fourth pew, where he joins them after escorting the bride.

When the groom's parents are divorced, they are seated in the same manner. The groom's mother, accompanied by close members of her family, sits in the first pew (or pews) on the right side of the aisle. The groom's father and family sit in the next pew behind the groom's mother's family.

Naturally, if the divorce is an amicable one and all are great friends, there is no reason that all the bride's or groom's divorced parents cannot share the first pew. It is only when relations are strained or sensitivities great that the etiquette of careful seating need be employed.

SEATING IMMEDIATE FAMILY

Behind the front pews, several pews on either side of the center aisle are reserved for the immediate families of the couple. The people who are to sit

Too Many Fathers

Q: I have a problem deciding who should walk me down the aisle. Naturally my father would be the logical choice, but my stepfather helped raise me and is an important part of my life. What do I do?

A: One of the greatest difficulties for brides today is choosing between a father and a stepfather as the person to "give her away." It is no easy choice, especially when she is close to both. The most diplomatic decision may be to fall back on tradition and ask her biological father to escort her up the aisle. However, it is acceptable for her to choose her stepfather if she feels she is closer to him. The decision may become cloudy again in the event that her father has stepped forward to pay for the wedding. Some brides take a different route and have their mothers escort them. Others choose to walk alone or to have a brother or uncle do the honors.

It is rare that both fathers escort their daughter, but it's not unheard of—as long as they are friendly and share affection for the bride. Under no circumstances, however, would a bride have her divorced mother and father escort her up the aisle if either has remarried. This would be inappropriate and confusing, not to mention potentially painful or threatening to the new spouses. If they are divorced but have not remarried, it would still be better for the bride to walk with her father and let her mother be seated before the ceremony.

there may have been sent pew cards to show their usher, or the usher may keep a list of guests to be seated in the first few pews.

❧ THE CEREMONY ❧

Places, Everyone

AISLE RUNNER AND PEW RIBBONS

Once the mothers are seated, it is time to place the aisle runner, if one is being used. Two ushers or the junior ushers pick up the runner, place it at the foot of the chancel steps, and carefully draw it back down the length of the aisle. A broad white ribbon may be put in place on either side of the aisle. The ribbons should be folded at the ends of the last reserved pews. The ushers walk with the ribbons to the back of the church, laying them over the end of each row. The ribbons should not be removed until the guests in the reserved pews leave. After they are escorted out, the ushers will indicate that the remaining guests should exit, starting at the front.

SEATING THE BRIDE'S MOTHER

After the bride's mother is taken to her place, no guest may be seated from the center aisle. If guests arrive after the bride's mother is seated, they must stand in the vestibule, go to the balcony, or slip into a pew from the side aisles. The ushers may assist them.

THE COUNTDOWN BEGINS

The bride and her father arrive at the precise moment for the wedding to start, and the procession forms in the vestibule at the back of the sanctuary. As soon as the attendants have taken their places, a signal is given, and the officiant, followed in order by the groom and the best man, enters the church. Many churches have a buzzer system in the vestry or study to announce to the groom and best man that all is ready. In others, the sexton or wedding coordinator goes to the vestry with the message; sometimes the opening bars of the "Wedding March" or another specific piece of music give the signal. In any case, the groom and the best man enter and take their places at the right side of the head of the aisle or, in some churches, at the top of the steps to the chancel. The best man stands to the groom's left and slightly behind him, and both face the congregation. As soon as they reach their places, the procession begins.

The Processional

1. The ushers lead the procession, walking two by two, the shortest men first. Junior ushers follow the adults.

2. Junior bridesmaids come next.

3. The bridesmaids follow, walking in pairs or singly. (See chapter 9, "Planning the Ceremony," for more details on processionals, ceremonies, and recessionals for both Christian and Jewish weddings.) The spaces between each couple or individual should be even and approximately four paces long. The hesitation step, which used to be very popular, is actually considered awkward and difficult these days. A slow, natural walk is the more graceful.

4. The arrangement of the attendants at the front of the church varies. The ushers may divide and stand on either side, as may the bridesmaids, or the ushers may line up on one side and the bridesmaids on the other. The minister or priest will help determine what looks best during the rehearsal. The ring bearer comes next, followed by the flower girl. In a Jewish ceremony the rabbi helps determine how many of the wedding party fit under the *chuppah*.

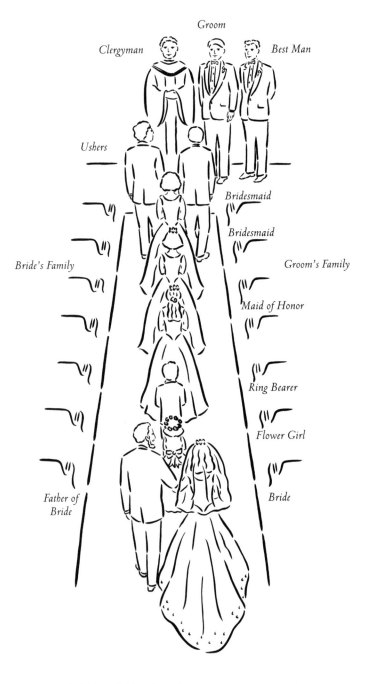

TRADITIONAL PROCESSIONAL FOR A
CHRISTIAN WEDDING

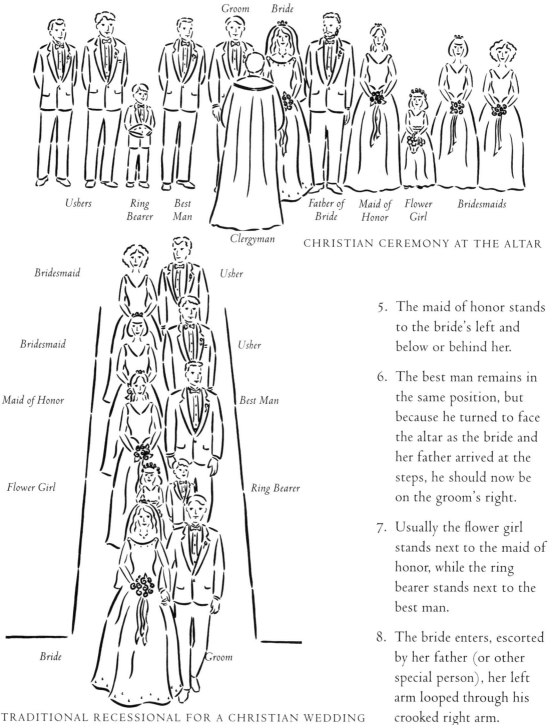

Groom   Bride

Ushers   Ring   Best   Father of   Maid of   Flower   Bridesmaids
          Bearer   Man   Bride   Honor   Girl

Clergyman   CHRISTIAN CEREMONY AT THE ALTAR

Bridesmaid   Usher

Bridesmaid   Usher

Maid of Honor   Best Man

Flower Girl   Ring Bearer

Bride   Groom

TRADITIONAL RECESSIONAL FOR A CHRISTIAN WEDDING

5. The maid of honor stands to the bride's left and below or behind her.

6. The best man remains in the same position, but because he turned to face the altar as the bride and her father arrived at the steps, he should now be on the groom's right.

7. Usually the flower girl stands next to the maid of honor, while the ring bearer stands next to the best man.

8. The bride enters, escorted by her father (or other special person), her left arm looped through his crooked right arm.

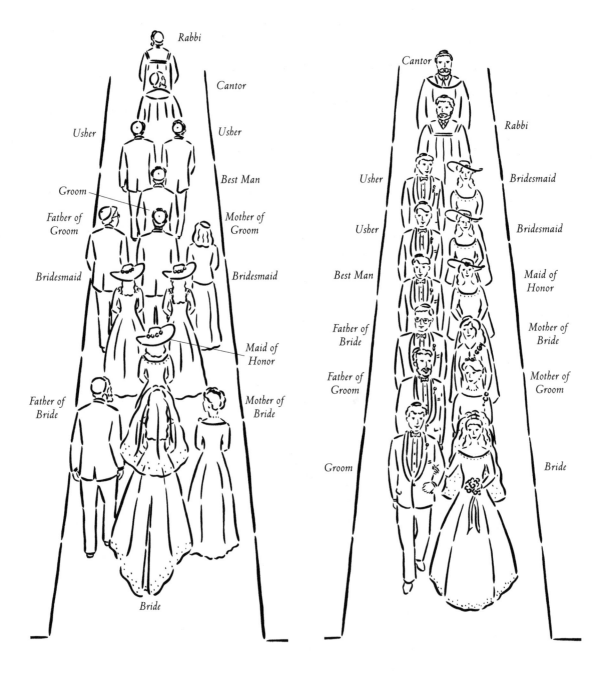

JEWISH PROCESSIONAL FOR A CONSERVATIVE
OR ORTHODOX CEREMONY

JEWISH RECESSIONAL

EMILY POST'S WEDDING ETIQUETTE

Maid of Honor

Best Man

Father of Bride

Father of Groom

Bridesmaids

Mother of Bride

Cantor

Bride

Groom

Rabbi

Mother of Groom

Ushers

CONSERVATIVE OR ORTHODOX JEWISH CEREMONY,
UNDER THE CHUPPAH

The Ceremony

1. When the bride reaches the groom's side, she lets go of her father's arm, transfers her flowers to her left arm, and gives her right hand to her groom. He puts it through his left arm, and her hand rests near his elbow. If the bride is not comfortable this way, they may stand hand in hand or merely side by side. The minister faces them from the top of the steps.

2. In a Christian ceremony the bride's father remains by her side or a step or two behind until the minister says, "Who will support and bless this marriage?" or "Who represents the families in blessing this marriage?" The bride's father reaches in front of her and puts her right hand into that of the minister and says, "Her mother and I do." He then turns and joins his wife in the front pew.

Sharing the Peace

When communion is offered at a Christian wedding, the minister or priest will often ask everyone to reach out and share a message of peace with one another, at the point in the service where he says, "Peace be with you." At this time, and especially if the guests are few in number, the wedding party may move out into the congregation, offering handshakes, hugs, and kisses to guests. It is but a small break in the ceremony, but it gives the bride and groom the opportunity to connect with their guests.

3. In a Jewish processional, the groom's parents follow the groom, who is then joined by his bride. The couple, their parents, and their attendants face the rabbi and the cantor, and the ceremony begins.

4. If there are children from the bride's or groom's previous marriages, the minister could ask, "Who will support this new family with their love and prayers?" In this instance the bride, groom, children, and often the guests may answer together.

5. At the conclusion of the ceremony, the officiant may say, "I now pronounce you husband and wife." Some clergypersons are still saying "man and wife." If you prefer, ask to be pronounced as "husband and wife."

6. The bride and groom kiss.

The Recessional

1. The maid of honor hands the bride back her bouquet and straightens her gown and train for her as she starts down the aisle.

2. The flower girl and ring bearer walk together behind the bride and the groom, followed by the maid of honor and the best man.

3. The other attendants step forward and recess behind the couple either singly or side by side, depending on their number. They may

walk together as they entered, groomsmen with one another and bridesmaids together, or a bridesmaid may walk with an usher. Each member of the wedding party should know how to fall in line, since this recessional will have been practiced during the rehearsal.

4. The Jewish ceremony ends with the recessional, led by the bride and groom, who are followed by the bride's parents, the groom's parents, the attendants, the rabbi, and the cantor.

❧ THE CELEBRATION BEGINS ❧

A Smashing Exit

PHOTOGRAPHS AND VIDEOS

The photographer, who has remained at the back of the sanctuary after taking pictures of the bride's arrival, may now catch the radiant couple as they come down the aisle. The videographer, who may have been taping from the back of the balcony, quickly descends and joins the photographer in catching the wedding party coming down the aisle. The bridal party may then gather for a formal wedding party portrait. If certain aspects of the ceremony are to be re-created for the photographer, the wedding party waits to the side and reenters the building for pictures to be taken *as quickly as possible*. The guests either wait, taking their cue from the parents, or depart for the reception if it is suggested they do so.

CEREMONY RECEIVING LINE

If a receiving line is not planned for the reception, the bride, the groom, their mothers, and the maid of honor and bridesmaids may form a receiving line and greet guests as they exit the ceremony site. If either the bride or groom has children, they may want to have them stand in the receiving line, too, as a part of the family.

BUBBLES AND ROSE PETALS

Rose petals or bubbles are distributed by someone designated to do so earlier to the guests looking on. Once the photography is completed, the wed-

The Officiant Asks: Who Cleans Up the Rose Petals?

Q: I am an officiant for a large church with frequent wedding services. We try to discourage couples from scattering rose petals, or anything for that matter, because of the cleanup involved. Who, indeed, is responsible for cleaning up after a wedding?

A: Any couple set on being showered with rose petals or some other celebratory symbol should first ask the officiant if this processional option is allowed—and if it is, they should then offer to pay extra for cleanup. Most churches don't permit guests to throw anything at the bride and groom as they leave the ceremony for the reception, because cleanup is too costly. If you have your heart set on having rose petals scattered before you during the processional, keep in mind that petals are notoriously slippery. Instead of rose petals, some couples provide their guests with tiny bottles of bubbles, used for blowing toward them during the recessional. One warning if you do consider celebrating with bubbles: If the bubbles float onto your gown, they could stain. Other options: colored streamers or confetti.

And do remember that many couples decide to forgo scattering anything, for practical reasons. Rice is rarely used anymore, even though as a symbol of fertility it is deeply rooted in tradition. Rice can be damaging to birds and other wildlife, who cannot digest uncooked grains of rice. It is also almost impossible to rake, scoop, or pick up from grass and flower beds.

ding party heads to the waiting cars and is properly showered with rose petals or bubbles by the guests.

TRANSPORTATION TO THE RECEPTION SITE

Cars taking the wedding party to the reception should be waiting at the entrance of the ceremony site. The bride and groom are placed into the first car by the best man and are the first to leave for the reception. The bride's parents ride together, and the maid of honor and bridesmaids depart in the same cars in which they arrived. The flower girl and ring bearer may travel with their parents or they may ride with either the bride's parents or the bridal attendants.

Signing the Papers

The bride and groom must at some point during the proceedings sign their wedding papers, witnessed by the maid of honor and best man. If this has not been done before the ceremony, it should be done before they leave for the reception.

CHAPTER NINETEEN

Your reception is a

AT THE

celebration, and you and

RECEPTION

your family are

the hosts.

No matter how large or how small, your reception is a celebration, and you and your family are the hosts. You are there to welcome guests, feed them, enjoy their company, and thank them. Let them know how happy and pleased you are that they are there to celebrate with you.

❧ THE ETIQUETTE OF THE ❧ RECEIVING LINE

A receiving line is a traditional way for the wedding party to greet guests, upon their arrival at the reception or at the ceremony before leaving for the

Guest Books

Q: What is the proper way to display a guest book for guests to sign at my wedding reception?

A: While it is not obligatory to have a guest book at the reception, as a memento of the occasion and a record of all present it's a very nice touch. Place the book on a table near the reception entrance or at the end of the receiving line. Delegate a friend, a member of the family, or an attendant to stand by the book and remind each guest to sign. Occasionally a guest book is placed instead at the entrance to the ceremony, and one of the ushers asks guests to sign it before entering the sanctuary. This is done when there are more guests attending the ceremony than the reception, such as the times an officiant extends to church members an open invitation to the nuptials. If a member of the family or a close friend is supervising the guest book, be sure to present him or her with a boutonniere, corsage, or nosegay to show your appreciation.

reception. *Whether you decide to have a receiving line or not is simply a matter of choice.* It is certainly not required; in the event of a small wedding, it even seems superfluous.

✣ *Why a receiving line?* Its purpose makes sense at a large wedding, where it is unlikely that the bride, the groom, and their parents will get a chance to speak to everyone. A rule of thumb: It is helpful to have a receiving line if there are seventy-five or more guests. If you choose to eliminate a receiving line, make sure that you greet every guest at your reception.

✣ *When do you have a receiving line?* Usually the wedding party completes the formal photographs at the ceremony site before leaving for the reception. If you choose to do so, take the pictures *quickly* so that guests won't have to wait a long time for you, your parents, and your attendants at the reception. Ideally you will have discussed the best place to form a receiving line with the club manager or caterer, one that permits guests to have a refreshment while they are waiting their turn or one that flows into the open area where the reception will take place. If you choose the latter, you may position a waiter at the end of the line with a tray of champagne or other beverages that are offered to guests as they pass on their way to the reception area.

The Bride's Mother Asks: What to Do with Garrulous Guests?

Q: *How do I tactfully deal with an excessively talkative guest in a long receiving line?*

A: No one should tie up the line with extended conversation. If a guest is talkative, it is up to the parents or the bride and groom to gently break in and say, "We're so glad you're here. Let me introduce you to . . ." to help move that person along.

ETIQUETTE FINE POINTS

Where to Put the Cocktail?

Guests should not go through the receiving line either eating or drinking, so a table should be placed near the beginning of the line for them to deposit glasses and plates or napkins.

✦ *Who stands where?* The traditional order, based on the custom of the wedding being hosted by the bride's parents, is for the bride's mother to stand first in line, to greet guests. The bride's father is next, followed by the groom's mother and father, followed by the bride, the groom, the maid of honor and, sometimes, the bridesmaids. Fathers are not *required* to stand in the receiving line, but it certainly gives them an opportunity to greet all the guests, something they might not otherwise be able to do at a large reception. A general guideline: If one father stands in the line, the other father does as well. A disabled parent or a parent in ill health may be in the line seated on a high stool, if possible, or in a chair or wheelchair.

✦ *Where do divorced parents stand?* Divorced parents do not stand in the line together. The parent and stepparent who are giving the

| Mother of
Bride | Father of
Bride | Mother of
Groom | Father of
Groom | Bride | Groom | Maid of
Honor | Bridesmaids |

RECEIVING LINE

reception, or with whom the bride or groom has spent the most time, are the ones who should normally be in the line. If neither parent has remarried and both are helping give the reception, it is easier to go by the rule of thumb that fathers needn't stand in the line and have only the bride's or groom's mother do so.

When divorced parents are friendly and accept one another's new spouses, or when both couples are giving the wedding, they may all stand in the receiving line, separated, however, by the groom's parents to avoid creating confusion. If the groom's parents are divorced and remarried as well, and you absolutely want everyone in the receiving line, then each set of parents should alternate: bride's family, groom's family, bride's family, and groom's family. Or, for the sake of not confusing guests with so many parents—and in the interest of having a line that isn't too long—the sets of parents may take turns standing in line.

The full lineup, then, would look something like this:

- ✦ Bride's mother
- ✦ Bride's stepfather
- ✦ Groom's mother
- ✦ Groom's stepfather
- ✦ Bride's stepmother
- ✦ Bride's father
- ✦ Groom's stepmother
- ✦ Groom's father
- ✦ Bride
- ✦ Groom
- ✦ Maid of honor
- ✦ Set the bridesmaids free—the line is long enough!

There are so many variables in the case of divorced and remarried parents. It is best that the bride and groom plan early with their parents to determine who stands where. Usually the traditional guideline—the hosts stand first in line—comes in handy for helping to diffuse any hurt feelings and questions. And sometimes the fathers circulate among the guests simply to make things easier.

- ✦ *Should bridesmaids and children stand in line?* Although it is quite correct for bridesmaids to stand in the receiving line, they don't have to, especially if the line is long. Doing so only prolongs the line and stretches the imaginations of guests thinking up a polite, clever

Are Cash Bars Acceptable at the Reception?

Q: My fiancé really wants to serve alcohol at our wedding reception, but it would put a crimp on our budget. Someone suggested a cash bar, where guests would pay for their own drinks. What are your thoughts?

A: You wouldn't think of asking someone to pay for a cocktail in your home, so don't have a cash bar at your reception. When you invite guests to your reception they are just that—your guests. If a bar is not in your budget, serve soft drinks, wine, or champagne. Or perhaps you'll cut back on the size of your guest list and serve a full array of drinks. Just do not let the hotel or club or reception site manager talk you into selling tickets for drinks or having guests pay their way!

comment for everyone. Young children—flower girls, ring bearers, pages, and train bearers—do not stand in the line, although the children of the bride and groom may be in line if they are old enough and want to do so.

✢ *How should guests pass through the line?* As quickly as possible, pausing only long enough to be greeted by the host and hostess, to wish the bride happiness, and to congratulate the groom. Close friends and family often accompany a congratulations with a kiss. Otherwise each person extends a hand to the person in line, who turns to introduce him or her to the next person in line before greeting the next guest. This eliminates the need for the guest to have to introduce himself or herself over and over again, and it also makes the process more personal.

✤ TOASTS ✤

Toasting the happy couple at the wedding reception is one of the event's most cherished traditions. The customary toasting drink is champagne, the effervescent, light-as-air libation that is a liquid expression of the giddy happiness shared by all at the celebration.

✢ *Pouring the champagne.* At a sit-down reception, champagne is poured as soon as everyone is seated. At a cocktail reception where guests are either seated at small tables or standing, it is poured after everyone has gone through the receiving line. (If champagne is not being served, toasts are then made with whatever beverage guests have in front of them, whether it's water, soft drinks, punch, or juice.)

✢ *Getting the guests' attention.* The best man attracts the attention of the guests, either from his table or from the microphone, and proposes a toast to the bride and groom.

The Wedding Consultant on Toasts: Short and Sweet!

A wedding reception is not the time for long anecdotes or jokes; those are usually told at the rehearsal dinner the night before or at bachelor or bachelorette parties. Short and sweet: that's what the best man's toast to the newlyweds should be. Here are three recommendations from wedding consultants:

- **From William Shakespeare's *The Tempest*:**
  "**Please join me in a toast to Mark and Cindy, first written by William Shakespeare: *Look down you gods and on this couple drop a blessed crown*. May all your days be blessed and crowned with joy and happiness. To Mark and Cindy!**"

- **A favorite Irish blessing:**

  May the wind be always at your back.
  May the road rise up to meet you.
  May the sun shine warm on your face,
  The rains fall soft on your fields.
  Until we meet again, may the Lord
  Hold you in the hollow of his hand.

- **A toast sometimes used in Moscow includes this couplet:**

  Two birds were sitting in the tree branches vis-à-vis.
  This is to the wind, which rose and joined their lips.

✢ *Who gives a toast?* It's perfectly fine for the best man's toast to be the only one offered; often, however, both fathers offer toasts welcoming each other's families and guests or simply express their happiness at their children's happiness. The maid of honor and other members of the bridal party may also propose toasts, and the groom often toasts his bride and new parents-in-law. If any telegrams or messages have been sent, they may be read by the best man.

✢ *Who stands, who sits?* Everyone should rise for the toasts to the newlyweds except the bride and groom, who remain seated. If a toast is directed to the bride only, the groom rises; if it is directed to their parents, both the bride and groom rise. If there is no seating and everyone is standing, including the bride and groom, then the newlyweds simply smile as toasts are made. They do not drink a toast to themselves.

✦ *When the bride and groom toast.* When making a toast together, the bride and groom do not speak in unison, but rather stand together while one speaks or take turns speaking.

BLESSING THE MEAL

If a meal is included in your reception, you might want to say grace before guests begin moving through a buffet line or before waiters begin serving. This is a good time to have a relative, a friend, or your officiant participate. No matter who gives the blessing, you should be sure to ask him or her ahead of time, so that a little thought can go into the prayer. If you have a DJ or bandleader, you might ask him or her to request everyone's attention, at which point the person giving the blessing goes to the microphone. If there is no microphone, the best man may call for quiet and introduce the person saying the blessing. The blessing done, the best man would then thank that person, signaling to all that guests can begin eating.

❧ DANCING ❦

Dancing is often an essential element of the reception. Indeed, almost every culture has a tradition of joyous dancing at the wedding celebration. As it was noted in *A Bride's Book of Wedding Traditions,* by Arlene Hamilton Stewart: "Italians do the tarantella; Irish dance a jig; Scots do the Highland fling; Greeks join hands in a chain dance they call the *kalamatianos;* and the Jewish people dance circles around the bride and groom in their famous dance, the *hora.*"

While there are surely many types of dances and a wide variety of customs, here are a few general guidelines for dancing at the wedding reception:

⚜ *When does the dancing start?* At a seated dinner, dancing should not start until after dessert has been eaten. If, however, the reception follows an afternoon wedding and the meal won't be served until later, guests may dance before the bridal party goes to its table. At a buffet reception, the newlyweds may start the dancing as soon as they have left the receiving line or after any group photographs have been taken.

⚜ *Who dances first?* The bride and groom dance the first dance, while guests watch and applaud.

⚜ *What is the following order of dances?* When the second song begins, the bride's father-in-law asks the bride for the second dance, and then the bride's father cuts in. The groom, meanwhile, dances with his mother-in-law and then with his mother. Next the bride's father may ask the groom's mother to dance, and the groom's father asks the bride's mother. As the groom dances with the maid of honor and the ushers with the bridesmaids, guests may begin dancing. When the family makeup is such that it complicates the order of dances—more than one father and mother, stepparents—then everyone is free to dance as soon as the newlyweds have danced the first dance. The bridal party joins the bride and groom on the dance floor, a signal to the guests that everyone else may join in. The bride and groom should make a point to dance with all of their parents during the reception.

✢ *When do the bride and her father dance?*   At some point during the dancing, perhaps a half hour or so before the bride and groom leave the reception, the bride and her father may have a special dance of their own. The bride may want to select the song ahead of time. They may either dance the entire song alone or be joined by the bride's mother and the groom. If the latter, halfway through the song, they may change partners and join their respective spouses, and the other guests may join them on the dance floor.

❧ CLOSING ACTIVITIES ❧

You most likely have formulated a general time to take your leave from the reception. Stick to it. You may be having so much fun that you want to stay forever, but because guests don't generally leave until you do, courtesy demands that you depart.

Cutting the Cake

At a seated meal, the cake is cut just before dessert is to be served. Slices can then be passed. Sometimes another dessert is served, which is passed also. If the reception is a buffet or cocktail reception, the cake is cut later, often shortly before the couple departs.

Tossing the Bouquet

Traditionally, just before the couple leaves the reception, the bride or her maid of honor gathers together the bridesmaids and all single women guests, often at the foot of a stairs, in the center of the dance floor, or by the door. The bride then turns her back and over her shoulder throws her bouquet or a facsimile of it, called a "tossing bouquet," if she wants to keep and preserve her original bouquet. Tradition has it that whoever catches the bouquet— who gets to keep it, by the way—will be the next one married.

A Grand Departure

Many couples believe in making a grand departure from the reception (and even the ceremony), whether by horse-drawn carriage, on horseback, or on a boat in water strewn with rose petals. Make sure to have someone recording the moment, in photographs or videotape, when you make your grand leap into a new life.

Throwing the Garter

In some communities it is traditional for the bride to wear an ornamental garter just below her knee, so the groom can remove it easily and tastefully with no fanfare. For this event the best man and the ushers gather, and the groom throws the garter over his shoulder. According to tradition, the man who catches the garter will be the next to marry. The throwing of the garter should never be done in a tasteless manner, with the groom fondling the bride's leg for all to see, for example. This can be embarrassing for both the participants and the guests.

And You're Off!

The bride and groom may leave in their bridal finery or change into "going away" clothes. If they decide to change clothes, the maid of honor and the best man generally attend the bride and groom in their separate changing rooms and collect the wedding finery. At some point parents and relatives join them for a good-bye.

When the newlyweds are ready to go, the attendants form a farewell line and are joined by the guests. The couple is often showered with rose petals, confetti, or the like as they dash to their departure vehicle, which may have been decorated by the ushers with "Just Married" written in shaving cream or something similar that is (hopefully) biodegradable and easy to clean.

Make sure

AFTER THE

postwedding loose ends

WEDDING: FROM THIS

are taken care of.

DAY FORWARD

One of your main responsibilities is to make sure postwedding loose ends

are taken care of, so that they don't become a burden to anyone else while you

are away on your honeymoon. These duties include making arrangements for

gift deliveries and delegating the mailing of wedding announcements, rental

returns, and the storage of wedding clothes. It goes without saying that if you

are leaving children or pets behind, you will have to make arrangements that

they be taken care of while you are gone. Many of these duties can be dele-

gated to members of the wedding party and friends and relatives.

Error

 371

THANK-YOUS

Ideally you have kept up with your thank-you notes throughout the prewedding period. You will most likely be inundated with more gifts, however, upon your return from your honeymoon—and thus have a whole new batch of thank-you notes to pen. Remember, grooms write thank-you notes these days, too, so make writing thank-you notes a shared task. It's a nice touch to send your parents a thank-you note and a gift, perhaps a souvenir picked out on your honeymoon travels. Don't forget to thank your attendants for being in your wedding when you're thanking them for their gifts.

HONEYMOON ETIQUETTE

The honeymoon is the romantic interlude bridging your past and future lives. It's the time to revel in your nuptial bliss and recuperate from the hectic planning and activities of the weeks and months before.

Because the honeymoon is as much the groom's vacation as it is the bride's, the planning should be shared by both of you. That includes doing research, meeting with travel agents, and making reservations. More important, you should both be involved in making arrangements so that all you leave behind runs smoothly without you—especially if you have children or own pets.

✣ Be sure to leave a written schedule of your trip, including telephone numbers, with the people who are responsible for maintaining any aspect of your home life while you're away, whether it's taking care of a pet, watering plants, or picking up mail. A very thoughtful gesture is to buy phone cards with prepaid minutes for your designated caretakers to use in the event that they have to call you. Be sure to give parents or other close relatives copies of your schedule as well.

Storing Wedding Attire

You will want to take as much care with your wedding clothing after the event as you did before. Here are some practical ways to store your wedding attire so that it will stay fresh and wrinkle-free for years to come.

Wedding gown. Have an attendant or relative hang up your gown as soon as you take it off and get it to a professional cleaner who specializes in wedding gowns as soon as possible, particularly in the event of spots or champagne spills. The cleaners will then clean and store the gown in a sealed box or container. Store the box or container in a high shelf in a closet or in the attic.

Headdress. Any headdress not attached to a veil should be cleaned professionally and placed in a hatbox.

Trains and veils. Have each cleaned professionally with the wedding gown and stored in the same manner.

Gloves. Cotton gloves: Launder. Wrap in tissue in a box and keep it in a drawer. Kid or leather: Have cleaned professionally.

Shoes. Carry to a shoe shop to have shoes cleaned professionally and stored in a box. For cloth shoes, sponge with a cloth and mild detergent; when dry, put them away in tissue in a box. For leather shoes, polish and store. If tough grass stains are on shoes, have them cleaned professionally, no matter what the fabric.

Bouquet. If your freezer is large enough, store your bouquet inside until you return from your honeymoon. When you return, have it freeze-dried by a florist or dry it yourself by hanging it upside down in a dry place.

✢ Take with you on the honeymoon the phone numbers of any caretakers.

✢ Leave written instructions for feeding pets, giving medication, or watering plants. Be sure to stock up on pet food and the like so that the caretakers are not obligated to spend money on supplies.

Taking the Kids Along

Many couples marrying for the second time bring children of their own into the marriage. Encore marriages can be unsettling for kids, especially young children who are dependent on their parent. They may feel that they are being abandoned or will become less important in your life. If your kids are

Wedding Announcements

Q: When do I send out wedding announcements?

A: It's a good idea to have your wedding announcements addressed and stamped before the wedding, either by you or someone helping you. They should go into the mail soon after your wedding day—traditionally announcements are mailed the day after the wedding. Ask a friend or relative to mail them if you are planning a long honeymoon. (For more on wedding announcements, see chapter 6.)

feeling threatened by your marriage plans, you may rightly be concerned about leaving them immediately after the wedding to go on a honeymoon. This is a clear conflict, as you and your new spouse may be eager—and certainly deserve—to share some private time together.

Some couples decide to take their kids on the honeymoon with them, making the trip a family vacation. This is fine, as long as you and your mate are enthusiastic and in complete agreement about this. Others find ways to divide their honeymoon, with the first part a time for the two of you alone and the second part a trip as a family. This gives your children something to look forward to during the few days you are away from them. Or you could plan a special kids' party after you get home from the honeymoon. If you do decide to take a honeymoon away from the kids, think of ways to remember them while you are gone (see "The Personal Touch: A Gift a Day," page 377). Call often and send plenty of postcards. You can even make videotapes or audiotapes to mail overnight to the kids, describing your vacation spot and sending your love.

THE TWO OF YOU: LIFE AFTER THE HONEYMOON

It's easy for couples who are swept up in countless wedding details and duties to become somewhat myopic about preparing for life *after* the wedding. Many newlyweds returning from their honeymoon will be living together for the first time. Make sure to set aside time during your wedding planning to discuss how to make the transition a smooth one for both of you.

Start with the practical details. It's a good idea to have made any *financial and name-change arrangements* before your wedding day (see chapter 3), particularly if you will be sharing a bank account. Discuss the *division of household duties:* who will be responsible for keeping a household budget, for example, or buying groceries or cleaning the house? Even though you may plan to share household duties, you may quickly discover that one of you naturally falls into the role of cook or cleaner or that you each have a distinct preference in household chores. Whatever you do, try to keep the balance of duties equal. There are also adjustments to be made for differing styles: he wants all the counters clear, for example, and you don't mind a little clutter. The key words, here, are flexibility and communication.

Other little sticking points you and your partner should discuss include the following:

+ Which side of the bed to sleep on.

+ Closet and drawer space.

+ Making sure each of you has a sacred private place.

+ How much and what to watch on television, and clicker control.

+ Music volume.

+ Privacy boundaries, such as always knocking before entering an occupied bathroom.

+ Drop-ins, such as in-laws popping in without calling first.

+ Pros and cons of pets. It would be a big disappointment to count on sharing a pet with your loved one only to find out after the fact that he or she is simply not interested in having the responsibility.

Selecting Wedding Pictures

One of the things you should set up with your photographer and videographer before the wedding day is a date to view and select wedding photos and videos. Both you and your mate should be present to select photographs; often other family members are included as well.

Once you've made your selections, you will want to decide the quantity to be printed of each photograph, their order in photo albums, and how many albums you will want to order, to present to family later.

Photo Gift List

Bride and groom	Bride's grandparents	Bridal party: *Best man,*
Bride's parents	Groom's grandparents	*Maid/matron of honor, Bridesmaids,*
Groom's parents	Other relatives	*Ushers, Flower girl, Ring bearer,*
		Special friends

Make sure the wedding negatives are stored in a safe place. You may want to have them scanned onto a disk or printed on a CD-ROM for safekeeping.

Finally, make sure you are both committed to *open communication.* If something is making either of you increasingly unhappy or irritated, you'll want to feel free to express that unhappiness in an open forum—and the sooner you deal with a problem, the less time it has to fester into resentment. Do so sensitively, however, without playing the "blame game." At the same time, you should both promise to openly and willingly listen to any complaints the other may have. It helps enormously to commit from the start to a certain flexibility and willingness to compromise—and stick to it. It's a lifelong pledge.

❧ ANNIVERSARIES ❧

*A*nniversaries are special milestones, honoring your commitment to each other, past and future. Your first anniversary is full of special traditions, such as sharing a bit of the wedding cake that has been frozen for the occasion (see "The Wedding Team: The Baker: Tips on the Anniversary Cake," page 378). Here is a list of traditional gifts given to couples on each subsequent anniversary of their wedding vows.

A Gift a Day

If you are leaving children at home—especially young children—while you and your new mate enjoy a honeymoon, here's a nice way to remember them and make them feel special. Before you leave, buy fun little toys or gifts, wrap them, and have the children's caretaker present one to your child every day that you're gone. The gifts don't have to be big or expensive; they are simply loving remembrances that let the child know he or she is in your thoughts every day. You could even make a scavenger hunt out of it, providing the child with a written clue each day on the whereabouts of that day's gift.

1. Paper or plastics
2. Calico or cotton
3. Leather or simulated leather
4. Silk or synthetic material
5. Wood
6. Iron
7. Copper or wool
8. Electric appliances
9. Pottery
10. Tin or aluminum
11. Steel
12. Linen (table, bed, and so on)
13. Lace
14. Ivory
15. Crystal or glass
20. China
25. Silver
30. Pearls
35. Coral and jade
40. Ruby
45. Sapphire
50. Gold
55. Emerald
60. Diamond
70. Diamond
75. Diamond

Anniversaries: Reaffirmation of Vows

Traditionally couples who reaffirm their vows do so on a big milestone anniversary, such as the twenty-fifth or an even higher one. This practice is becoming more and more popular, as a way for couples to celebrate earlier anniversaries. In addition to wanting to recommit to each other publicly, they may want to have the no-holds-barred celebration they may have missed out on the first time around. A large party will usually suffice—as it may have to, given that some clergy will not perform a duplicate of the first wedding ceremony. Most, however, will conduct a simple reaffirmation of vows. The ceremony can occur during a regular Sabbath service or at a separate

Wedding Party Get-Together

A postwedding party hosted by the newlyweds is a great excuse for reuniting with loved ones and close friends to remember and celebrate a shared momentous event. Whether held a month or six months after the wedding, the gathering of the wedding party and family and close friends can also be an occasion to view wedding videos and photo albums. It can be the most casual of affairs but can also be a chance to show loved ones your new home, wedding gifts, and entertaining skills as a couple.

time. The form of the service varies, depending on the wishes of the officiant and the tenets of the place of worship. The couple may be joined by any members of the original wedding party, plus their children. The ceremony is generally followed by a celebratory party. (See chapter 9 for more on reaffirmation of vows.)

The Baker: Tips on the Anniversary Cake

It's a special tradition to freeze part of your wedding cake and share it with your partner on the first anniversary of your wedding. Often it is the top tier of the wedding cake that is saved and frozen. There are variations, however:

- Keep in mind that some icings hold up better in the freezer than others; ask your baker for suggestions if you are planning to save some wedding cake to eat on your first anniversary.

- Many couples choose to freeze only one piece of cake and save the pretty top layer to be eaten at the reception.

- Often couples don't like the idea of eating a year-old, possibly freezer-burned cake, preferring to take it out of the freezer and share it on their one-month anniversary.

- If you are going the one-year in-the-freezer route, be sure to freeze the cake (delegate someone to be responsible for doing this) as soon as possible after the reception. Ideally it should be taken out of the cake box and placed in plastic wrap and then aluminum foil.

INDEX

A

A-line gown, 242, 243
Abbreviations, in printed matter, 108
Absentee shower, 153, 175
Accessories, printed, 146–47
Addressing envelopes, 131–32
Admission cards, 133
African American traditions, 219, 267
After the wedding, 371–78
    anniversaries, 376–78
    anniversary cake, 378
    communication, 37, 376
    division of household duties, 374–75
    duties, 371
    freezing the wedding cake, 378
    guests, 182–83
    honeymoon, 371, 372–74
    life together, 374–76
    name change notifications, 64, 374
    reaffirmation of vows, 377–78
    returning rentals, 372
    selecting wedding pictures, 376
    sending announcements, 374
    storing wedding attire, 373
    thank-you notes, 372
    wedding party get-together, 378
Afterglow festivities, 182–83

Age, 53–55
    of bride, 53
    restrictions, 54
Aisle runner, 180, 344–45
Alcohol information, on wedding invitation, 144
Altar, fashioning outside a house of worship, 192
Ancient Greece, wedding traditions in, 24
Anniversaries, 376–78
Anniversary cake, 378
Announcement of engagement
    newspaper, 6–11
    printed announcements, 30, 44
    telling families and close friends, 3–4
    timing of, 6
Announcements, wedding, 128–30
    newspaper, 147–48
    ordering, 30, 44
    variations of, 129–30
    when to mail, 129, 374
    wording, 129–30
Annulment, 56
Apache wedding poem, 203
Appreciation party, 177
Arm bouquets, 297

Arnand Karaj, 208
At-Home cards, 133–34
Attendants, 71–86. *See also* specific attendant
  appearances, 75
  average number of, 72
  backing out, 82
  best man, 79–80
  bridesmaids, 80–81
  budget and, 72, 251
  choosing, 73–75, 86
  destination weddings and, 75
  difficult choices, 74
  duties and responsibilities, 77–86, 342,
    343
  in farewell line, 79, 80
  financial obligations of, 74
  flower girl, 84
  gifts from, 78, 80, 82
  gifts to, 77, 159–60
  honor attendants, 77–80, 86
  information required, 76
  junior bridesmaids, 83–84,
    252
  maid/matron of honor,
    78–79
  other honor roles, 75, 86
  preparation for ceremony, 341–42
  in processionals, 78, 81, 84, 85
    Christian weddings, 349–51, *350*
    Jewish weddings, 201, 204, 350,
      352
  religious restrictions, 72–73
  replacing, 82
  ring bearer, 85
  traditions, 86
  train bearers and pages, 85–86, 252
  treating, 77
  ushers, 81–83
  wedding attire, 241, 249–55
  when to ask, 74

Attire, wedding, 239–56
  bridal, 241, 243–49. *See also* Bridal gown
    and accessories
    accessories, 244–49
    attendants' attire, 241,
      249–51
    bridal gown and accessories, 241,
      242, 243–49
    getting dressed, 248
    gown, *242*, 243
    hair, 247, 298
    headdresses, 246–47, *247*
    makeup, 248
    veil, *244*, 244–46, *245*
  bridal attendants, 241, 249–51
    accessories, 250–51
    budget and, 72, 251
    dresses, 241, 249–50
    flowers, 250, 282, 295–300
  bridal party, 241, 243–56
  dressing tips, 248, 341–43
  encore weddings, 235, 240
  fabrics by season, 243
  fathers of the bride and groom, 241,
    255–56
  gloves, 248–49
  groom and his attendants, 241,
    252–55, *253*
    best woman, 252
    comfort factor, 255
    formal-wear rental, 254
    shoes, 254
    tuxedo, 252, *253*, 254
  guests, 241, 251
  jewelry, 249
  mothers of the bride and groom,
    241, 255
  shoes, 248
  traditional guidelines, 240–41
  young attendants, 252

ℬ

Bachelor dinner/party, 176–77
Bachelorette party, 177
Baguette stones, 19
Baker. *See* Cake, wedding
Ball gown, 242, 243
Bank(s)
    accounts, 68
    name change notification and,
        64, 374
Banns, 59
Bar, at reception, 274, 276, 363
Bartenders, 50
Basque gown, 242, 243
Bathroom shower, 174. *See also* Shower(s)
Belated reception, 183–84
Beneficiaries, 68
Best man
    attire of, 241, 252–55
    duties and responsibilities of, 79–80,
        343
    expenses paid by, 80
    getting ready, 343
    groom's gift to, 160
    in receiving line, 80
    traditions, 81
Best woman, 252
Betrothal, 4. *See also* Engagement
Beverages, at reception, 274, 276, 363
Bezel setting, 17
Birth month flowers, 286
Birthstones, 18
Blessing, at reception, 366
Blood tests, 53
Blusher veil, 244, 244
Book of Common Prayer, The, 197
Bouquet, 295–98, 297, 300
    additions to, 298
    after the wedding, 373
    alternatives, 298

    arm, 297
    bride's, 282, 295–98
    bridesmaids', 282, 295–300
    carrying, 298
    cascade, 297
    nosegays, 297
    preserving, 299, 373
    shapes of, 296–97
    sprays, 297
    styles, 295–96
    tossing, at reception, 368
    traditional beliefs, 279–80
Boutonnieres, 82, 282, 299
Breaking the glass, 219, 221
Bridal gown and accessories, 242, 243–49,
        244, *245*, *247*
    after the wedding, 373
    alterations to, 52
    dressing tips, 248
    encore weddings, 235, 240
    expense of, 44
    fabrics by season, 243
    getting dressed, 248
    gloves, 248–49
    hair, 247, 298
    headdresses, 246–47, *247*
    jewelry, 249
    makeup, 248
    seasonal, 243
    shoes, 248
    shopping for, 243
    storing, 373
    styles, 243
    traditional guidelines, 241
    traditions, 239–40
    trains, 246
    undergarments, 240
    veils, 244–46
Bridal party. *See* Attendants
Bridal registry. *See* Gift registry; Gift(s)

Bride
   bridal gown. *See* Bridal gown and accessories
   engagement announcement variations, 7–11
   expenses paid by family and, 23
   getting ready, 341–42
   gift to attendants, 160
   gift to groom, 160–61
   "giving away of," and multiple fathers,
      348
   groom's gift to, 160–61
   preparation for ceremony, 341–42
   in receiving line, 361–63
   seeing before wedding, 218
Bride's Book of Wedding Traditions, A, 367
Bride's parents/family
   belated reception hosted by, 184
   engagement announcement made by, 6–7
   father's wedding attire, 241, 255–56
   gifts for, 161
   mother's wedding attire, 241, 255
   in receiving line, 361–63
Bridesmaids. *See also* Attendants
   accessories, 250–51
   attire of, 241, 249–51
   budget and, 72, 251
   dresses, 241, 249–50
   duties and responsibilities of, 80–81, 342
   expenses paid by, 81
   flowers, 282
   getting ready, 341–42
   gift to bride, 80
   hosting shower, 80
   junior, 83–84, 252
   luncheon, 175–76
   in receiving line, 81, 361–63
   replacing, 82
   traditions, 86
   treating, 77
Broken engagement, 12
Broken gifts, 159

Browning, Elizabeth Barrett, 203
Budget, 23, 45–51
   categories, 47–49
   ceremony fees, 51
   comparison shopping and, 46
   economy vs. value, 46–47
   guest list and, 22, 88
   number of attendants and, 72
   tipping, 50–51
Buffet, at reception, 267–70
Bulletin board invitations, 143–44

C

Cake, wedding, 331–39
   anniversary cake, 378
   baker, 332, 334, 335
   contracts, 335
   cost-cutting, 332
   cutting of, 337–39, *338,* 368
   dessert and, 336
   displaying, 336–37
   flowers and, 335
   freezing, 378
   groom's cake, 222, 339
   helping the baker, 334
   toppers, 337
   types of, 222, 332–36
   when to order, 336
Cancellation of wedding, 139
Candid photos, 325
Capacity to consent, 55
Carat, defined, 15–16, 18
Caribbean wedding cake, 222
Cascade bouquets, 297
Cash bar, 363
Caterer, 31, 269–74
   costs and, 259, 271
   helping, 259
   interviewing, 270–73

tastings, 271–72, 273
tips, 50, 51
wedding cake from, 272, 273–74
Cathedral train, 246
Cathedral veil, 244, *245*
Celtic music, 223
Ceremony, 185–87, 349. *See also* Planning the
    wedding
  aisle runner, 344–45, 348–49
  at the altar, *351*, 351, 353–54
  at-home tips, 194
  attire, 189, 239–56. *See also* Attire, wedding
  beginning of, 349
  best man preparations, 343
  bridal preparations, 341–42
  ceremonies of commitment, 210–12
  children from a previous marriage in, 214
  choosing date and time, 186
  church documents and, 187
  civil, 58, 193, 207, 208, 215–16
  clergy from out of town, 191
  commitment, 210–12
  details, confirming, 186
  double weddings, 213–14
  escorting guests, 345
  family, seating of, 346–47
  fees, 51
  flowers and decor, 189, 290–93, 344
  "giving away of bride," and multiple fathers,
    348
  greeting guests, 345
  groom preparations, 23, 343
  guest behavior during, 99–100
  guests arrive, 345
  Holy Communion, 191, 195
  honoring the deceased during, 214–15
  interfaith, 194, 195–207, 221
  kiss, at end of, 219, 354
  last-minute details, 345
  leaving for reception, 355–57

  location, 186
    aisle runner, 180
    other ceremonies on same day, 188
    questions to ask at, 188–92
    at site other than house of worship, 192
    specifics on, 188–89
    traffic officer, 44
  military, 212
  music, 302–7
    checklist, 302–3
    house organist, 180, 303
    prelude, 304
    processional, 180, 304–5
    recessional, 306–7
    sample selections, 190, 305, 306–7
  officiant, choosing, 186
  personalizing, 190–92
  pew cards, 344
  pew ribbons, 348–49
  photographs, 190, 321–22, 355
  planning, 185–87
  processional, 304–5, 349–52
  programs, 344
  pronouncing husband/man and wife, 354
  readings for, 202–3
  reaffirmation of vows, 216
  receiving line, 355
  recessional, *351*, *353*, 354–55
  religious ceremonies, 58, 193–210
    Eastern Orthodox, 200–201
    Episcopal, 196–99
    Hindu, 59, 207–8
    Islamic (Muslim), 205–7
    Jewish, 201, 204, 219, 350, *352*, 354
    Judaism, 59
    Lutheran, 59
    Mormon, 205
    Presbyterian, 59
    Protestant, 197–99
    Quaker, 59, 210

Ceremony (*continued*)
    Roman Catholic, 59, 195–96, 198–99
    Sikh, 208–10
    Unitarian-Universalist, 210
  reservation for rehearsal, 187
  rose petals, 102, 355–56
  seating at, 346–49
    bride's mother, 349
    divorced parents, 346–47
    immediate family, 347–48
    parents, 346
    widowed parents, 346
  setting the date, 24, 25–26
  sharing the peace, 354
  signing the papers, 357
  tributes, 214–15
  unity candles, 215, 290, 292
  ushers arrive, 343
  ushers' demeanor, 346
  videotape of, 329–30, 355
  vows, personal, 206, 211
Certificate of Dissolution of Marriage, 56
Channel setting, 17
Chapel train, 246
Chapel veil, 244, *245*
Chauffeurs, 50, 51
Checks, displaying, 157–58
Child custody, 67
Child support, 67
Children
  buffet for, 270
  encore wedding and, 230–33, 236
  entertaining, 94, 270
  honeymoon and, 236, 373–74, 377
  informing of engagement, 4, 15
  invitations and, 120, 134, 143
  name changes and, 63–64
  from previous marriage, 66, 67
  from previous marriage, in ceremony, 214
  at reception, 270, 363

Chuppah, 204, 219, *352*
Civil ceremonies, 58, 193, 207, 208, 215–16
Clergy, 29, 58. *See also* Officiant
  additional, 58
  availability of, 29
  fee paid to, 51, 79
  out-of-state, 58, 59
  out-of-town, 191
Clothing, 239–56. *See also* Attire, wedding
  rehearsal, 179
Coat check, 50, 51
Communication, 37, 376
Comparison shopping, 46
Compromise, 37
Consent, 55
Consideration, 37
Consultant, wedding, 32–34
  budget and, 50
  cost of, 33–34
  destination weddings and, 34, 62
  questions to ask, 33
  services provided by, 33
  value of, 50
Consumption bar, 274
Contracts, 52
  domestic partnerships, 60
  hidden costs in, 52
  musicians, 312
  photographers, 317, 325
  postnuptial, 65–68
  prenuptial, 65–68, 237
  videographers, 325, 329
Corinthians (I), reading, 202
Counseling, premarital, 29, 61, 195–98
County clerk's office, 53, 58
Coupe de marriage, 221
Court clerk, authority to perform marriage, 58
Court train, 246
Credit accounts, name change notification and,
  64, 65

Credit card companies, name change notification
    and, 64
Credit unions, name change notification and,
    64
Crossing sticks, 219
Cultural traditions
    African American, 219, 267
    American South, 222
    Caribbean, 222
    Chinese, 187, 218, 220–21, 304
    combining, 221
    Danish, 222
    Egyptian, 42
    food and drink, 220–22
    French, 221
    German, 100, 222, 224
    Greek, 24, 224
    Indian, 224
    Irish, 221, 222, 223
    Japanese, 225
    Jewish, 204, 219, 221, 223
    Latin American, 42
    marriage cup, 221–22
    Mexican, 42, 220
    Scottish, 220, 223
    Spanish, 225
    Swedish, 223
    wedding favors, 162
Cup, marriage, 221–22
Cutaway, 253

D

Dancing, at reception, 367–68
    bride and father, 367
    dinner dance, 308–9
    first wedding dance, 367
    order of, 367
Danish wedding cake, 222
Date of wedding, 24

change of, and invitations, 140
day of the week, 26
Deceased, honoring at ceremony, 214–15
Decisions to make, 21–40. *See also* Planning the
    wedding
Decor, at reception, 262, 283, 293–94
Decree of Divorce, 56
Defense of Marriage Act, 60
Delegating, in wedding planning, 38
Delivery truck drivers, 50
Destination weddings, 34. *See also* Honeymoon
    attendants and, 75
    flowers and, 294
    guests, 34
    reception and, 264
    residency requirements, 62
    travel agent, 34, 62
    wedding consultant, 34
Diamond(s)
    engagement ring, 15–17
    four C's of, 15–16
Dinner dance reception, 308–9
Dinner napkins, monogramming, 167–68
Diplomacy, and divorced parents, 14
Disapproval of engagement, by family or friends,
    13–15
Disc jockey, 307, 310–11
Disclosure, 67
Displaying gifts, 157–58
Divorced bride and groom
    engagement announcements, 3, 56
    religious factors, 59
    Roman Catholics and, 59
Divorced parents
    engagement announcement wording, 7–8
    getting acquainted with, 5
    in receiving line, 361–63
    seating arrangements
        at ceremony, 346–47
        at reception, 275

Domestic partnerships, 60
Double wedding
    ceremony, 213–14
    invitation wording, 127
Drinks, 274–77
    types of bars, 274, 276, 363

E

Eastern Orthodox wedding ceremony, 200–201
Ecclesiastes, 202
Economizing, 46–47
Egypt, wedding traditions in, 42
Emerald cut diamond, 20
Emily Post's Wedding Planner, 38
Empire gown, 242, 243
Employer payroll department, name change
        notification and, 64
Enclosures, 30, 44
Encore weddings, 227–41
    attire, 235
    children and, 230–33, 236
    etiquette for, 230–37
    ex-spouse and, 231, 234
    gift registry and, 150
    gifts for, 156, 234–35
    giving the bride away, 228, 229
    guidelines for, 229–30
    honeymoon, 236
    invitations, 230, 233
    monogrammed items, 235
    prenuptial agreement, 237
    showers, 153, 156, 171, 237
    veil, 236, 244
    wedding party, 236
    wedding rings and, 232
Engagement, 1–20
    addressing future in-laws, 5–6
    announcements, 6–11, 30, 44
    broken, 12

divorce and, 3, 56
divorced parents and, 7–9, 14
family reactions
    diplomacy and, 14
    disapproval, 13–15
    welcome, 4–6
gifts, 11–13, 152
guidelines, 2–3
length of, 2, 4
parents meeting divorced parents, 5
parents meeting parents, 5
party, 11–13
photographs, 319
ring. *See* Engagement ring; Wedding rings
sharing the news, 3–4
spreading the news, 6–11
timing of, 6
Engagement, disapproval of, 13–15
Engagement ring, 15–20
    birthstone, 18
    diamond, 15–17
    gemstone, 17–18
    heirloom, 18
    metal used for, 18
    origins of, 17
    returning, after broken engagement, 12
    selection of, 15
    settings, 17, 18–19
    stone shapes, *19*, 19–20
    wearing, 16, 18, 19
Engraved items, from first marriage, 235
Engraving
    gifts, 167–68
    of wedding band, 36
Envelopes, 130–32
    addressing, 131–32
    one or two, 130–31
    stuffing, *138*
Episcopal wedding ceremony, 196–99
Ethnic traditions. *See* Cultural traditions

Exchanging the tartan sash, 220
Expenses, 41–51
    average U.S. wedding costs, 41
    bridal gown, 44
    budget, determining, 23, 45–51
        categories, 47–49
        economy vs. value, 46–47
        fixed costs, 46
        tips on saving, 47
    ceremony fees, 51
    comparison shopping, 46
    contracts, 52
    division of costs, 44–45
    flowers, 44
    hidden costs, 52
    lowering, 47
    nontraditional trends, 43
    photography, 315
    rehearsal dinner, 44
    responsibilities of
        bride and her family, 42, 43, 44
        bridesmaids and honor attendants, 45
        groom and his family, 43, 44
        out-of-town guests, 45
        ushers and best man, 45
    sharing, 43
    tipping, 50–51
    traditional trends, 43, 44–45
    wedding consultants, 50

F

Family. See also Bride's parents/family; Divorced
        parents; Groom's parents/family
    flowers for, 283
    informing of engagement, 3–4
    restrictions, on marriage within, 55
    widowed parents, 9, 346, 361–62
Favors, wedding, 146–47, 162
Fees, 51, 79. See also Expenses

Finances, 65–68. See also Budget
Financial planner, name change notification and,
        64
Fingertip veil, 244, 244
Fireman's Fund, 69
First dance songs, 311
Floral designer, 288
Florists, 287–90. See also Flowers
    contracts, 52
    helping, 291
    interviewing, 288–90
    tips, 50
Flower girl, 84, 252
Flowers, 279–300, 344
    after the celebration, 300, 373
    allergies to, 281
    bouquets, 295–98, 297, 300
        additions to, 298
        alternatives, 298
        bride's, 282, 295–98
        bridesmaids', 282, 295–300
        carrying, 298
        as decorations, 296
        freeze-dried, 299, 373
        preserving, 299, 373
        shapes of, 296–97
        styles, 295–96
        to toss, 368
        traditions, 279–80, 300
    boutonnieres, 282, 299
    at ceremony, 283, 290–93, 344
    checklist, 282–83
    for children, 299–300
    choosing, 280–82
    cutting costs of, 287, 288
    delivery details, 289
    for destination wedding, 294
    for family, 283
    floral designer, 288
    floral themes, 284–87

Flowers (*continued*)
  birth month flowers, 286
  fragrant flowers and herbs, 287
  language of color, 286
  language of flowers, 285
florist, 287–90, 291
as gifts, 283
for groom and his attendants, 282, 299
for hair, 298
poetry of, 285
at reception, 283, 289, 293–94
seasonal, 284
theme weddings, 282
traditions, 279–80, 300
wedding cake and, 335
wreath of, for bride's hair, 247, 298
Foreign countries, U.S. citizen marriage in, 62
Foreign nationals, marriage to U.S. citizen in
    U.S., 59
Forgiveness, 39
Formal wedding, 27
  age of bride and, 53–54
  budgeting, 44–47
  daytime attire, 27, 241. *See also* Attire, wedding
  evening attire, 27, 241. *See also* Attire, wedding
  military, 212
French (sit-down) service, 267
Friends. *See also* Guests
  informing of engagement, 3–4
  videotape of wedding for, 326

G

Garter, throwing, 369
Gay marriage. *See* Same-sex marriage
Gemstone engagement rings, 17–18
Gender restrictions, on same-sex marriage, 56,
    60
George, Chief Dan, 202
German measles, 57

Gift registry, 150–52. *See also* Gift(s)
  choosing gifts, 151–52
  information on wedding invitation, 152
  on the Internet, 151
  letting others know, 152
  registering at stores, 150–52
  registry form, 151
  when to register, 151
Gift(s), 12, 149–68. *See also* Gift registry
  for attendants, 159–60
  from attendants, 154, 159–60
  broken, 159
  for children, 161
  delivery, 155–57
  displaying, 157–58
  displaying checks, 157–58
  duplicate, 158
  for each other, 160–61
  encore weddings, 156,
      234–35
  engagement, 11–13, 152
  engraving, 167–68
  exchanging, 158–59
  homeowners' insurance for, 158
  for hosts, 166
  information on wedding invitation,
      152
  keeping record of, 156–57
  monogramming, 167–68
  for parents, 161
  registry. *See* Gift registry
  returning, 158–59
  returning, if engagement is broken, 12
  safekeeping, 158
  shower, 153. *See also* Shower(s)
  thank-you notes for, 161–67
  wedding, 152–59
  wedding favors, 146–47, 162
  from wedding guests, 154–59
  when to send, 156

where to send, 155–56
wish list, 150–51
Gloves
    bridal, 248–49
    worn by mothers, 255
Godparents, in Mexican weddings, 220
Gold, durability of, 18
Good-luck charms, 223–25
    coins in shoes, 223
    evil eye, 224
    gifts for guests, 225
    horseshoes, 223
    Jordan almonds, 224
    Mehndi, 224
    orange blossoms, 225
    plates, 224
Gourmet cook shower, 173. *See also* Shower(s)
Great outdoors shower, 173. *See also* Shower(s)
Greece, ancient, wedding traditions in, 24
Groom
    attire of, 241, 252–55, *253*
    expenses paid by family and, 42–45
    getting ready, 343
    preparation for ceremony, 23
    in receiving line, 361–63
    seeing bride before wedding, 218
    wedding ring for, 19, 36
Groom's cake, 222
Groom's parents/family
    belated reception hosted by, 184
    engagement announcement made by, 8, 9–10
    father's wedding attire, 241, 255–56
    making acquaintance with parents of the bride,
      5–6
    mother's wedding attire, 241, 255
Guest book, 360
Guest list, 22, 87–102
    budget, 22, 88
    children and, 90, 93–95
    cutting down, 91–92

for destination wedding, 91
engagement party, 11–13
master list, 92–93
necessary inclusions, 89
organizing, 92–93
out-of-town guests, 96–98
rehearsal party, 178
showers, 92
special considerations, 95–96
standby list, 90, 92
survival guide, 88–89
Guests
    arrival at ceremony, 345
    behavior of, 99–102
    children, 94
    etiquette for, 98–102
    greetings from, 100–101
    lodging for, 97–98
    noisy, 99–102
    out-of-town, 96–98
    passing through receiving line, 100–101, 361,
      364
    during reception, 100–101, 361, 364
    responsibilities of, 98–102
    RSVP, 98
    sending gifts, 98
    talkative, 361
    wedding attire, 241, 251

H

Hair
    bride's, 298
    flowers for, 247, 298
Handwritten formal reply, 136
Happy Holidays shower, 173. *See also* Shower(s)
Head coverings required in house of worship,
    providing, 251
Headband, 247, *247*
Headdresses, bridal, 246–47, *247*

Health care centers, name change notification
    and, 65
Health certificates, 57
Health considerations, 57
Health insurance, same-sex couples and, 60
Heirloom rings, 18
Herbs, 287
Hindu marriage poem, 203
Hindu wedding ceremony, 59, 207–8
HIV/AIDS virus, 57
Holiday weddings, 35
Holy Book, The, 209
Holy Communion, 191, 195
Holy Union, 210
Homeowner's insurance, 158
Honeymoon, 40, 371, 372–74, 377–78. *See also*
    Destination weddings
    children and, 236, 373–74, 377
    encore weddings and, 236
    expenses, 40
    planning, 40, 372
    shower, 173. *See also* Shower(s)
    tradition, 375
Honor attendants, 77–80
    best man, 79–80
    expenses paid by, 79, 80
    maid/matron of honor, 78–79
Honor roles, 75, 86
Hosts
    gifts to, 166
    thanking, 166–67
Hotel, as reception site, 263–64

I

Illusion ring setting, 18
Immigration and Naturalization Service, 59
In-laws, addressing future, 5–6
Infectious disease, health requirements and, 57
Informal receiving line, 201

Informal wedding, 28–29
    attire, 28–29, 241. *See also* Attire, wedding
Insurance
    health, 60
    homeowners', 158
    photography, 325
    videography, 325
    wedding, 69
Interfaith marriages, 194, 195–207, 221
International Gemological Institute, 16
Internet Web sites, 151
Invitations, 103–48. *See also* Guest list
    alcohol information and, 144
    alternatives to traditional, 105, 106
    awkward questions concerning, 95–96, 134
    bulletin board, 143–44
    cancellation of wedding after mailing of, 139
    to ceremony and reception, 112
        belated reception, 114, 184
        at someone's home, 114
    children and, 120, 134, 143
    date change, 139–40
    do's and don'ts, 141–45
    envelopes, 130–32
        addressing, 131–32
        one or two, 130–31
        stuffing, *138*
    formal, 107–11
    gift registry and, 143
    handwritten, 106
    insertions, 132–39
        admission cards, 133
        at-home cards, 133–34
        handwritten formal reply, 136
        maps, 137
        pew cards, 133
        rain card, 138
        reception cards, 113, 134
        response cards, 135
        tissues, 137

labels, 144
ordering, 30, 44
organizing, 141–42
personal notes, 111
postage, 142
printing of, 144–45
printing options, 105–7
reception cards, 113, 134
to reception only, 113
rehearsal dinner, 181–82
RSVP, 108, 112
sample, 115–28
 belated reception, 114, 184
 bride and groom issue invitation, 118–19
 bride has a stepfather, 117
 bride has one living parent, 115–16
 bride is a widow or divorcée, 121
 bride is an orphan, 117–18
 bride with one living parent, 115–16
 bride with professional name, 124
 bride's mother is divorced, 116
 bridegroom's family gives the wedding, 122
 ceremony and reception, 112
 couples who have been living together, 119
 divorced parents giving wedding together, 116–17
 double weddings, 127–28
 foreign traditions, 123
 groom's family included on invitation, 122–23
 grown children giving wedding, 120
 home ceremony and reception, 114
 mature couples, 119
 military titles, 124–25
 other relatives issue invitations, 120
 reception cards, 113
 reception only, 113
 same-gender unions, 126–27
 titles other than military, 125, 143

shower, 172
spellings, 142
styles, 104–12
titles, 125, 143
wording, 107–12
 encore weddings, 230, 233
 less formal, 109–11
 personal notes, 111
 for special cases, 112
 traditional, 107
Irish blessing, 365
Irish wedding cake, 222
Islamic wedding ceremony, 205–7

J

Japanese wedding traditions, 225
Jewelry, worn by bride, 249
Jewish wedding ceremony, 201, 204
 under the Chuppah, 204, 219, 350, 352
 processional, 201, 204, 350, 352, 354
Judge, with authority to perform marriage, 58
Juliet cap, 247, *247*
Jumping the broom, 219
Jumping the Broom, 267
June weddings, 24, 25
Junior bridesmaids, 83–84, 252
Junior ushers, 252
Justice of the peace, 58

K

Kiss, at end of, 219, 354
Kitchen shower, 173, 174. *See also* Shower(s)

L

Labels, printed, 144
Labor of love shower, 173. *See also* Shower(s)

Latin American countries, wedding expenses in, 42
Legal factors, 52–69
  age restrictions, 53–54
  capacity to consent, 55
  contracts, 52
    domestic partnerships, 60
    hidden costs in, 52
    limousine, 52
    musicians, 312
    photographers, 317
    pre- and post-nuptial, 65–68
    reception, 162
    videographers, 329
  familial restrictions, 55
  finances, 65–68
  gender, 56
  health certificates, 57
  homeowners' insurance for gifts, 158
  marriage in another country, 62
  marriage license, 53, 56–57
  marriage to a foreign national, 59
  officiants, 58
  officiating at ceremonies, 58
  postnuptial agreement, 65–68
  prenuptial agreement, 65–68, 237
  religious factors, 59
  remarriage, 56
  wedding insurance, 69
  wills, 68
  witnesses, 60
Leisure-time shower, 173. *See also* Shower(s)
Lesbian marriage. *See* Same-sex marriage
Life together, 374–76
Limousine
  contract, 52
  drivers, 50, 51
  to reception, 277
Linen, monogramming, 167–68

Location
  for ceremony
    aisle runner, 180
    other ceremonies on same day, 188
    questions to ask at, 188–92
    at site other than house of worship, 192
    specifics on, 188–89
    traffic officer, 44
  for reception
    club, hotel, or wedding facility, 263–64
    contract for site, 261
    home, 263, 266
    restaurant, 264–65
    tented, 265
Luncheons, bridesmaids'
  hosts of, 175
  types of, 175–76
  when to hold, 175–76
Lutheran wedding ceremony, 59

M

Madrinas, 42
Maid/matron of honor
  duties and responsibilities of, 78, 342
  expenses paid by, 79
  gift to bride, 78, 154, 160
  in processional
    Christian ceremony, 350–51
    Jewish ceremony, 201, 204, 350
  in receiving line, 79, 361–63
Mail deliveries, name change notification and, 64
Makeup, 248
Mandaps, 208
Mantilla veil, 244, *245*
Maps, included in invitations, 137
Marquise cut diamond, 19
Marriage in another country, 62
Marriage license, 53, 54, 56–57
  age restrictions, 53–54

familial restrictions, 55
 premarital examinations, 57
Marriage to a foreign national, 59
Master of Ceremonies, 310–11
Matron of honor. *See* Maid/matron of honor
Memory books, 360
Mental illness, and capacity to consent, 55
Mexican traditions, 42, 220
Military weddings, 212
Money tree, 224
Monogrammed dinner napkins, 167–68
Monogrammed items, from first marriage, 235
Monogramming, 167–68
Mormon wedding ceremony, 205
Mortgage company, name change notification
 and, 64
Motor vehicles department, name change
 notification and, 64
Multicultural weddings, 217–25
 combining traditions, 221
 food and drink, 220–22
 good-luck charms, 223–25
 music and dancing, 222–23, 367–68
 symbolic acts, 219–20
Music, 301–12
 at ceremony, 302–7
  checklist, 302–3
  cutting costs of, 312
  house organist, 303
  musicians, 302
  order of, 303–7
  participation in, 305–6
  payment for, 303
  planning, 302–3
  postlude, 307
  prelude, 304
  processional, 180, 304–5
  program for, 303
  recessional, 306
  sample selections, 305, 306

at reception, 307–9
 afternoon, 307–8
 brunch, lunch, or tea, 307
 cutting costs of, 312
 dancing, 367–68
 details, 307–11
 dinner dance, 308–9
 disc jockey, 307, 310–11
 first dance songs, 311
 helping musicians, 308–9
 interviewing musicians, 311–12
 making requests, 310, 312
 musicians, 307, 312
 selecting musicians, 309–11
 time of day and, 307–8
 tips, 308–9
 traditions, 304
Music and dancing, 222–23, 367–68
 bagpipes, 223
 Celtic music, 223
 circle dance, 223
 money dance, 222
Muslim wedding ceremony, 205–7

N

Name changes, 62–65, 374
 children and, 63–64
 nontraditional choices, 62, 65
 official notifications, 64–65
 professional vs. social, 63
Newspaper announcements
 engagement, 6–11
  basic content, 6–7
  timing of, 6
  variations, 7–11
 wedding, 147–48
Nonreligious ceremonies, 58
Nosegays, 297
Nuptial Mass, 195

O

Officiant, 58
  additional clergy, 58
  availability of, 29
  fee paid to, 51, 79
  out-of-state, 58, 59
  performing ceremonies, 58
Online gift registries, 151
Open bar, 274
Orange blossoms, 225, 235, 280
Organist, 180
  fee paid to, 51
Organization, importance of, 38–39
Out-of-town guests, 96–98
  events for, 96–97
  lodging for, 97–98
  parties for, 96–97, 178
  post-wedding festivities and, 97, 182–83
  travel information for, 98, 139
Outdoor weddings/receptions
  flowers and, 293
  tents, 293
Oval cut diamond, 20

P

Padrinos, 42
Pages, 85–86, 252
Parents
  bride's
    belated reception hosted by, 184
    engagement announcement made by, 6–7
    father's wedding attire, 241, 255–56
    gifts for, 161
    mother's wedding attire, 241, 255
    in receiving line, 361–63
  consent of, for underage bride or groom, 55
  divorced, and engagement announcement, 7–8
  groom's
    belated reception hosted by, 184
    engagement announcement made by, 8, 9–10

    father's wedding attire, 241, 255–56
    making acquaintance with parents of the bride, 3–6
    mother's wedding attire, 241, 255
  in receiving line, 361–63
    divorced parents, 361–63
    widowed parents, 361–62
  seating of, at reception, 275
Parking
  attendants, 50, 51, 263
  security, 263
Parties and celebrations, 169–84
  appreciation, 177
  bachelor and bachelorette, 176–77
  belated reception, 183–84
  engagement, 11–13, 152
  luncheons, 175–76, 177–78
  for out-of-town guests, 96–97, 178
  post-wedding, 182–83
  rehearsal dinner, 181–82
Party, bachelor and bachelorette, 176–77
Party, engagement, 11–13
  gifts at, 11–13, 152
  guest list, 11
Passed-tray receptions, 269
Passport agency, name change notification and, 64
Pavé stones, 19
Pear cut diamond, 20
Personal stationery, 147
Pew cards, 133, 344
Photography, 313–25. See also Videography
  black and white vs. color, 320
  candid, 325
  ceremony photographs, 321–22
  contract negotiations, 317, 325
  engagement photographs, 319
  equipment, 319
  "getting ready" photographs, 325
  helping photographer, 316
  insurance, 325
  interviewing, 318–19

photographer, selection of, 315–18
photos not turning out, 325
planned events, 324–25
portrait photographs, 320–21, 323–24
price comparisons, 315
reception photographs, 323–25
selecting wedding pictures, 376
style, choosing, 314–15
    classical, 314
    commercial, 314–15
    photographic artist, 315
    photojournalistic, 314
    traditional, 314
timing of, 321
Place cards, 146, 148, 267, 277
Planning the wedding, 21–40
booking vendors, 30
budget, 22, 23
ceremony location, 27–29
coping, 36–40
date and time, 24, 25–26
day of the week, 26
decision-making, 22–32
delegating, 38
destination weddings and, 34
formal wedding, 27
guest list, 22, 87–102
honeymoon, 40
informal wedding, 28–29
officiant, availability of, 29
organization, 38–39
prewedding counseling, 29, 61
reception location, 29–30, 31
semiformal wedding, 28
staying calm, 39
style of wedding, 27–29
taking care of self, 40
theme weddings, 35
three C's of, 37
time of day, 26
time of year, 24, 25–26
wedding consultants, 32–34, 50

Plated service, 267
Portrait photographs, 320–21, 323–24
Posies, 297
Postage, 142
Postnuptial contract, 65–68
Postwedding details, 371–78
Postwedding party, 378
Powder room attendants, 50, 51
Pre-wedding luncheon, 177–78
Prelude, 304
Premarital counseling, 29, 61, 195–98
Prenuptial contract, 65–68, 237
Presbyterian wedding ceremony, 59
Printed accessories, 146–47
Private club, as reception site, 263–64
Processional, 180
    Christian wedding, 349–51, 350
    Jewish wedding, 201, 204, 350, 352
    music, 180, 304–5
    walking down the aisle, 305, 349–50
Programs, 145, 344
    music credits in, 303
Protestant wedding ceremony, 197–99

Q

Quaker (Society of Friends) weddings, 59, 210

R

Rain card, 138
Readings, 202–3
Reaffirmation of vows, 216, 377–78
Receiving line, 359–64, 362
    at ceremony, 355
    informal, 201
    reception
        bridesmaids in, 361–63
        children in, 363
        disabled parents in, 361
        divorced parents in, 361–63
        passing through, 361, 364

Reception, 257–78, 336, 359–69
  after the celebration, 371–78
  afternoon, 307–8
  arriving at, 359–60
  belated, 184
  the blessing, 366
  bouquet, tossing, 368
  bride and groom departure from, 369
  bride's table, 275–76
  brunch, lunch, or tea, 307
  buffet meals, 267–70
  cards, 113, 134
  closing activities, 368–69
  cutting the cake, 337–39, 338, 368
  dancing at, 367–68
  decor, 262, 283, 293–94
  dessert, 336
  destination weddings and, 264
  dinner dance, 308–9
  expenses, 44, 46–47, 260–61, 271
  first dance songs, 311
  flowers, 283, 293–94
  food and drink, 266–77
    bars, 274, 276, 363
    buffet, 267–70
    caterers, 259, 269–74
    cuisine trends, 271
    drinks, 274
    passed-tray, 269
    sit-down or seated meal, 266–67, 275
  garter, throwing, 369
  guest book, 360
  guests' behavior during, 100–102, 361
  leaving, 369
  leaving for, 355–57
  location, 258–62
    checking, 261–62
    choosing, 258, 260–61
    club, hotel, or wedding facility,
      263–64
    contract for site, 261
    home, 263, 266
    out-of-the-ordinary, 264
    restaurant, 264–65
    tented, 265
  memory books, 360
  menus, 259, 266
  money tree, 224
  music, 307–12
    details, 307–11
    disc jockey, 307, 310–11
    first dance songs, 311
    making requests, 310
    time of day and, 307–8
  packages, 263
  parking security, 263
  photographs, 323–25
    candid, 325
    planned events, 324–25
  place cards, 146, 148, 267, 277
  receiving line, 201, 359–64, 362
  seating arrangements, 266–69, 275–77
  time of day, and cost of, 260–61, 271
  toasts, 364–66
  tossing the bouquet, 368
  transportation to, 44, 277–78, 356
  videotape of, 330
  wedding cake
    cutting of, 337–39, 338, 368
    displaying, 336–37
    freezing, 378
  wedding favors, 146–47, 162
Recessional, 351, 353, 354–55
Recipe shower, 173. See also Shower(s)
Registry. See Gift registry
Rehearsal, 178–80
  attire for, 179
  duties during, 179–80
  when to hold the, 179
  who attends, 178

Rehearsal dinner, 181–82
   guest list, 181–82
   host of, 181
   invitations, 182
   presentation of attendants' gifts, 182
   toasts, 182
   when to hold the, 181
Religious ceremonies, 58
   Eastern Orthodox, 200–201
   Episcopal, 196–99
   guest participation in, 305–6
   head coverings required in, 251
   Hindu, 59, 207–8
   Islamic (Muslim), 205–7
   Jewish, 201, 204, 219, 350, 352
   Lutheran, 59
   Mormon, 205
   Presbyterian, 59
   Protestant, 197–99
   Quaker, 59, 210
   Roman Catholic, 59, 195–96, 198–99
   Sikh, 208–10
   Unitarian-Universalist, 210
Religious factors, 59
Remarriage, 56. See also Encore weddings; Second
      marriage
Rentals
   groom's and attendant's clothing, 254
   returning, 372
Residency requirements, foreign marriages and,
      62
Response cards, 135
Rice, throwing, 102
Ring bearer, 85, 252
Rings. See Engagement ring; Wedding rings
Rite of blessing, 210
Roman Catholic wedding ceremony, 59, 195–96,
      198–99
Rose petals, 102, 355–56
Round cut diamond, 20

RSVP, 98, 108, 112
Rubella, 57
Russian (sit-down) service, 267

S

Same-sex marriage, 56, 60
   ceremonies, 210–11
   domestic partnerships, 60
   invitation wording, 126–27
   restrictions, 60
Samuel, Book of, 211
Scottish traditions, 220, 223
Seating arrangements, at ceremony,
      346–49
   bride's mother, 349
   divorced parents, 346–47
   immediate family, 347–48
   parents, 346
   widowed parents, 346
Seating arrangements, at reception, 266–69,
      275–77
   bride's table, 275–76
   place cards, 146, 148, 267, 277
   seating parents, 275
Second marriage, 56, 150. See also Encore
      weddings
   gift registry and, 150
   showers, 153, 156, 171, 237
   wedding gift for, 156
Semiformal wedding, 28
   attire, 28, 241. See also Attire, wedding
Serbala, 206
Setting the date, 24, 25–26
Settings, for engagement rings, 17, 18–19
Seven Steps, 208
Shakespeare, William, 365
Sharing the peace, 354
Sheets, monogramming, 167–68
Shoes, bridal, 248

Shower(s), 153, 170–75
    absentee, 153, 175
    from attendants, 154
    encore weddings, 153, 156, 171, 237
    etiquette of, 172–74
    gift for host, 174
    gifts, 153
        etiquette of, 172–74
        to hosts, 166
        opening, 153, 174
        returning, if engagement is broken, 12
        thanks for, 174
        theme, 172–73
    guest list, 171, 176
    hosts of, 170–71, 174
    invitations, 172
    opening gifts at, 153, 174
    origin of, 153
    second-marriage, 153, 156, 171
    size, 171
    style, 170
    thank-you notes, 153
    thanking guests and hosts, 166–67
    theme, 173
    traditions, 172
    wedding guests and, 176
    when to hold, 170
    wishing well, 155
Sikh wedding ceremony, 208–10
Silver, engraving, 167–68
Simulated train, 179
Social Security Administration, name change
        notification and, 64
Soloist, fee paid to, 51
Southern wedding cake, 222
Spa shower, 173. *See also* Shower(s)
Sprays (bouquets), 297
Standby guest list, 90, 92
Stationery
    ceremony programs, 145

    personal, 147
    place cards, 146
    printed accessories and favors, 146–47, 162
    thank-you notes on, 147, 162
Style of wedding, 27–29
Suit, 253
Sweep train, 246
Sweep veil, 244, 245
Symbolic acts, 219–20

T

Table captain, 50
Tablecloths, monogramming, 167–68
Tailcoat, 253
Taxes, included in wedding expenses, 52
Tempest, The, 365
Thank-you notes, 147, 161–67
    for acts of kindness, 161, 165–66
    content of, 162, 163–67
    engagement gifts, 13
    to hosts, 166–67
    money gifts, 164
    not received, 165
    preprinted, 162, 163
    promptness of, 161–62, 165
    samples, 163–67
    stationery for, 147, 162
Theme showers, 173. *See also* Shower(s)
Theme weddings, 35
Third marriage, 150. *See also* Encore weddings
    gifts for, 150, 153, 171, 234–35
    showers, 237
Throwing rice, rose petals, etc., after ceremony,
        102, 355–56
Tiara, 247, 247
Tiffany ring setting, 18
Time of wedding, 24, 25–26
    day of week, 26
    favorite months for weddings, 24

religious restrictions, 25
time of day, 26
time of year, 24, 25–26
Tipping, 50–51
Tissues, enclosed in invitations, 137
Titles, 124, 125, 143
Toasts, at the reception, 364–66
    getting guest's attention, 364–65
    made by bride and groom, 366
    offering of, 365
    pouring the champagne, 364
    samples, 365
    standing, 365–66
    tradition of, 366
    wedding cup, 221–22
Toppers, for wedding cake, 337
Towels, monogramming, 167–68
Traditions
    African American, 219, 267
    American South, 222
    Caribbean, 222
    Chinese, 187, 218, 220–21, 304
    combining, 221
    Danish, 222
    Egyptian, 42
    food and drink, 220–22
    French, 221
    German, 100, 222, 224
    Greek, 24, 224
    henna painting, 224
    Indian, 224
    Irish, 221, 222, 223
    Japanese, 225
    Jewish, 204, 219, 221, 223
    June weddings, 24, 25
    Latin American, 42
    marriage cup, 221–22
    Mediterranean, 224
    Mexican, 42, 220
    Scottish, 220, 223
    Spanish, 225
    Swedish, 223
    Victorian, 17–18, 24
    wedding favors, 162
Traffic officer, 44
Train bearer, 85, 252
Train styles, 246
Transportation, to and from ceremony, 44
Transportation, to reception, 44, 277–78, 356
Travel agents, destination weddings and, 34, 62
Travel clubs, name change notification and, 65
Trousseau, 43, 44
Tussy-mussies, 297
Tuxedo, 252, 253, 254

U

Underage bride or groom, 53–54
Unitarian-Universalist wedding ceremony, 210
Unity candles, 215, 290, 292
Universal Fellowship of Metropolitan
    Community Churches, 210
U.S. Department of State Visa Office, 59
Ushers
    arrival at ceremony, 81, 343
    boutonnieres for, 82
    in Christian ceremonies, 349
    demeanor of, 346
    duties and responsibilities of, 81–83, 343
    escorting guests, 345
    expenses paid by, 83
    groom's gift to, 159–60
    in Jewish ceremonies, 204
    junior, 252

V

Valet parking, 50, 51, 263
Veils, 244, 244–46, 245
    lifting, 246

Venereal disease, 57
Victoria, Queen of England, 239, 280
Victorian traditions
    gemstone rings, 17–18
    time of wedding, 24
    time to marry, 24
Videography, 313, 326–30.
            See also Photography
    of ceremony, 329–30
    choosing a videographer, 327–28
    contracts, 325, 329
    discretion and, 330
    insurance, 325
    interviewing, 328–29
    of reception, 330
    video not turning out, 325
    videotape for faraway friends, 326
    what to expect, 326
Visas, 59
Voter registration, name change notification and,
        64
Vows
    reaffirmation of, 216, 377–78
    same-sex marriage, 210
    writing, 206, 211

Waistcoat, 253
Wait staff, 50
Watteau train, 246

Wedding announcements, 128–30
    newspaper, 147–48
    ordering, 30, 44
    variations of, 129–30
    when to mail, 129, 374
    wording, 129–30
Wedding cake. *See* Cake, wedding
Wedding consultant, 32–34, 50
Wedding gifts. *See* Gift registry; Gift(s)
Wedding gown. *See* Bridal gown and accessories
Wedding insurance, 69
Wedding rehearsal, 178–80. *See also* Rehearsal
Wedding rings, 35–36
    choosing, 35–36
    engagement ring worn with,
        36
    engraving, 36
    for groom, 19, 36
    types of, 35–36
Wedding showers. *See* Shower(s)
White, as traditional wedding color, 239–40
White bar, 274
Widowed bride or groom
    invitation wording, 121
    marriage license and, 56
Widowed parents, seating at ceremony, 346
Wills, 68
Wishing Well, 155
Witnesses, 60
Wreath of flowers, 247
Writing marriage vows, 206, 211